DIRECTING STAFF EDITION

> **RESTRICTED**
> The information given in this document is not to be communicated either directly or indirectly to the Press or to any person not authorised to receive it.

BRITISH ARMY OF THE RHINE

BATTLEFIELD TOUR

OPERATION TOTALIZE

2 CANADIAN CORPS OPERATIONS ASTRIDE THE ROAD
CAEN-FALAISE 7-8 AUGUST 1944

The Naval & Military Press Ltd

Published by

The Naval & Military Press Ltd
Unit 5 Riverside, Brambleside
Bellbrook Industrial Estate
Uckfield, East Sussex
TN22 1QQ England

Tel: +44 (0)1825 749494

www.naval-military-press.com
www.nmarchive.com

In reprinting in facsimile from the original, any imperfections are inevitably reproduced and the quality may fall short of modern type and cartographic standards.

BATTLEFIELD TOURS

Headquarters, British Army of the Rhine, compiled Battlefield Tours during 1947, covering the following operations in the Campaign in North-West EUROPE (June 1944—May 1945).

Name of Operation	Action covered
GOODWOOD	Operations of 8 Corps East of the River ORNE (NORMANDY) 18–22 July 1944, with particular reference to 11th Armoured Division.
BLUECOAT	Operations of 8 Corps South of CAUMONT (NORMANDY) 30–31 July 1944, with particular reference to 15th (Scottish) Infantry Division.
TOTALIZE	Operations of 2 Canadian Corps astride the road CAEN-FALAISE (NORMANDY) 7–8 August 1944, with particular reference to 51st (Highland) Infantry Division.
NEPTUNE	Assault crossing of the river SEINE by 43rd (Wessex) Infantry Division 25–28 August 1944.
VERITABLE	Operations of 30 Corps between the Rivers MAAS and RHINE 8–10 February 1945, with particular reference to 15th (Scottish) Infantry Division.
PLUNDER	Assault crossing of the River RHINE by 12 Corps 24–25 March 1945, with particular reference to 15th (Scottish) Infantry Division.
VARSITY	Airborne operations of XVIII United States Corps (Airborne) in support of the crossing of the River RHINE 24–25 March 1945, with particular reference to 6th British Airborne Division.

A similar book was written on each of these operations, of which four hundred copies were printed, one hundred of these containing notes for Directing Staff. A further fifty Directing Staff copies and two hundred and fifty Spectator's copies have been distributed to various libraries, original speakers and certain other individuals.

Directorate of Military Training, War Office, or Headquarters British Army of the Rhine, can supply information as to where these books are kept.

FOREWORD

By

Lieutenant General Sir Richard L. McCREERY, KCB, KBE, DSO, MC
General Officer Commanding-in-Chief The British Army of the Rhine

In June 1947, British Army of the Rhine conducted a battlefield tour in NORMANDY with the dual purpose of studying four operations with the assistance of officers who had been present in these battles and of recording the information obtained for the benefit of future students. The results are set out in these books, which have been arranged with a view to facilitating the conduct of future tours.

We were fortunate in collecting on the tour many officers who commanded formations and units carrying out these operations, before time had blurred their memories of events. Consequently, their personal accounts of these battles are accurate and introduce, as far as this is possible, the atmosphere of war.

When a battlefield is revisited at a later date, in full possession of all the information and with a clear picture of the situation, it is comparatively easy to say what should have been done. In war, the situation is rarely clear, the information is never complete and actions must be considered in the light of the situation as it was known to the commanders at the time. The view of the commander on the spot in each of the various situations is supplied in the personal accounts.

These past operations must be studied with an eye to the future if full benefit is to be derived from them. In studying the problems, constant consideration must be given to the conditions which are likely to be met and the material and equipment which is likely to be available in the next war. It is certain, however, that whatever form land warfare may take in the future, certain fundamental factors which constantly stand out in these operations, such as morale, training, junior leadership, and surprise, will retain their pre-eminent importance.

R. L. McCreery,
Lieutenant General

THE OBJECT OF THE BOOK

The Book describes the operations of 2 Canadian Corps astride the road CAEN-FALAISE on 7/8 August 1944. It is especially concerned with the air plan and the part played by 51st Highland Division with particular reference to :–

(a) The use of armoured personnel carriers

(b) Maintenance of direction during a night advance.

It forms the necessary background to a detailed study of the battle carried out on the ground.

This edition cancels the one issued in June 1947.

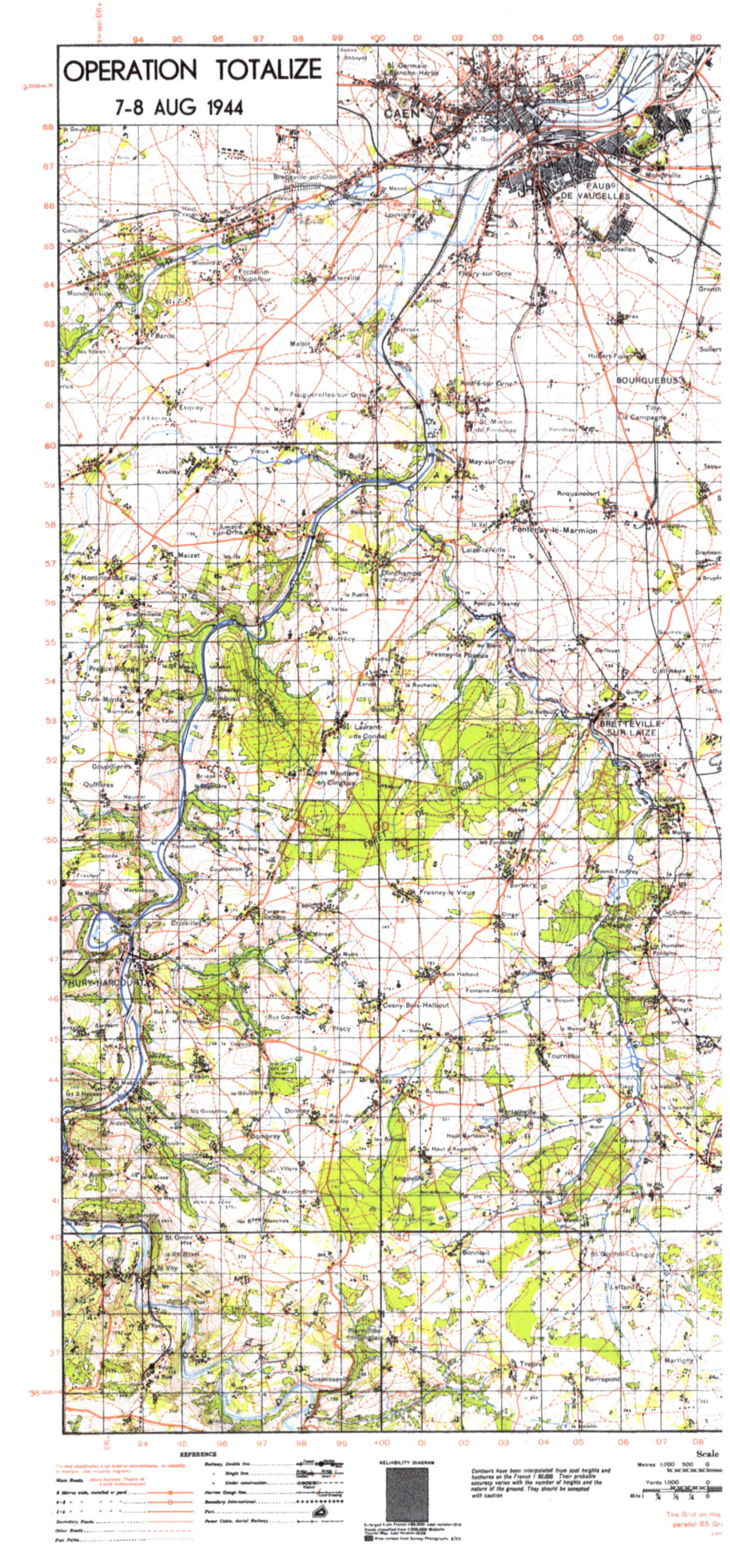

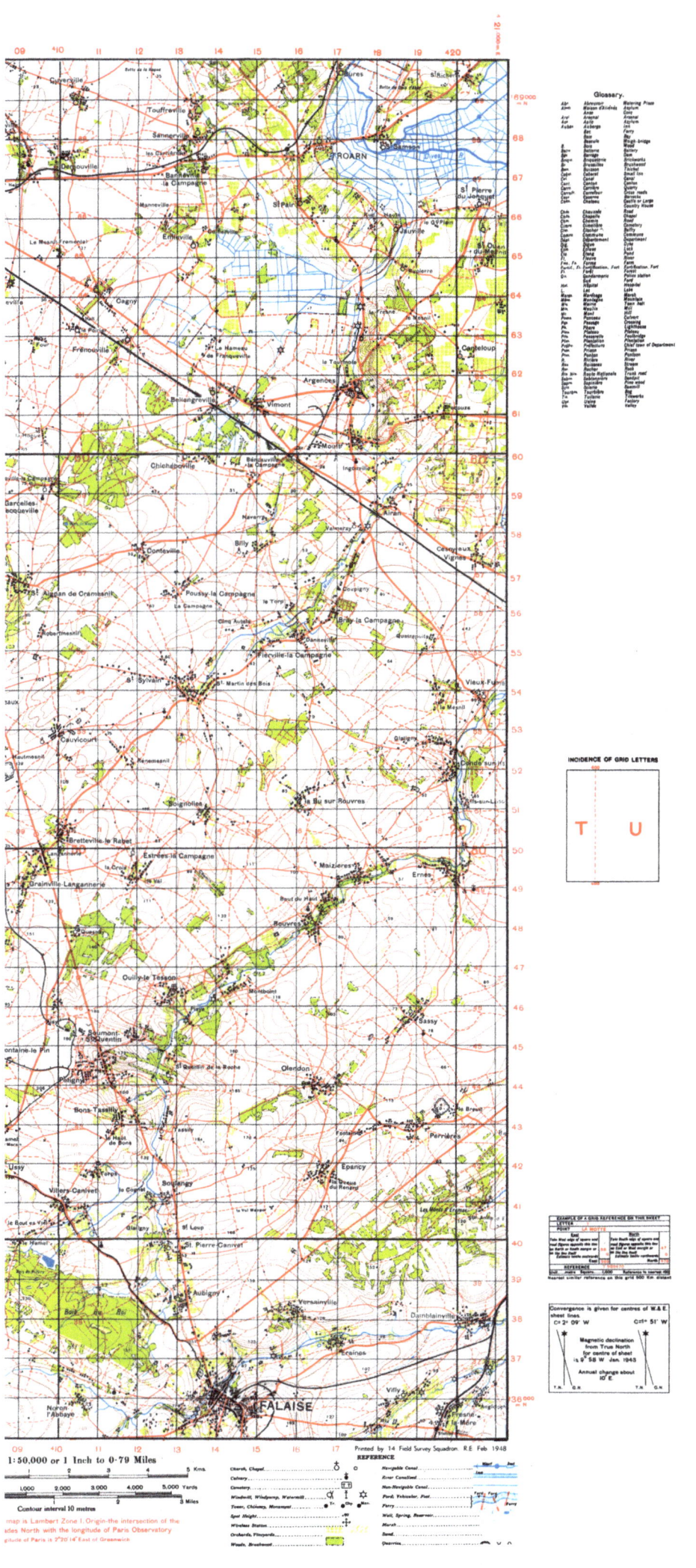

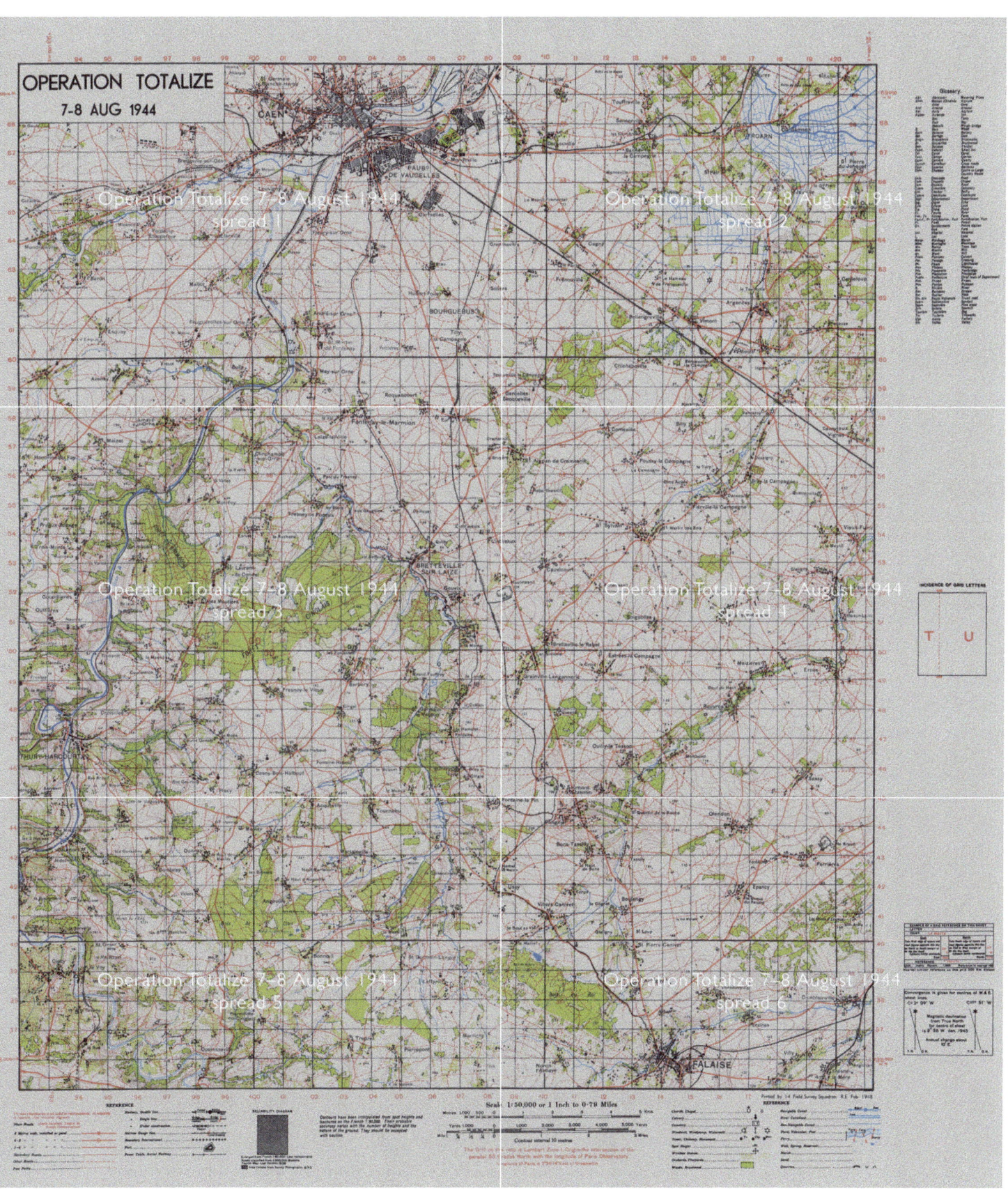

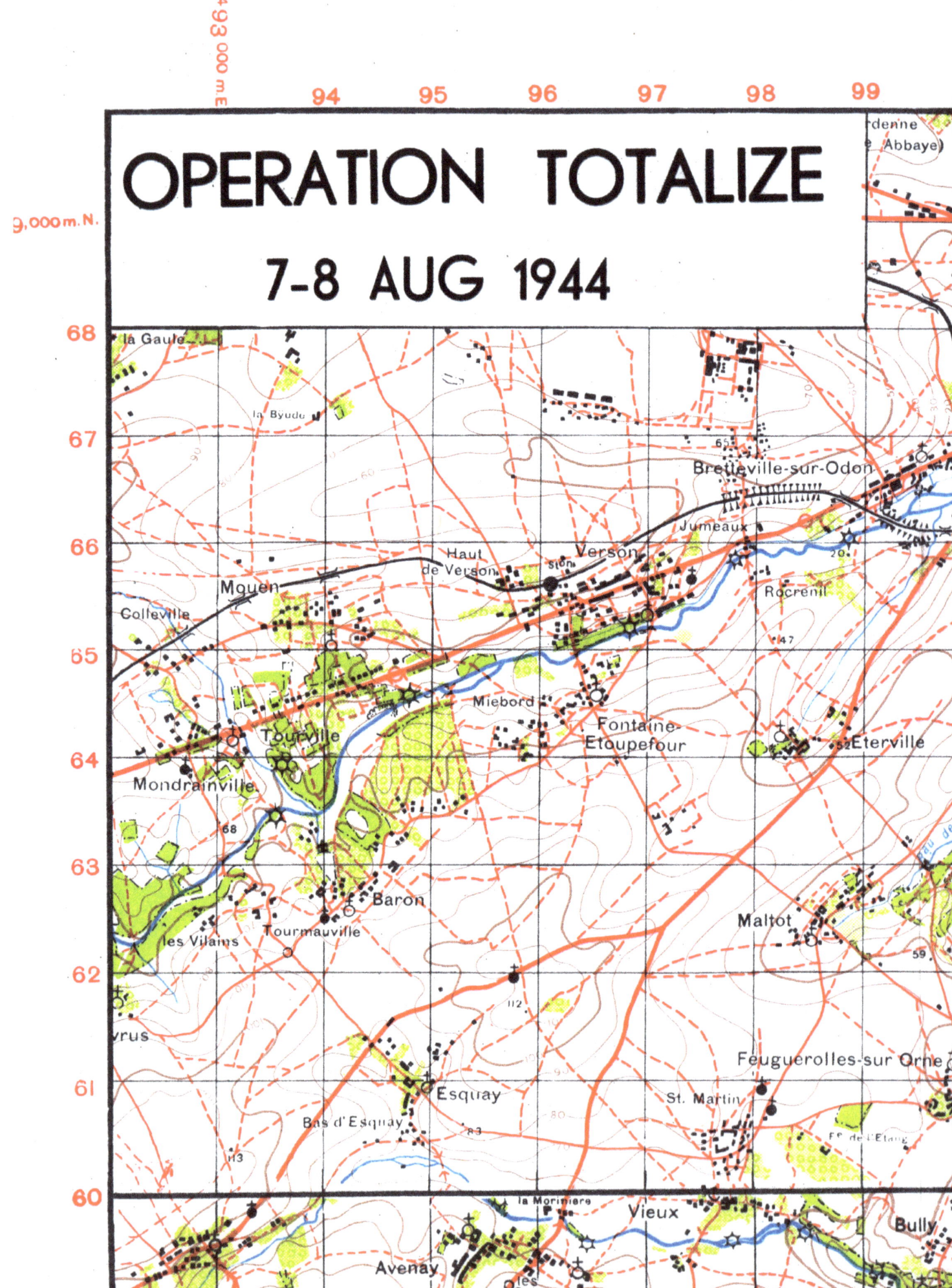

Operation Totalize 7–8 August 1944 — spread 1

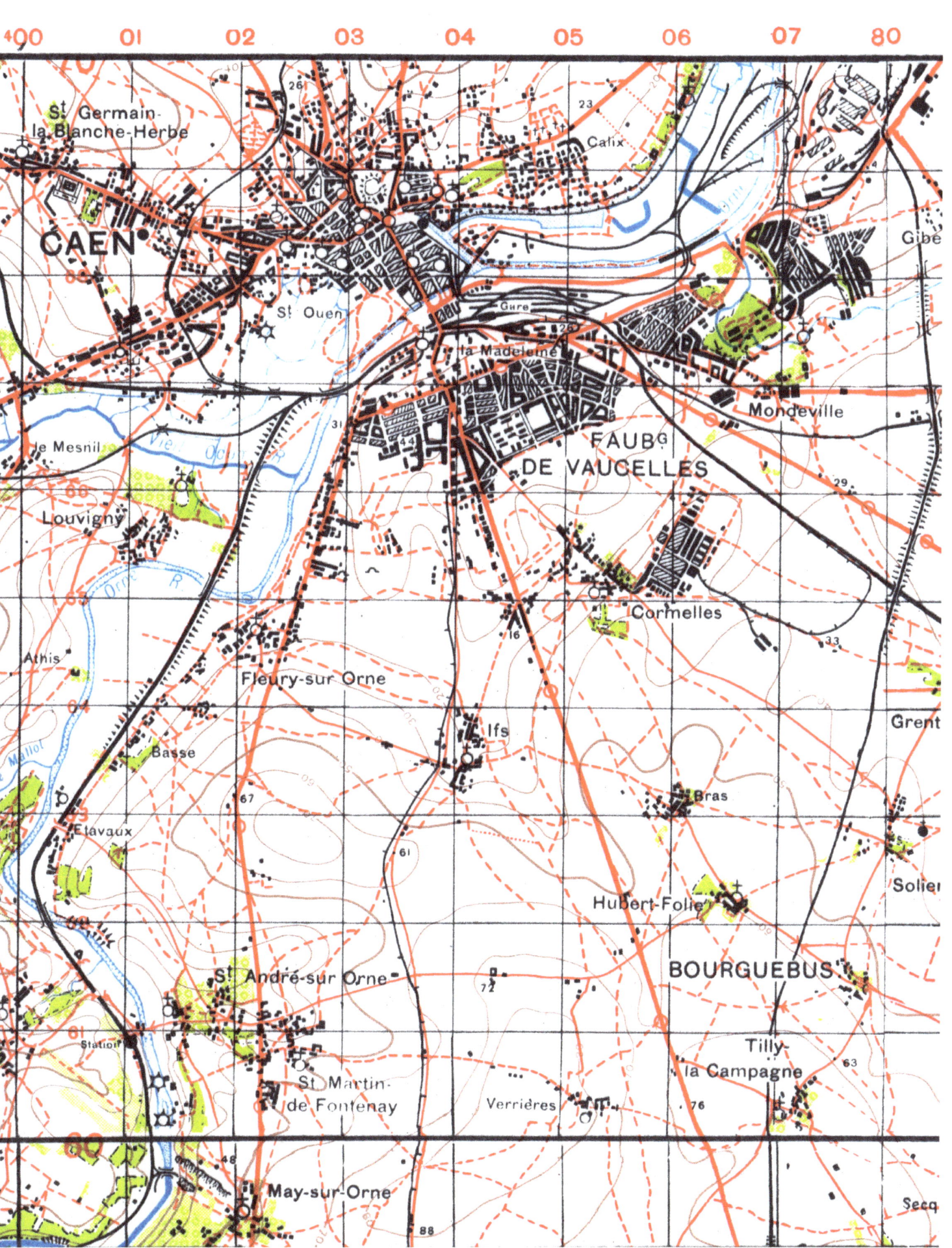

Operation Totalize 7–8 August 1944 — spread 2

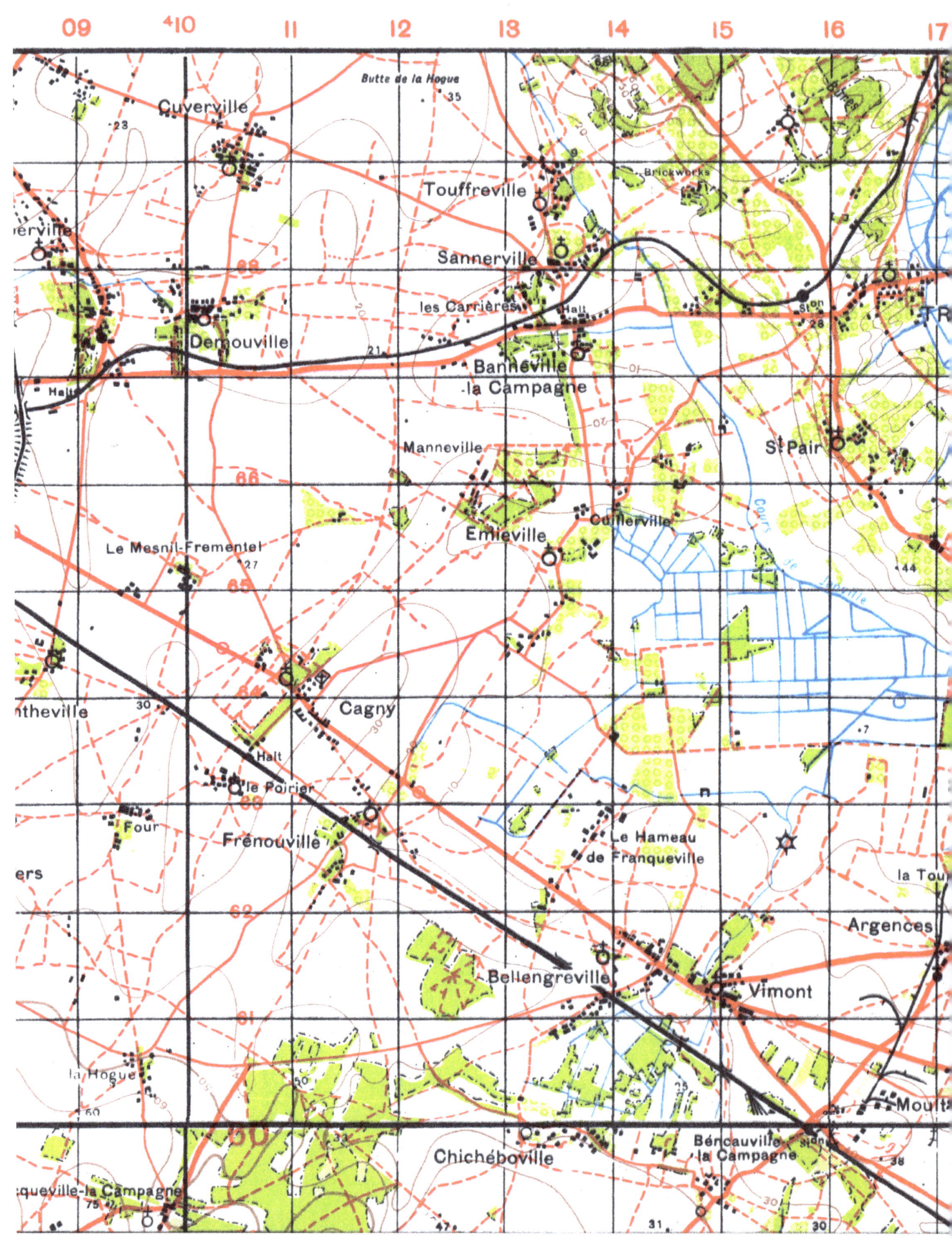

Operation Totalize 7–8 August 1944 — spread 2

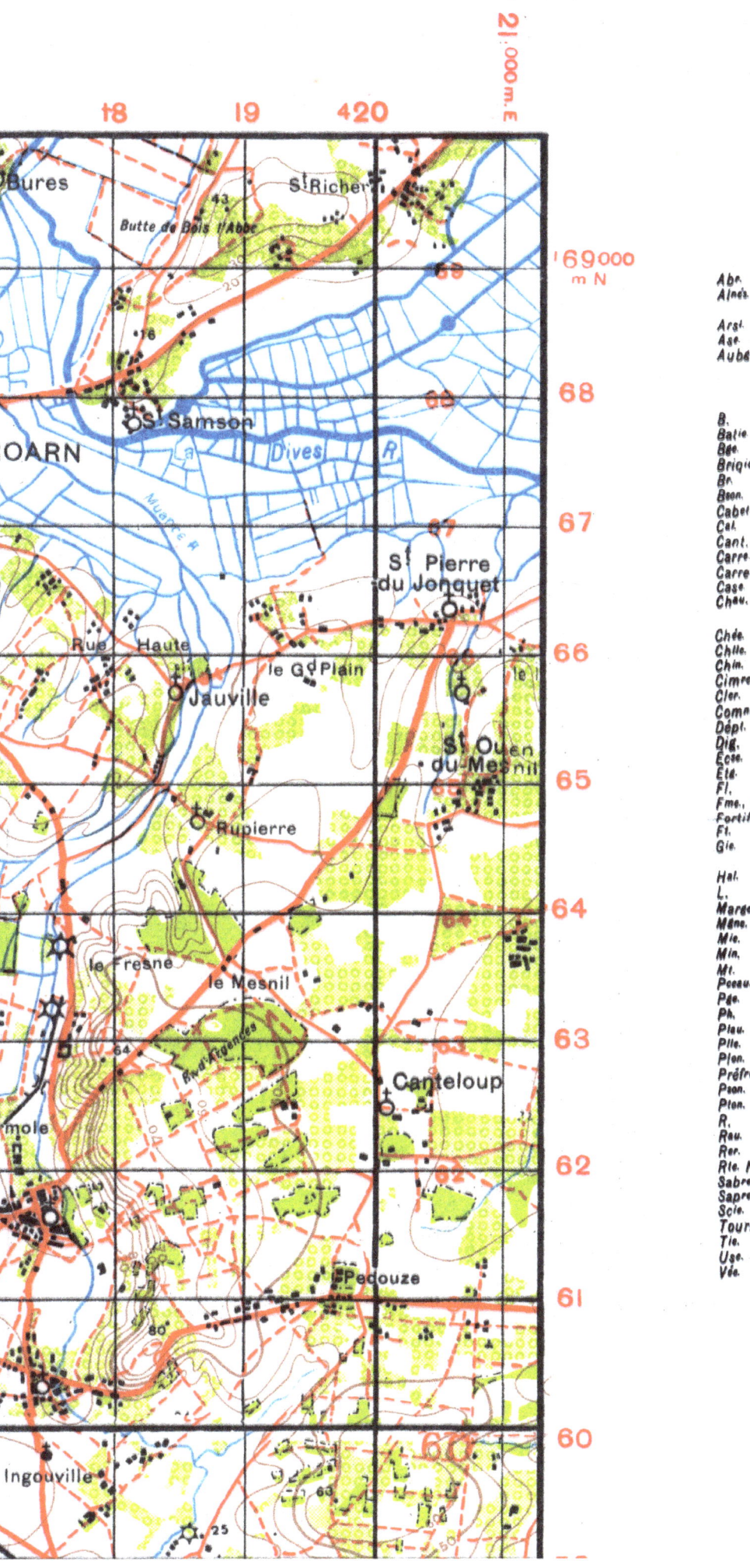

Glossary.

Abr.	Abreuvoir	Watering Place
Alnés.	Maison d'Aliénés	Asylum
	Anse	Cove
Arsl.	Arsenal	Arsenal
Ase.	Asile	Asylum
Aubge.	Auberge	Inn
	Bac	Ferry
	Baie	Bay
	Bascule	Weigh-bridge
B.	Bois	Wood
Batie.	Batterie	Battery
Bge.	Barrage	Dam
Briqie.	Briqueterie	Brickworks
Br.	Brusailles	Brushwood
Bson.	Buisson	Thicket
Cabet.	Cabaret	Small Inn
Cal.	Canal	Canal
Cant.	Canton	Canton
Carre.	Carrière	Quarry
Carrefr.	Carrefour	Cross roads
Case.	Caserne	Barracks
Chau.	Chateau	Castle or Large Country House
Chée.	Chaussée	Road
Chlle.	Chapelle	Chapel
Chin.	Chemin	Road
Cimre.	Cimetière	Cemetery
Cler.	Clocher	Belfry
Comne.	Commune	Commune
Dépt.	Département	Department
Dig.	Digue	Dyke
Ecse.	Ecluse	Lock
Etg.	Etang	Pond
Fl.	Fleuve	River
Fme., Fe.	Ferme	Farm
Fortif., Ft.	Fortification, Fort	Fortification, Fort
Ft.	Forêt	Forest
Gie.	Gendarmerie	Police station
	Gué	Ford
Hal.	Hôpital	Hospital
L.	Lac	Lake
Marge.	Marécage	Marsh
Mne.	Montagne	Mountain
Mie.	Mairie	Town hall
Min.	Moulin	Mill
Mt.	Mont	Hill
Poeau.	Ponceau	Culvert
Pge.	Passage	Crossing
Ph.	Phare	Lighthouse
Plau.	Plateau	Plateau
Plle.	Passerelle	Footbridge
Pton.	Plantation	Plantation
Préfre.	Préfecture	Chief town of Department
Pson.	Prison	Prison
Pton.	Ponton	Pontoon
R.	Rivière	River
Rau.	Ruisseau	Stream
Rer.	Rocher	Rock
Rte. Nle.	Route Nationale	Trunk road
Sabre.	Sablonnière	Sandpit
Sapre.	Sapinière	Pine wood
Scie.	Scierie	Sawmill
Tourbre.	Tourbière	Bog
Tle.	Tuilerie	Tileworks
Use.	Usine	Factory
Vée.	Vallée	Valley

Operation Totalize 7–8 August 1944 — spread 3

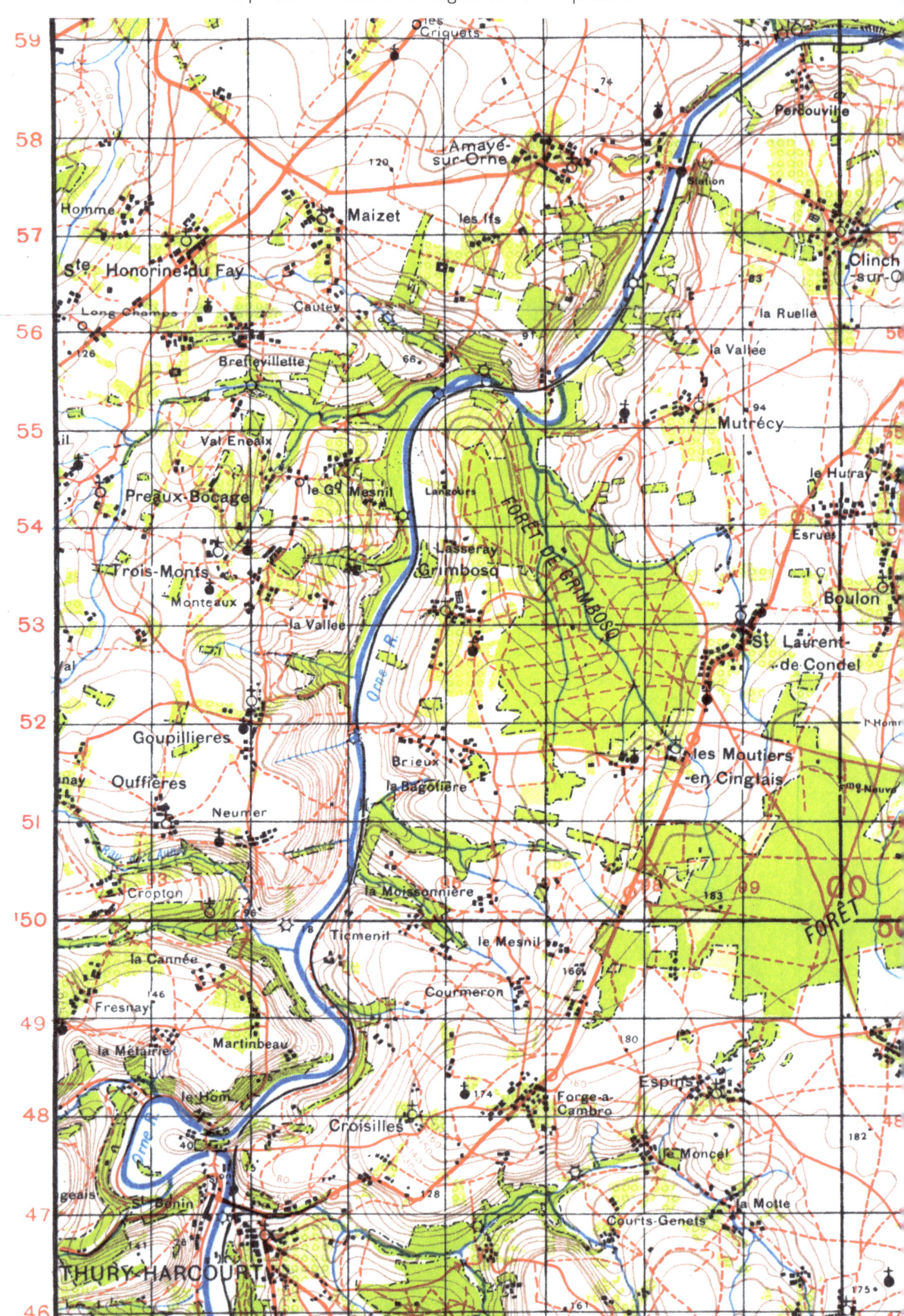

Operation Totalize 7–8 August 1944 — spread 3

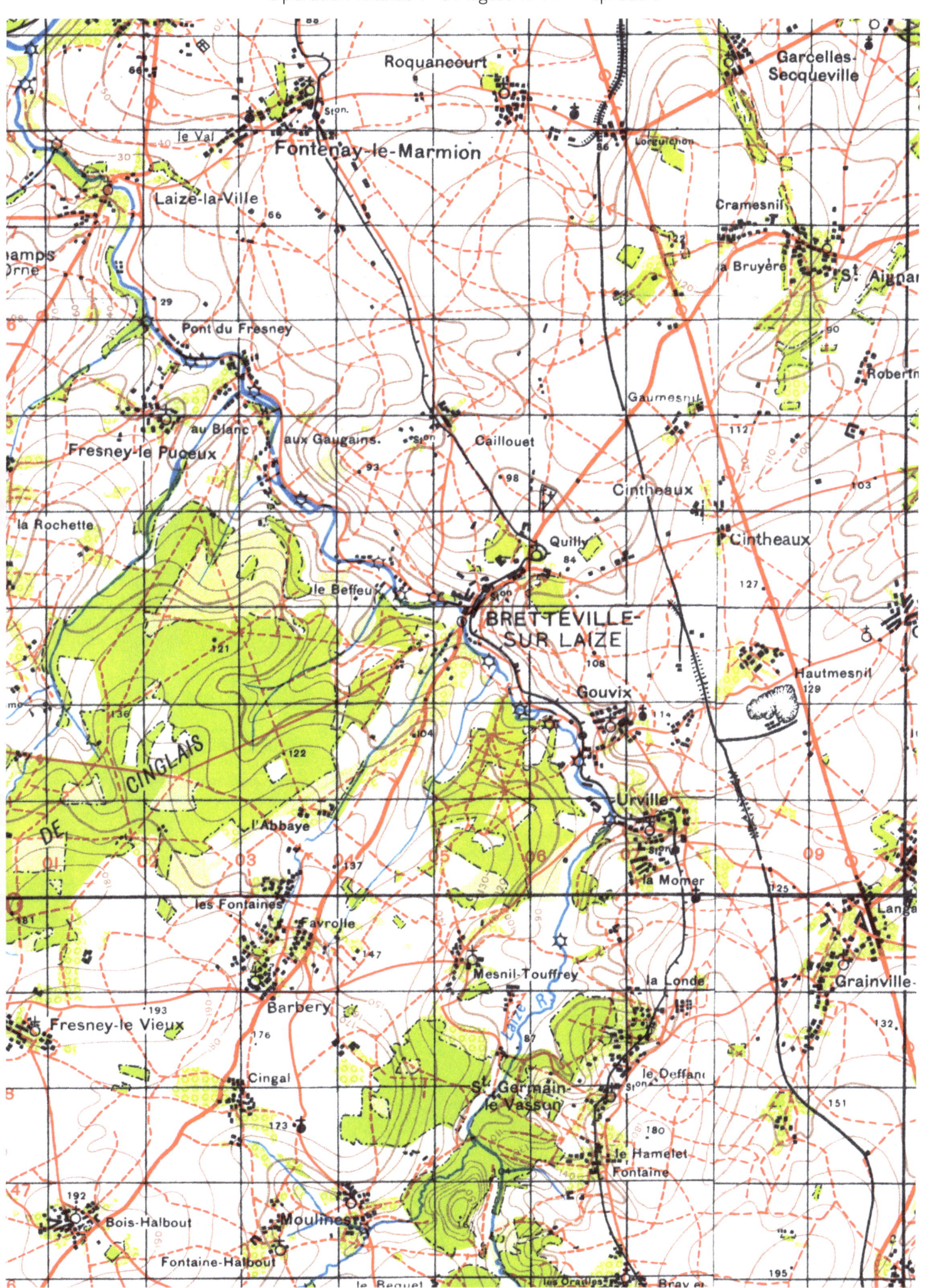

Operation Totalize 7–8 August 1944 — spread 4

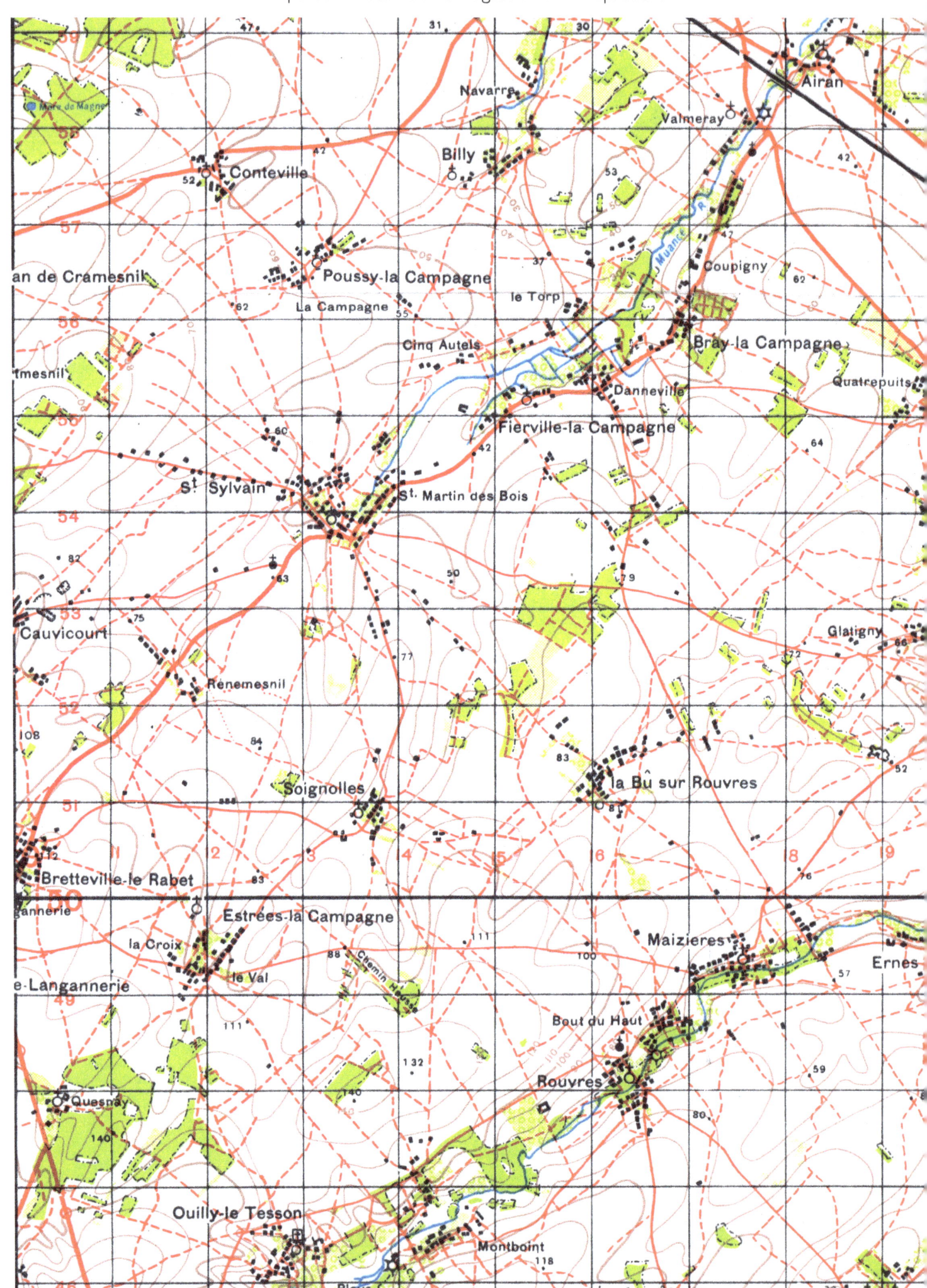

Operation Totalize 7–8 August 1944 — spread 4

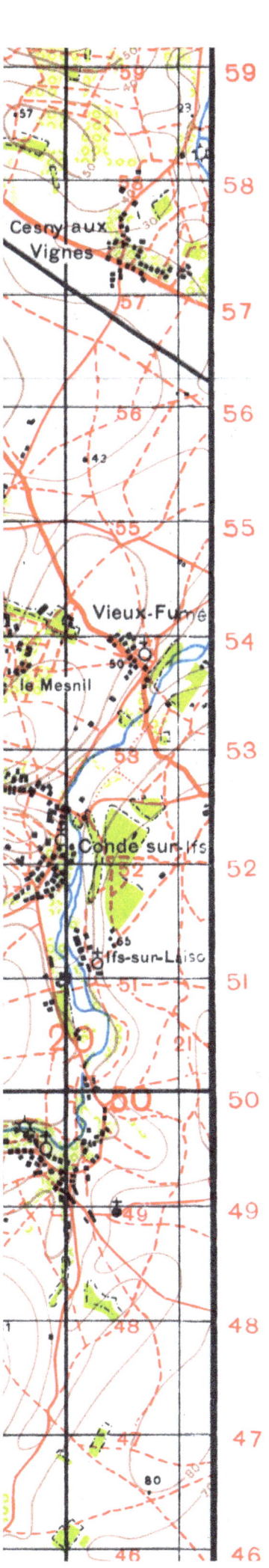

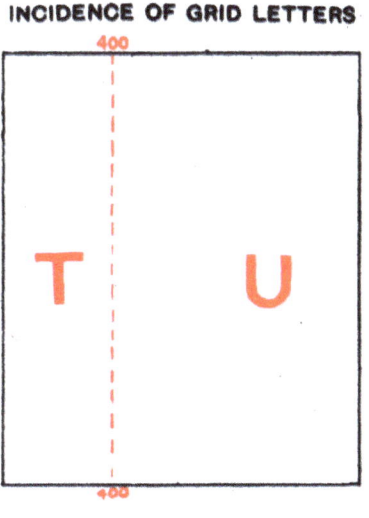

INCIDENCE OF GRID LETTERS

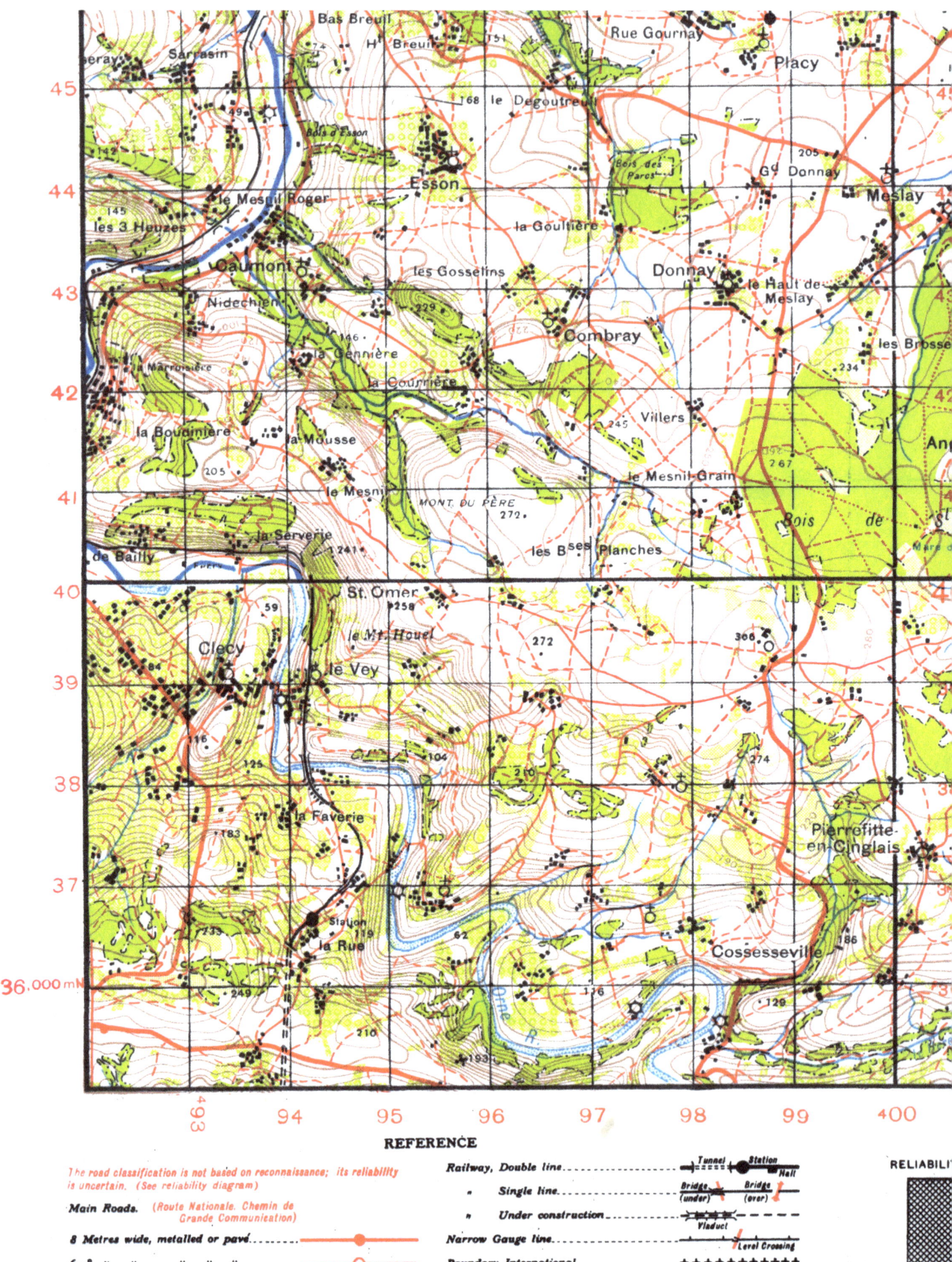

Operation Totalize 7–8 August 1944 — spread 5

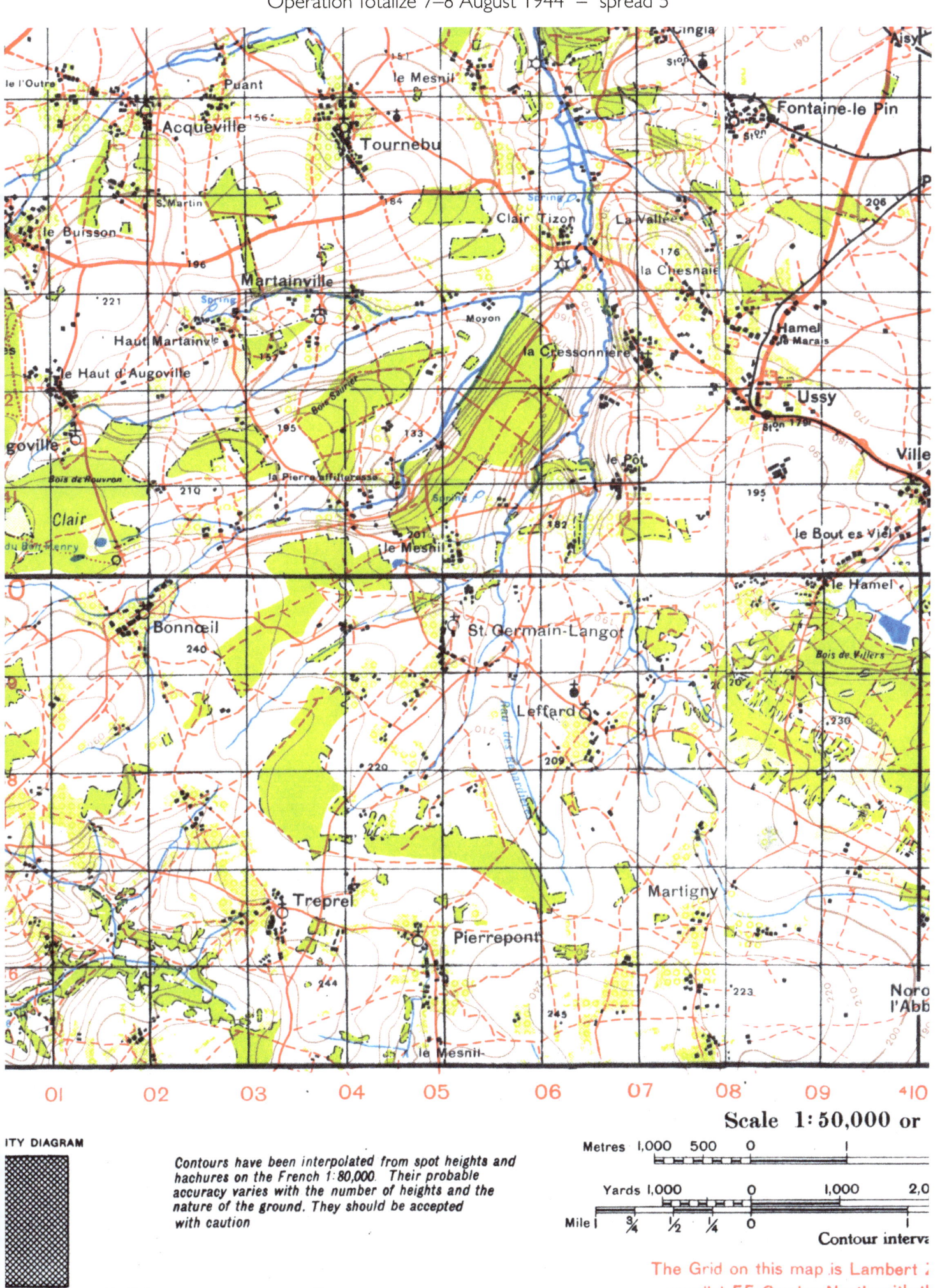

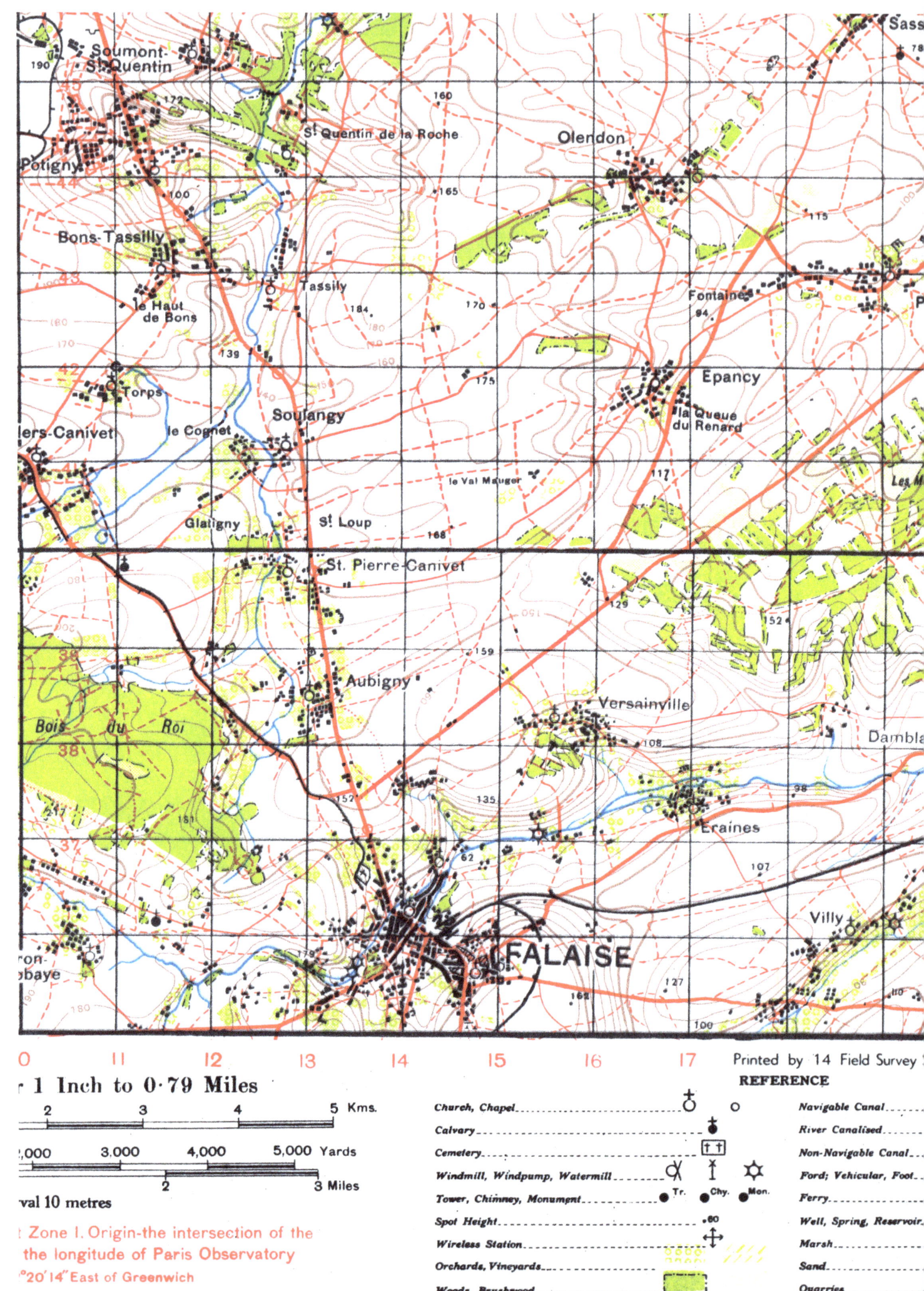

Operation Totalize 7–8 August 1944 — spread 6

Operation Totalize 7–8 August 1944 — spread 6

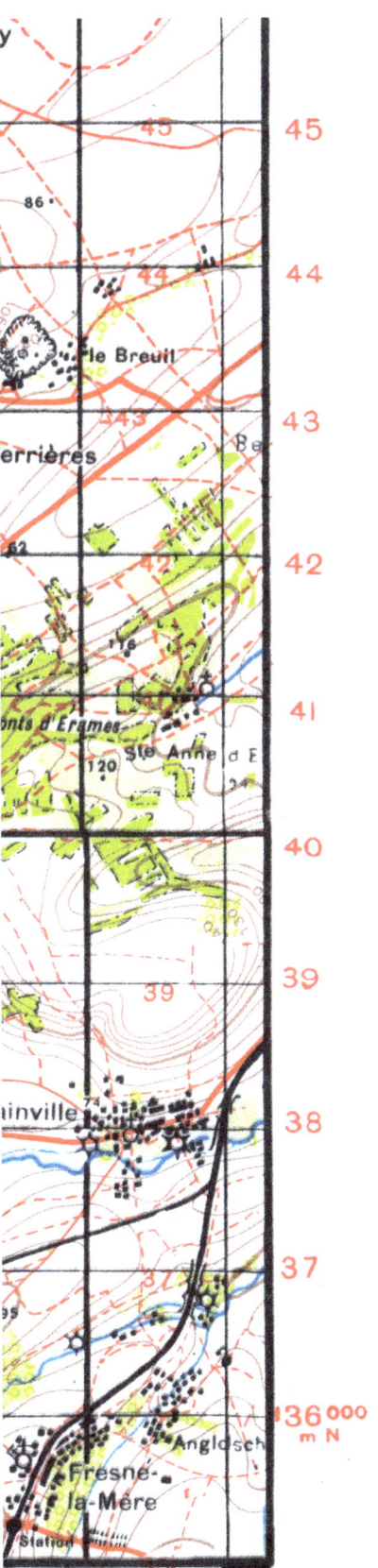

Squadron. R.E. Feb 1948

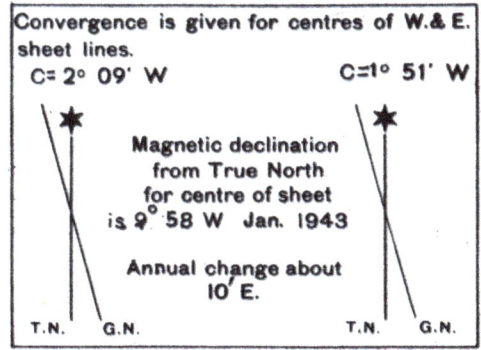

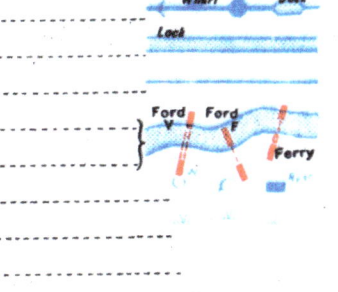

CONTENTS

PART I—PLANNING THE OPERATION

		Page
SECTION I.	Introduction	1
SECTION II.	Topography	3
SECTION III.	The Enemy	5
SECTION IV.	Planning Operation TOTALIZE	9
	A. Appreciation by Corps Commander	9
	B. Flank Formations	10
	C. The Corps Plan	10
	D. The Air Plan	12
	E. Divisional Outline Plans	13
SECTION V.	Training	15
SECTION VI.	Final Assembly	17

PART II—ACCOUNT OF THE BATTLE

SECTION I.	Account of the Night Attack 7/8 August	21
SECTION II.	Attack on Areas by-passed by Armoured Columns	23
SECTION III.	Daylight Operations 8 August	25
SECTION IV.	A Short Account of PHASE II	27

PART III—PERSONAL ACCOUNTS OF ACTIONS FOR STUDY

SECTION I.	Extracts from Introductory Lecture	31
SECTION II.	Itinerary	35
SECTION III.	Personal Accounts	37
SECTION IV.	The Problem	59
SECTION V.	Major Lessons from the Battlefield Tour	61
SECTION VI.	Notes for the guidance of Conducting Officers	63

MAPS

PART I

		Facing page
No. 1.	Situation in Normandy before Operation TOTALIZE	1
No. 2.	Enemy situation mid-July 1944	5
No. 3.	Enemy situation 22 July 1944	5
No. 4.	Enemy situation 7 August 1944	7
No. 5.	Corps Plan	9
No. 6.	Fire Plan PHASE I	11
No. 7.	Air Plan	13

PART II

No. 8.	Situation at first light 8 August 1944	23
No. 9.	Situation at last light 8 August 1944	26

ix

PART III

No. 10.	Battlefield Tour operation TOTALIZE	35
	1 : 50,000 Map of General Area	*End pocket*

APPENDICES

		Page
A.	Order of Battle 2 Cdn Corps	67
B.	Equipment and Organisation (Allied and German)	71
C.	List of Reference Maps	73
D.	2 Cdn Corps Operation Instruction No. 4	73
E.	Addendum to 2 Cdn Corps Operational Instruction No. 4	79
F.	2 Cdn Div Operation Order No. 2 (less trace 'P')	81
G.	51 (H) Div Operation Order No. 6	85
H.	Addendum No. 1 to 51 (H) Div Operation Order No. 6	89
J.	Addendum No. 2 to 51 (H) Div Operation Order No. 6	91
K.	RCA 2 Cdn Corps Operation Instruction No. 5	93
L.	Addendum to RCA 2 Cdn Corps Operation Instruction No. 5	99
M.	Account by Brigadefuehrer KURT MEYER, Commander 12 SS Pz Div	101

PHOTOGRAPHS

Allied Equipment

No. 1. A Sherman Vc with 17 pr gun
No. 2. An AVRE
No. 3. A Crocodile
No. 4. A Flail
No. 5. Priest
No. 6. Priest
No. 7. An M. 10

German Equipment

No. 8. An 88 mm dual purpose gun
No. 9. A "Tiger" Tank
No. 10. A "Panther" Tank

Following Page 103

PART I

Planning the Operation

SECTION I

INTRODUCTION

The Allied break-out operation from the NORMANDY beach-head was launched on 25 July 1944. Second Army, following the offensive East of the ORNE, regrouped with great speed and it was found possible to commence the thrust Southwards from the CAUMONT area on 30 July. The main weight of the attack was developed by 8 and 30 Corps on a narrow front, and directed on VIRE and MOUNT PINCON. Meanwhile First United States Army continued its drive to the foot of the COTENTIN peninsula with Eastern thrusts in conformity.

The enemy was unable to reform his Left flank. As the American armour approached AVRANCHES, he attempted to hold a hinge between PERCY and TESSY, but was frustrated by First United States Army pressure and by the Second Army attack towards VIRE. By 4 August, American forces were on the general line LANDIVY-MORTAIN-FORET DE SEVER and the Northern outskirts of VIRE, ready to advance East towards ARGENTAN. Second Army had by this time joined the Americans at VIRE thence MONTCHAMP-ONDEFONTAINE-VILLERS BOCAGE-EVRECY.

Field Marshal MONTGOMERY, in his book "NORMANDY to the BALTIC" states :—

"The general situation was now very good. We had broken out of the bridgehead and had destroyed the first hinge on which the enemy had tried to pivot. We were now pressing hard against the next "key rivet" of his line on the slopes of the PINCON massif. Meanwhile, the American drive was beginning to swing towards the East according to plan and at the same time Third United States Army had turned VIII United States Corps Westwards into BRITTANY.

The time had now come to deliver the major attack towards FALAISE, which had so long been the fundamental aim of our policy on the Eastern flank. I planned that the Canadians should drive South East from CAEN to gain as much ground as possible in the direction of FALAISE, in order to get behind the enemy forces facing Second Army, and to continue the process of wearing down the enemy formations in the sector. I envisaged this operation as a prelude to subsequent exploitation of success.

My orders of 4 August provided for the First Canadian Army attack to be launched as quickly as possible. Meanwhile, Second British Army was to continue pivoting on 12 Corps, swinging down towards THURY HARCOURT, CONDE and FLERS; subsequent operations were to be developed towards ARGENTAN. I provided that the Northern flank of Twelfth United States Army Group should operate on the axis DOMFRONT-ALENCON.

I was continuing with my broad strategy of swinging the Right flank round towards PARIS, so as to force the enemy back against the SEINE. Plans were under preparation for the use of airborne forces in advance of the American columns in order to hasten the closure of the ORLEANS gap."

By 7 August, the German counter attack against the American VII Corps at MORTAIN was taking place. Elsewhere considerable advances had been made. American forces were in MAYENNE, twenty miles to the South of DOMFRONT, whilst in the North VIRE had been captured. On Second British Army front, 30 Corps tanks had reached the top of MONT PINCON and 12 Corps had secured a small bridgehead over the River ORNE to the North of THURY HARCOURT.

This was the situation prior to the attack by 2 Cdn Corps astride the road CAEN-FALAISE on 7/8 August (Operation TOTALIZE). This Corps had been fighting in the CAEN sector since it was first committed on 11 July. It had taken part in the bitter fighting during Operation GOODWOOD (18-21 July) and thereafter had carried out one major and a number of minor actions, large scale patrolling and a continuous fire fight in order to retain strong enemy forces East of the ORNE. By 7 August, the line of forward defended localities was ST ANDRE SUR ORNE-BOURGUEBUS, with 1 Corps, on the Left, continuing the line through FRENOUVILLE-EMIEVILLE and thence Northwards to the sea.

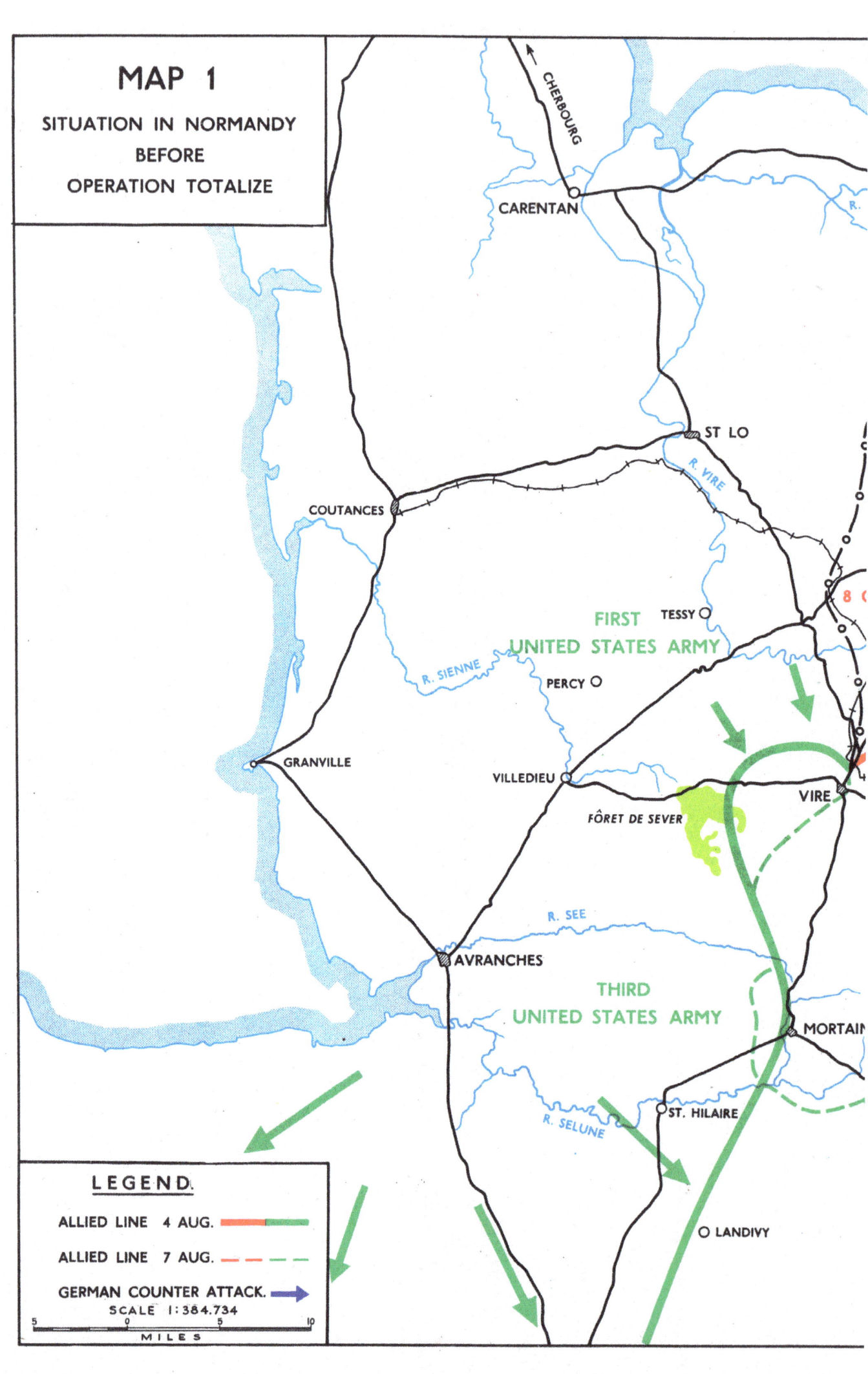

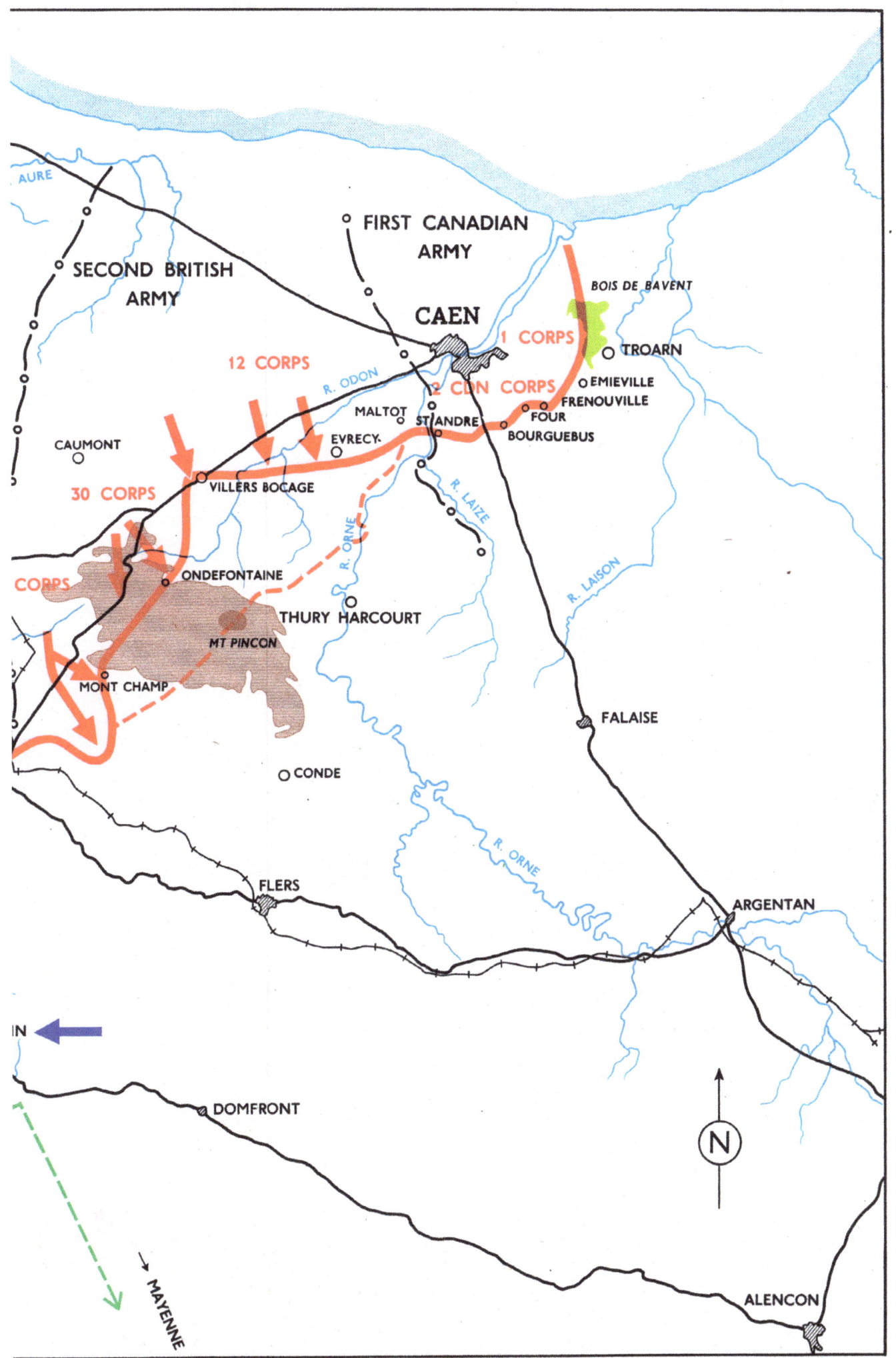

SECTION II

TOPOGRAPHY

For the first five miles after leaving the Southern outskirts of CAEN, the countryside is completely open arable land. The FALAISE road climbs without a curve in a succession of gentle slopes to Point 122. The acres of waving corn are only broken by the walled-in Norman villages with their surrounding orchards, and the occasional hedgerow and belt of trees lining the by-roads.

Just beneath the first intermediate crest lies the village of IFS, whilst East of the main road the tall trees of HUBERT FOLIE make an unmistakable landmark. From the top of this crest, the ground rises more gradually and in the distance the mine tower at ROQUANCOURT, point 122, LORGUICHON Wood, and the trees surrounding GARCELLES SECQUEVILLE can be seen. To the West of the road is the village of VERRIERES lying on the bare Northern slopes of a flat topped ridge. From the top of this ridge, which runs in a South Westerly direction almost to the River ORNE, a view is obtained of some three miles of open countryside bounded by Point 122 on the East and the wooded area above BRETTEVILLE SUR LAIZE to the South.

At Point 122, the dominating feature astride the main road, a magnificient view of the ground to the North and West can be obtained. The bare ridge above VERRIERES is very striking with the villages of FONTENAY LE MARMION and ROQUANCOURT beneath it. Further away lies CAEN. To the East and North East, between ST AIGNAN DE CRAMESNIL, GARCELLES SECQUEVILLE and SECQUEVILLE LA CAMPAGNE, woods and thick hedges surround the villages and small fields. From the village of ST AIGNAN, the ground slopes down to the South East to the river MUANCE.

Further South, the ground is more varied. Long stretches of open countryside are interspersed with wooded areas, which in the main are found in the river valleys and near the villages. From the quarry at HAUTMESNIL, the best viewpoint, the ground falls and then rises to a prominent ridge on which are the mine buildings at AISY, Points 206 and 195. To the East of the road, the QUESNAY wood, with the belt of trees at OLENDON above it on the skyline, and Point 140 can be clearly seen.

Although this ground provides excellent tank going and has few obstacles apart from the railway, it favours the defence much more than the attack. The villages are strongly built and the woods and hedges which surround them and the outlying farm buildings, provide excellent positions for anti-tank weapons sited to cover the open ground.

SECTION III

THE ENEMY

General situation mid-July 1944

In order to obtain an accurate picture of the German defences facing 2 Cdn Corps and the many moves of formations which took place prior to Operation TOTALIZE, it is necessary to give a brief narrative of events from the middle of July.

The front from MALTOT to the West was held by 2 SS Pz Corps with 10 SS Pz Div on the Left of the German front and 9 SS Pz Div on its Right. Astride the River ORNE as far as the road CAEN-VIMONT was 272 Inf Div of 1 SS Pz Corps, which had both 1 SS Pz Div and 12 SS Pz Div in reserve. Further North from the VIMONT road to the mouth of the River ORNE was 86 Corps. This front was held by 16 GAF Div, 346 Inf Div centre and 711 Inf Div in the North. Positioned in rear of the weakened 16 GAF Div, about CAGNY and VIMONT, was 21 Pz Div on loan to 86 Corps.

In brief there were three reasons for the presence of a large proportion of German armour in this sector. First, the High Command attached the greatest importance to this Northern hinge. Should the Allies gain ground in the West, the defensive line must pivot on CAEN and the River ORNE. Secondly, repeated thrusts by Second Army, designed to hold the German armour in this area, had produced the required result. The enemy reacted strongly every time and had been forced to plug the holes with Panzer troops who had taken over a sector of the front, or who were retained at immediate call for this purpose. Thirdly, the ground East of the River ORNE and in particular between CAEN, VIMONT, FALAISE and BRETTEVILLE SUR LAIZE, was open rolling country eminently suitable for the employment of tanks.

Colonel General SEPP DIETRICH, Commander 1 SS Pz Corps, appreciated that sooner or later a series of Allied attacks would be launched against FALAISE. He therefore ordered three defence lines to be prepared covering the approaches to this town. The work was to be done by the two SS divisions in reserve and all available men from 21 Pz Div. The first line ran from ST ANDRE SUR ORNE through TILLY LA CAMPAGNE to LA HOGUE, and crossed the road CAEN-VIMONT halfway between the latter town and CAGNY. The second was some three thousand yards further back and included Point 122, the dominating feature on the FALAISE road, and VIMONT. The third line ran from BRETTEVILLE SUR LAIZE to CAUVICOURT, North of ST SYLVAIN and thence followed the course of the River MUANCE.

Events from 18 July to 7 August 1944

Preparation of these defence lines was seriously interrupted by the 8 Corps attack East of the ORNE which started on 18 July. Both 1 SS and 12 SS Pz Divs were moved against this thrust, as were also some of the tanks from 2 SS Pz Corps. By 22 July 1 SS Pz Corps front had again stabilized and 272 Inf Div, with 503 Hy Tk Bn in support, now held from South of MALTOT to the road CAEN-FALAISE: further East came 1 SS Pz Div from the FALAISE road to LA HOGUE and on its Right 12 SS Pz Div linking up with 21 Pz Div South East of CAGNY. 16 GAF Div had been virtually destroyed in the above battle and had faded out of the picture.

It had been intended that 2 SS Pz Corps should take over up to the River ORNE but 9 SS Pz Div was unable to do this. The Panzer Divisions, and in particular 12 SS Pz Div, had for a long time been feeling the drain on their resources, resulting from the constant necessity of making counter-attacks against Allied thrusts and from wastage in the line. Very few reinforcements had been received and the infantry fighting strengths were down to 2,000 or less, whilst the number of runners in the tank regiments varied between a half and a third of the total. SEPP DIETRICH had complained many times of the shortages, and had suggested that the German Fifteenth Army in the PAS DE CALAIS could well afford to send some of its formations to NORMANDY.

However, far from being made up, the Panzer Corps were to suffer further losses during the next ten days. The sagging of the German Left flank during the period 25 July—4 August, in face of the onslaught by the First United States Army, left Field Marshal VON KLUGE with no alternative but to move additional armour West and thus further expose himself South of CAEN. Further, on 25 July the Canadian holding attack towards FALAISE inflicted severe casualties on 1 SS Pz Div and 272 Inf Div, so that it was found essential to move the latter with 503 Hy Tk Bn to a quieter part of the front. As a result, 10 SS Pz Div from 2 Pz Corps was sent to meet the Western threat, whilst 272 Inf Div came under command 86 Corps and occupied the line from EMIEVILLE to the South-West in place of 21 Pz Div. 9 SS Pz Div stretched East to fill the gap left by 272 Inf Div.

Following this came the Second Army attack South from CAUMONT, and the momentous decision from BERLIN to mount a large scale counter attack at MORTAIN. SEPP DIETRICH took over command of Fifth Panzer Army and its responsibility for the CAEN-FALAISE hinge, from General EBERBACH, who was required to lead the Panzer Gruppe in the West. The proposed

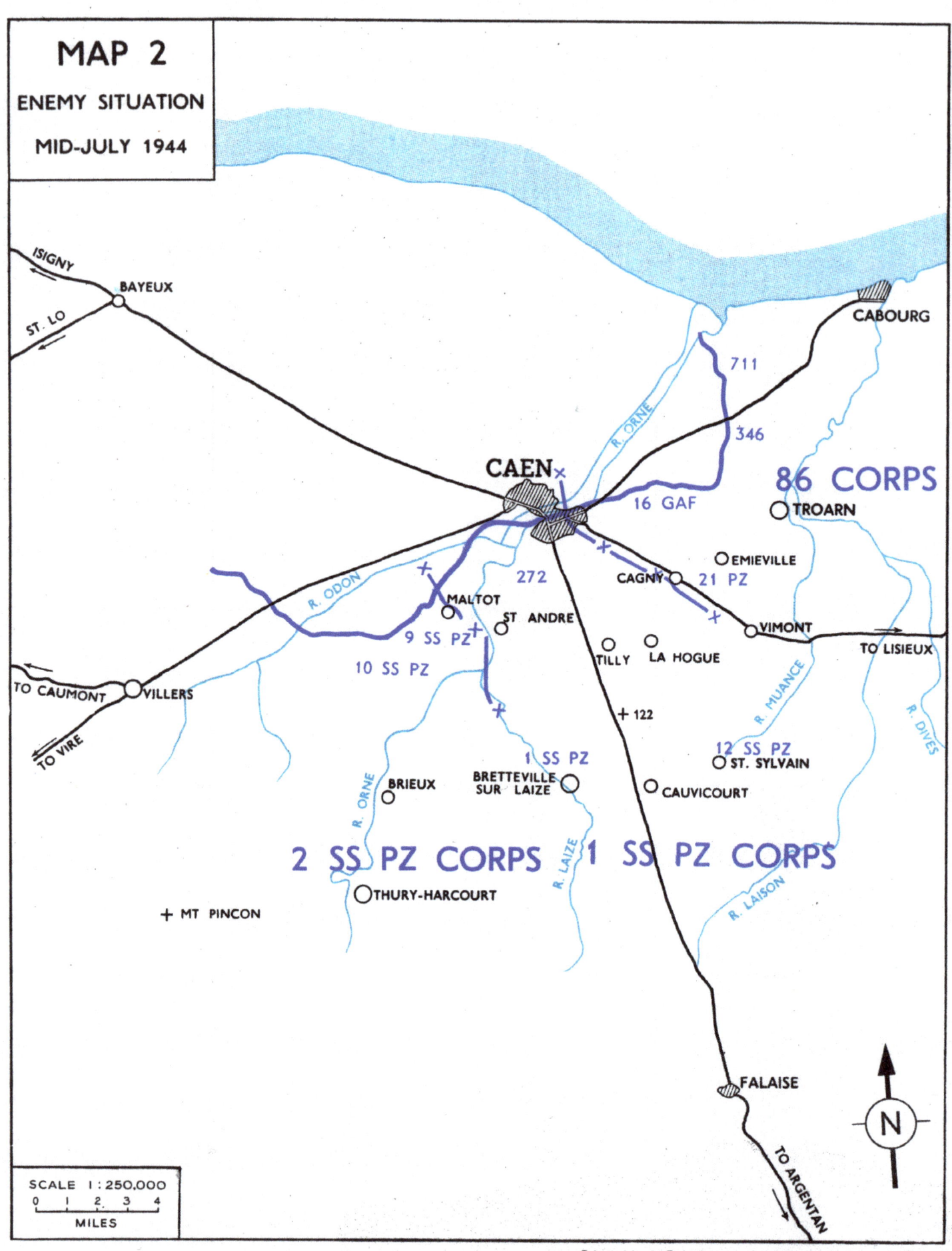

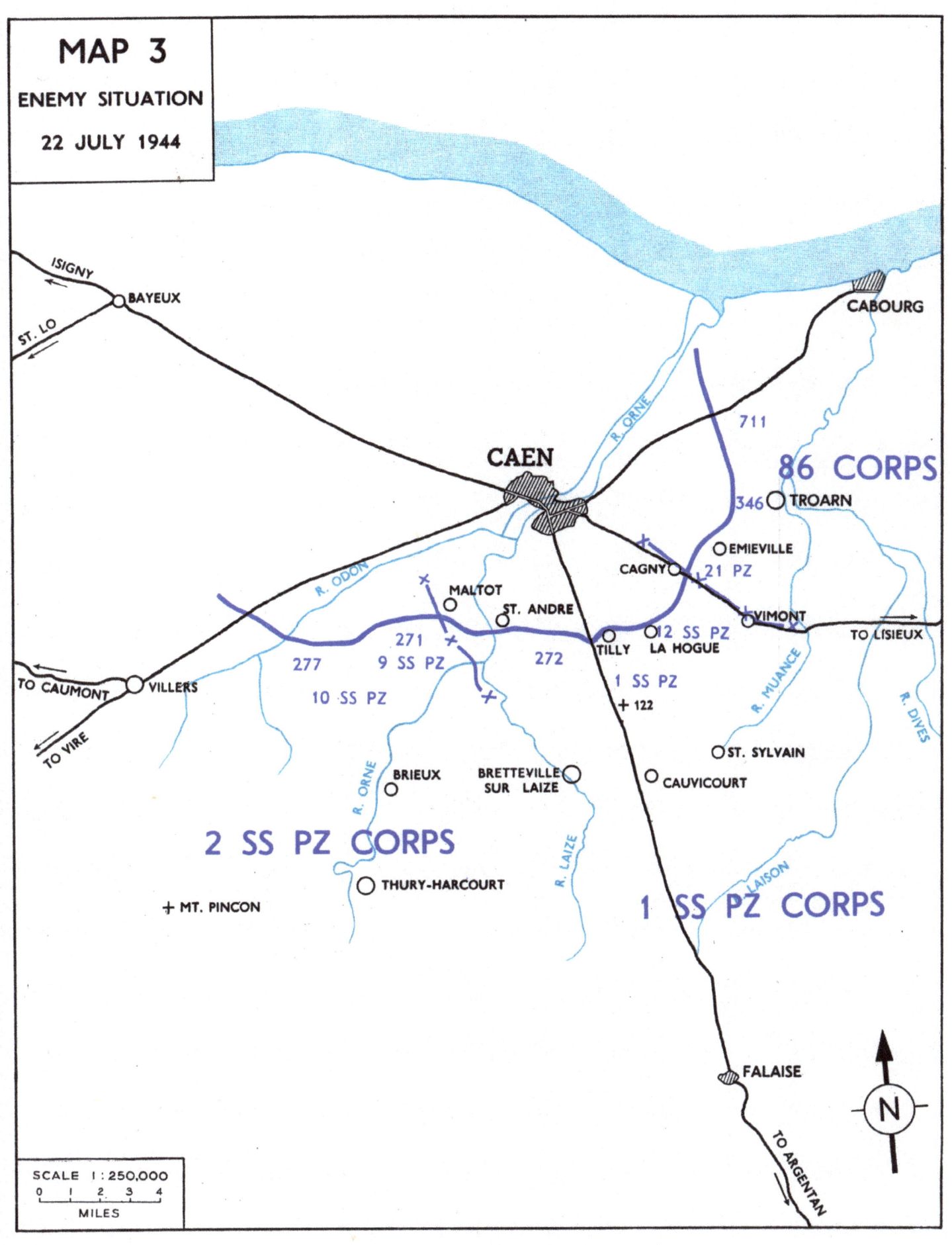

counter-attack raised a series of protests from almost every German commander and SEPP DIETRICH, in his capacity as Army Commander, claims he used every argument with VON KLUGE to convince him of the impracticability of such an operation. To each argument VON KLUGE had only one reply "It is Hitler's orders". Knowing that if the bulk of his armour was moved it would be impossible to hold FALAISE, SEPP DIETRICH says, "There is only one person to blame for this stupid, impossible operation—that madman Adolf Hitler."

In rapid succession 9 SS Pz Div and 21 Pz Div together with 503 Hy Tk Bn moved West. As a result the front was reorganized with 277 and 271 Inf Divs West of the River ORNE: 1 SS Pz Div holding from the river to LA HOGUE, and 272 Inf Div with a battalion from 711 Inf Div to assist it, took over from LA HOGUE to its original Northern boundary with 346 Inf Div about EMIEVILLE. 12 SS Pz Div was now pulled back into reserve on the River LAISON to refit and do some much needed work on the third defence line.

On the nights 4/5 and 5/6 August, quietly and without fuss, 1 SS Pz Div slipped away to join the Panzer formations assembling for the MORTAIN counter-attack and its place was taken by a new arrival, 89 Inf Div. This division had not seen action before and had marched over 150 miles from the PAS DE CALAIS to arrive just in time for Operation TOTALIZE.

The Enemy Defences and Layout

Although stronger in infantry than 1 SS Pz Div, 89 Div was forced to adopt its methods and garrison the tactically important features. Until the moves West started, two divisions had been deployed in this sector from the River ORNE to LA HOGUE, where a mass of weapon pits and machine gun posts had been constructed. It was now impossible to man all these defences, so, basing the deployment on the greater battle experience of their predecessors, 1056 Grenadier Regiment (1056 GR) took over the Western sector and 1055 the Eastern, each with two battalions up. The inter-regimental boundary ran East of VERRIERES and West of ROQUANCOURT. The defences, where possible, had been dug in the hedgerows and orchards on the outskirts of the villages, and the infantry occupying them were intimately supported by heavy machine guns, SP anti tank guns and mortars whose fire covered the inevitable gaps between the occupied localities. MAY SUR ORNE, the spur running North East towards VERRIERES, and ROQUANCOURT were all strongly held, as were TILLY LA CAMPAGNE, the wood fifteen hundred yards to the South East, and LA HOGUE. The third battalion in each Grenadier regiment was positioned to protect the forward gun areas and was available for patrolling and counter-attack. It was planned that in the event of penetration of the forward defences requiring a withdrawal, both regiments would fall back on the BRETTEVILLE-ST SYLVAIN line.

Two SP anti-tank battalions of 1 SS Pz Corps had been left in situ and 89 Div anti-tank battalion was used to thicken up the anti-tank defences. Besides the Divisional artillery and that of 12 SS Pz Div which was operating from 8 August onwards, there were two heavy artillery battalions equipped with 12 and 14 cm gun howitzers. The main gun areas were FONTENAY LE MARMION, the wooded area North East of BRETTEVILLE SUR LAIZE, CRAMESNIL, ST AIGNAN, ROBERTMESNIL and the SECQUEVILLES. One Werfer regiment and elements of another with their six-barrelled projectors added to the divisional total of seventy-eight mortars.

A Flak Brigade of three Flak Sturm Regiments equipped with between sixty and seventy 88 mm AA/A Tk guns and approximately the same number of 2 cm anti-aircraft guns was deployed on this front. This brigade was a Luftwaffe formation and did not come under the Army. It was a constant source of annoyance to the commander directing the immediate battle, who wished to employ the guns forward as effective anti-tank weapons; whereas their commander, General PICKARD, as often as not countermanded the Army orders and moved the guns back to protect administrative sites. As a result, these 88 mms were mainly deployed on the BRETTEVILLE–ST SYLVAIN line and further South.

12 SS Pz Div was the only armoured formation between the ORNE and the sea. Its strength was down to fifteen hundred infantry and sixty tanks—twenty panthers, twenty Mk IVs and twenty Panzer IVs belonging to the anti-tank battalion. 101 Hy Tk Bn was attached to the division and had ten Tiger tanks. Hardly had 12 SS Pz Div arrived in the reserve position when it was called on to provide support for the infantry struggling against the 12 Corps bridgehead East of the ORNE.

The Enemy Situation as known to 2 Cdn Corps

During the three weeks prior to Operation TOTALIZE, one major action, many minor ones and much active patrolling by 2 Cdn Corps had enabled an accurate forecast to be built up of what was likely to be found once the advance began. It had been appreciated that, unless a fresh formation arrived, the shortage of infantry must result in only some of the thick defences shown on the overprint being occupied. It had been established that important localities in the forward defences were strongly held, supported by an anti-tank screen in depth. It was estimated that 1 SS Pz Div had left one anti-tank battalion deployed on the front.

The rapid moves of enemy formations had completely altered the situation since planning started. However, the difficulties of identification were overcome after a struggle and a remarkably clear picture emerged. Prior to this, such remarks as: "Any attempts to clarify the situation have been frustrated by the elusiveness of live Germans and the abysmal ignorance of deserters and prisoners, who travel at night and are apparently told nothing by their superiors" were common in intelligence summaries. The arrival of an 89 Inf Div ambulance and a deserter in 6 Cdn Inf Bde lines gave away the relief of 1 SS Pz Div. From the information obtained, 1055 and 1056 GRs were placed astride the road CAEN–FALAISE between the divisional boundaries, which were known. Further East, another identification had established the fact that a battalion of 711 Div and a battalion from 272 linked up about 2,000 yards North East of LA HOGUE. The whereabouts of 1 SS and 12 SS Pz Divs were not so clear. The lack of prisoners from 12 SS and the reception of wireless messages from a set specially left in the VIMONT area, placed them in reserve on the 2 Cdn Corps Left flank at VALMERAY North East of ST SYLVAIN. 1 SS was thought to be in BRETTEVILLE SUR LAIZE. The deduction was, that apart from the immediate counter-attack force of tanks in support of 89 Inf Div, 2 Cdn Corps would meet stiffer resistance on the BRETTEVILLE–ST SYLVAIN line in the shape of 1 and 12 SS Pz Divs. On 7 August, news was received that large elements of 1 SS, and at least a battle group of 12 SS were fighting further West at VASSY and the FORET DE GRIMBOSQ respectively.

It was estimated that a total of fifty 88 mm guns was deployed against the Corps. Furthermore one Werfer regiment and a heavy artillery battalion were known to be in action. From counter-battery, air observation and other sources, the main gun areas had been located.

A great deal of accurate information was available concerning the organisation, strength and fighting value of 89 Inf Div. It was known that it was a low-category division composed largely of foreigners and Germans under 18 or over 40 years old. Based on the previous experience of the two other pocket divisions, 77 and 91 Inf Divs, its fighting value would not approach the quality of the Panzer troops. But with the latter behind them, and, with a stiffening of battle-experienced units of the anti tank companies, 89 Div was expected to fight hard for the positions it held.

The estimated strengths of 1 SS and 12 SS Pz Divs were as follows :—

    1 SS Pz Div   One thousand, seven hundred Infantry.
                           Eighty tanks (Twenty Mk Vs).

    12 SS Pz Div   One thousand, eight hundred Infantry.
                           Eighty tanks (Thirty five Mk Vs).

Opinion varied as to the possibility of encountering any Tiger tanks. It was thought that 503 Hy Tk Bn had left the sector with 21 Pz Div. The optimists were prepared to argue that, in view of the situation in the West, all heavy tank battalions had been rushed in that direction; the more wary were considering the whereabouts of 101 Hy Tk Bn and its number of runners.

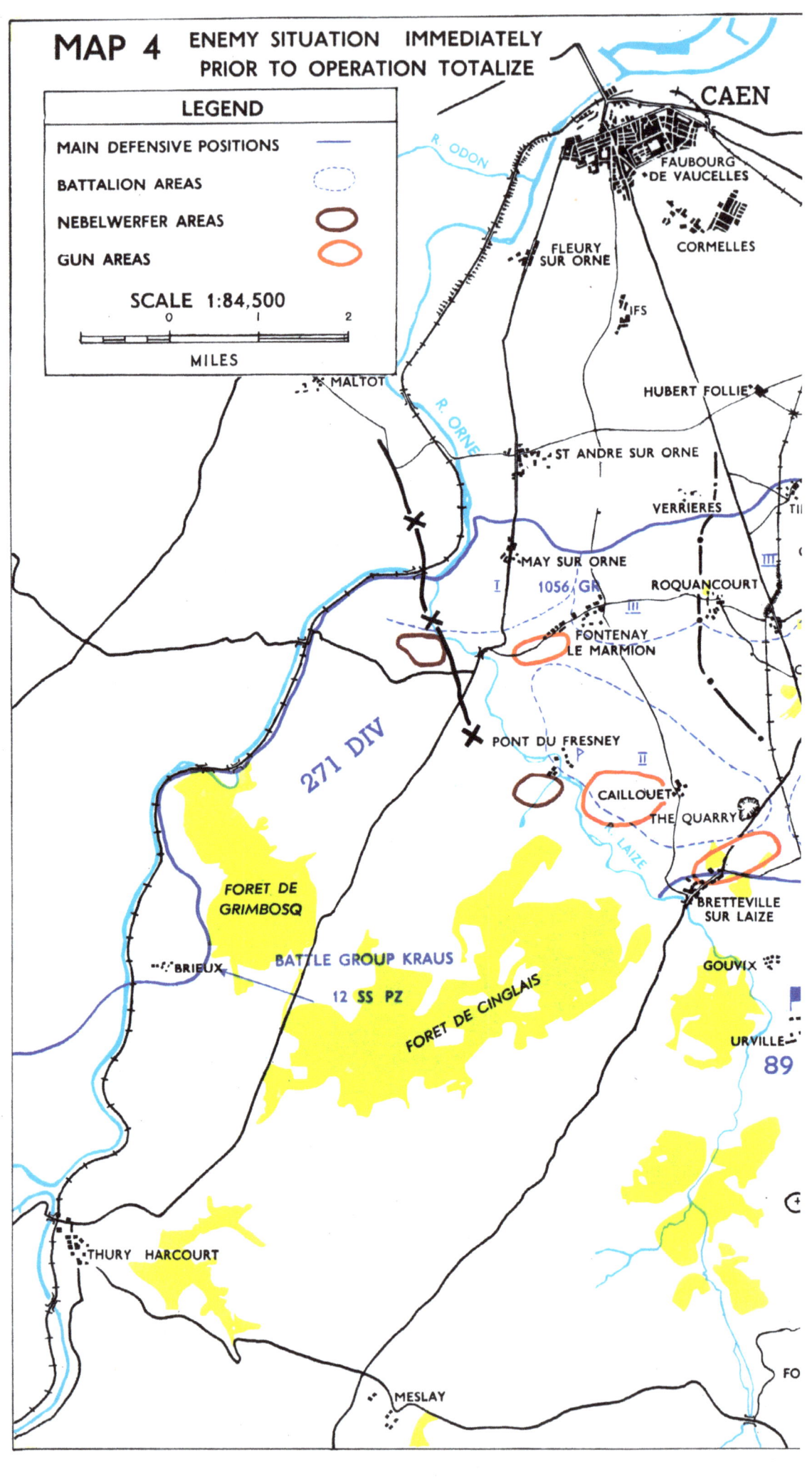

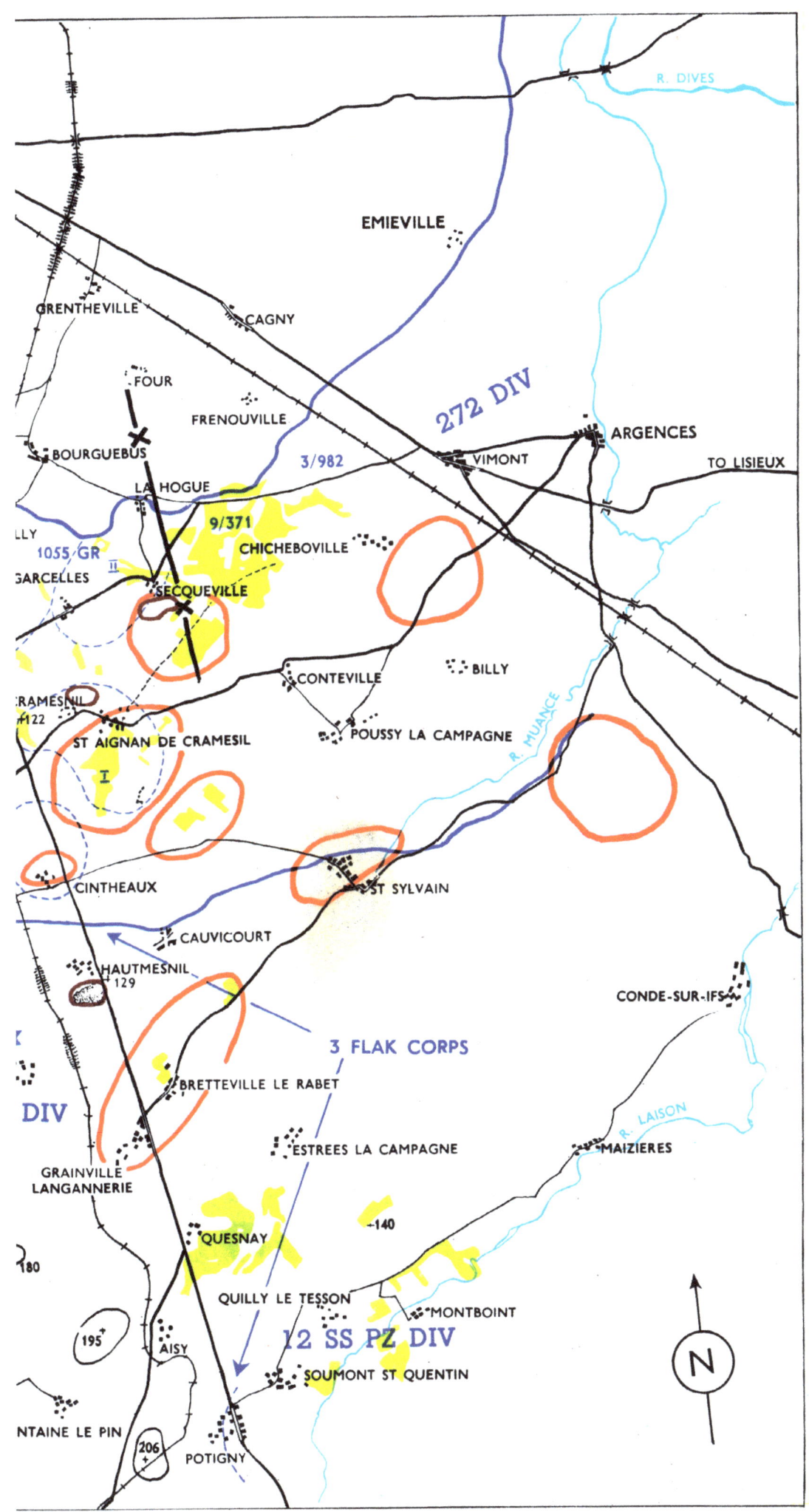

SECTION IV

PLANNING OPERATION TOTALIZE

A. APPRECIATION BY CORPS COMMANDER

The break out towards FALAISE was to be carried out by 2 Cdn Corps. The Corps Commander considered that his task, though difficult, could be achieved provided sufficient force was employed. His appreciation of the Problem, written on 1 August, is given below :—

1. "*Object*—To break through the German positions astride the road CAEN–FALAISE."

2. The Germans have a forward prepared defensive position with its FDL on the general line MAY SUR ORNE 0259–TILLY LA CAMPAGNE 0760–LA HOGUE 0960 and a rearward partially prepared position on the general line HAUTMESNIL 0852–ST SYLVAIN 1354. The high ground point 122 in 0756 is the key to the first and the high ground about HAUTMESNIL 0852 the key to the second. Both are obvious objectives and ones for which the Germans will fight very hard.

3. The positions are manned by as good troops as the German Army possesses. The area is the pivot, which, from the German point of view must be held so long as they fight West of, or on the line of the River ORNE. The position is at present manned by 1 SS Right and 9 SS Left. Available information indicates that each division has one infantry regiment forward, supported by all the tanks and SPs, whilst the other infantry regiment works on the rear position, and is available to form the nucleus of a defence in the event of a "break in" forward. The Germans apparently rely on being able to get tanks and SPs back, but ensure that some infantry will be available in the rearward positions from the outset, in the event of forward positions being over-run. Two "break in" operations are required to penetrate the German defence. 12 SS Div may be regarded as in close reserve opposite our front and counter-attack against our East flank must be expected.

4. The ground is ideally suited to full exploitation by the enemy of the characteristics of his weapons. It is open, giving little cover to either infantry or tanks and the long range of his anti-tank guns and mortars, firing from carefully concealed positions, provides a very strong defence in depth. This defence will be most handicapped in bad visibility—smoke, fog or darkness, when the advantage of long range is minimized. The attack should therefore be made under such conditions.

5. During the last few days we have attacked, and done everything possible to indicate that we intend to continue attacking, the positions opposite to us. Tactical surprise in respect to objectives or direction of attack is therefore impossible. Tactical surprise is still possible in respect to time and method, but very heavy fighting must be expected.

6. If all available air support is used for the first "break in" there will be nothing for the second except diminished gun support, unless a long pause is made with resultant loss of speed. If on the other hand the first "break in" is based upon limited air support (heavy night bombers), all available gun support and novelty of method, the heavy day bombers and medium bombers will be available for the second "break in" at a time when gun support begins to decrease, and it should be possible to maintain a high tempo to the operations.

7. In essence, the problem is how to get the armour through the enemy gun screen to sufficient depth to disrupt the German anti-tank gun and mortar defence, in country highly suited to the tactics of the latter combination. It can be done by :—

(a) Overwhelming air support to destroy or neutralize enemy tanks, anti-tank guns and mortars.

(b) Infiltrating through the screen in bad visibility to a sufficient depth to disrupt the anti-tank gun and mortar defence.

It requires practically the whole day-bomber lift to effect (a) and if two defence zones are to be penetrated, a pause with loss of speed and momentum must be accepted. It is considered that this may be avoided if the first zone is penetrated by infiltration at night but this can only be attempted with careful preparation by troops who are to do the operation.

8. The plan is submitted on the assumption that the Right wing of Second Army has secured, or imminently threatens to secure, a bridgehead East of the River ORNE, thus loosening the enemy grip on his Northern pivot."

(Sgd) G. G. SIMONDS, Lt General,
GOC 2 Canadian Corps.

1 August 1944.

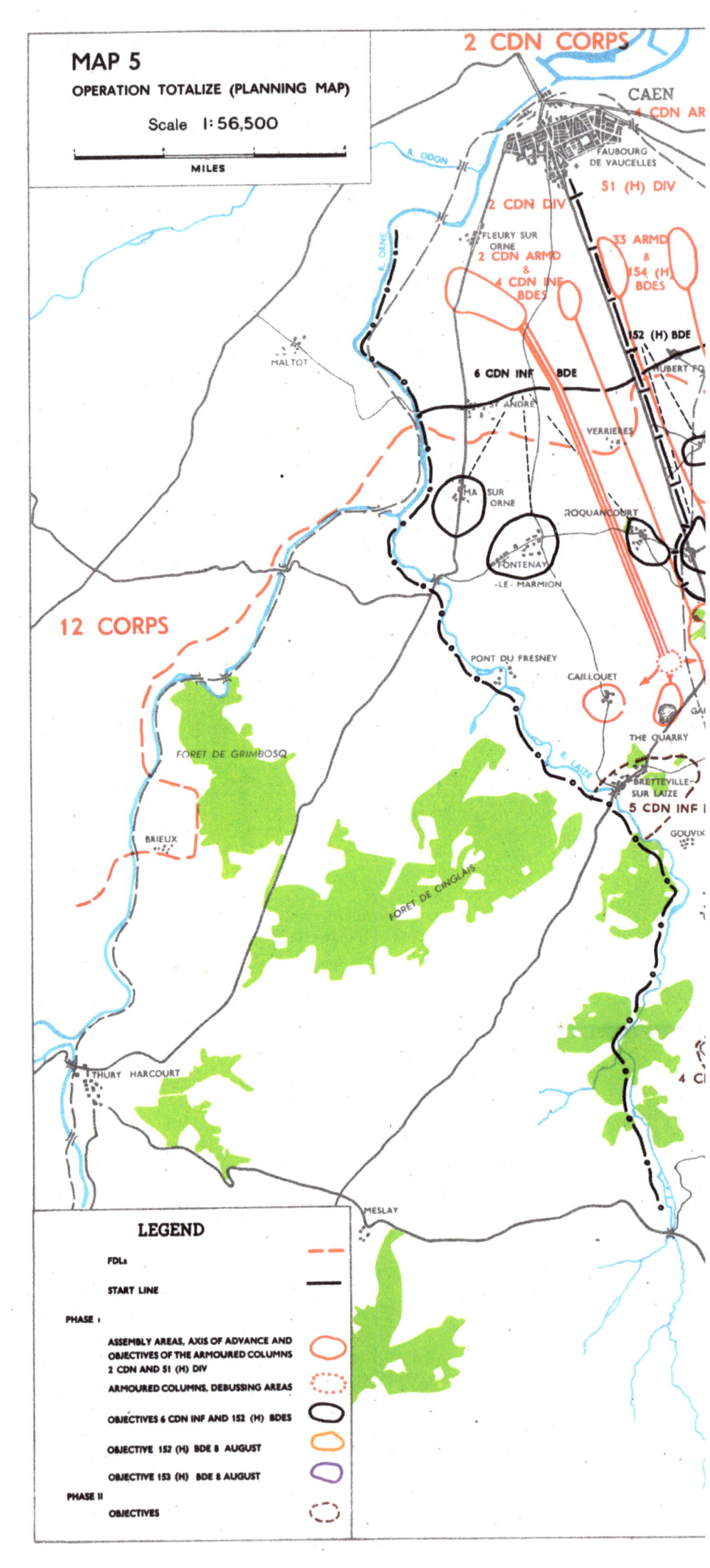

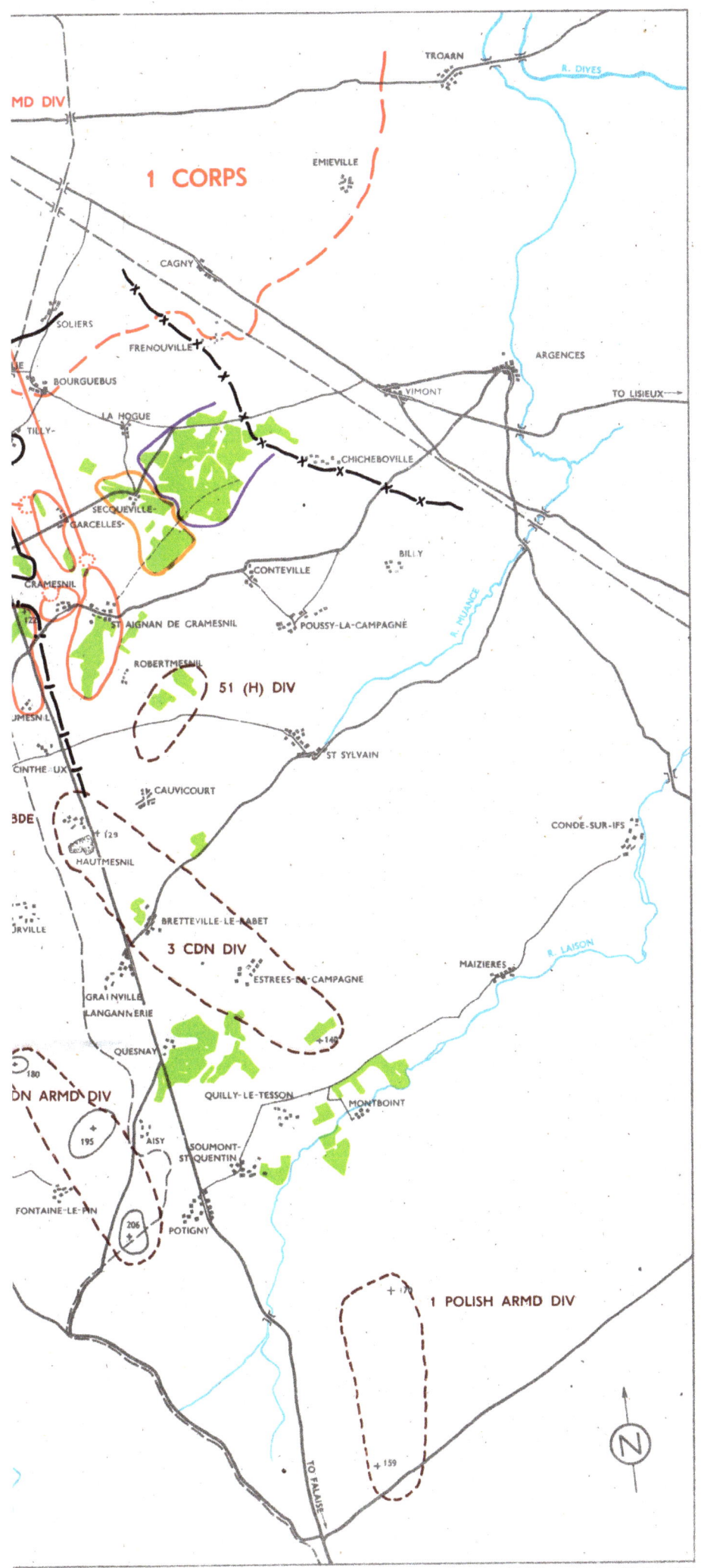

The Corps plan, given in subsequent paragraphs, was thus to attack under cover of darkness after a preliminary action by heavy bombers. General SIMONDS was insistent that infantry accompanying the armour in the initial phase must go straight through with the armour and themselves be protected. He therefore arranged that all available Priests should be stripped of their armament (less Browning machine guns) and made available as armoured personnel carriers: these vehicles had recently become available on the reconversion of some artillery regiments from SP to towed guns. There were approximately sixty, and the balance of assaulting brigades would therefore have to be carried in half-tracks and scout cars.

The conversion of Priests began at once. The gun, mantlet, seats and ammunition boxes were removed and a piece of armour plate welded over the front opening: when all available armour plate had been used up, a substitute was made by welding on two mild steel plates about two inches apart, and filling the space between them with sand. Engines were overhauled and the first armoured personnel carrier was ready on 3 August.

Finally, the Corps Commander laid down the following minimum requirements for the operation:—

(a) Two armoured divisions.

(b) Three infantry divisions.

(c) Two independent armoured brigades.

(d) One Searchlight battery for movement light.

(e) Two squadrons Flails—one for each armoured brigade.

(f) Crocodiles to assist mopping up during darkness.

(g) The whole of the available air effort (heavy night and day bombers as well as tactical air forces).

(h) Two AGsRA in addition to divisional artilleries and support of two additional AGsRA one each with 1 and 12 Corps respectively.

The operation was provisionally fixed to start on the night 8 August. This would allow the infantry divisions and armoured brigades to carry out special training in deep advance by night and give time to study ground and special equipment. A firm date and choice of H Hour could not be decided until after detailed planning and agreement had been reached regarding the air plan.

B. FLANK FORMATIONS

The situation on the Allied front to the West, and on the enemy front of 2 Cdn Corps was rapidly changing and it was not until 6 August that final details of Operation TOTALIZE were settled. 12 Corps had then met the requirements of the Corps Commander in securing his Right flank by gaining a bridgehead over the River ORNE West of the FORET DE GRIMBOSQ at BRIEUX.

On the Left, two divisions had been withdrawn from 1 Corps during the first week in August which left it very thin on the ground. Although this Corps was not directly involved in Operation TOTALIZE, except for fire support, it was important that this flank be firmly held. Further, as the operation developed, and when CRAMESNIL, SECQUEVILLE LA CAMPAGNE and the woods to the South East were secured, 1 Corps was to take over that part of the front, pushing its Right flank up to ST SYLVAIN.

C. THE CORPS PLAN

The following formations took part in Operation TOTALIZE:—

2 Cdn Div	2 Cdn AGRA
3 Cdn Div	3 AGRA
4 Cdn Armd Div	4 AGRA
51 (H) Div	9 AGRA
1 Polish Armd Div	
2 Cdn Armd Bde	
33 Armd Bde.	

As has already been stated, the Corps intelligence staff on 6 August placed 89 Inf Div with 272 Inf Div next to it in the enemy FDLs and 1 SS Pz back on the BRETTEVILLE SUR LAIZE–ST SYLVAIN position, with 12 SS Pz on the River MUANCE to the North East of ST SYLVAIN. As a result of this information, a conference was held at Corps HQ at 1000 hours, at which the Corps Commander explained the modifications that he had made to his original plan. He considered that counter attacks by either 89 or 272 Inf Divs were most unlikely and if they took place, at best would be half-hearted efforts. Therefore the two infantry divisions attacking in the first phase could be handled more boldly than had been originally planned. On the other hand, the second break through attack might meet stronger resistance than originally anticipated, as in the redisposition of the enemy forces, it was possible that neither 1 SS Pz nor 12 SS Pz Divs would be involved on the MAY SUR ORNE—LA HOGUE position, but would be found on the next defensive line. Consequently a widening of the frontage and an increase in the weight of attack for Phase II was required. He had decided therefore to launch the Polish Armd Div simultaneously and parallel with 4 Cdn Armd Div, and to direct these two divisions straight to their final objectives. Because this second "break through" operation had been foreseen and had been planned to take place in daylight during D+1, the weight of the air support had been disposed to deal with it during the second phase. No alteration was therefore considered necessary to the air plan in consequence of this new information.

The operation was to be carried out as follows:

(a) Phase I — Break through the FONTENAY LE MARMION–LA HOGUE position.

(b) Phase II — Secure the high ground West of the main road–Point 180–Point 195–Point 206 and East of the road at Point 170–Point 159.

(c) Phase III — Exploit as ordered by Commander 2 Cdn Corps.

For Phase I, 2 Cdn and 51 (H) Divs, each with an armoured brigade under command and with their leading infantry brigades carried in Armoured Personnel Carriers, were to move by night on the Right and Left respectively of the road CAEN–FALAISE. The following tasks were laid down:—

(a) *2 Cdn Div*

  (i) Capture as first objective CAILLOUET–GAUMESNIL and woods Point 122.

  (ii) Mop up area MAY SUR ORNE–FONTENAY LE MARMION–CAILLOUET–GAUMESNIL–ROQUANCOURT.

  (iii) Reorganise in the above area: protect the Right flank and form a firm base for launching Phase II.

(b) *51 (H) Div*

  (i) Capture as first objective LORGUICHON Wood–CRAMESNIL–ST AIGNAN DE CRAMESNIL and woods to the South–GARCELLES SECQUEVILLE.

  (ii) Capture in succession SECQUEVILLE LA CAMPAGNE and the wooded area to the East.

Meanwhile 4 Cdn Armd and 1 Polish Armd Divs were to move up behind the assaulting divisions so as to be positioned on the Corps Start Line (road ST ANDRE–SOLIERS) by the morning D plus 1.

3 Cdn Div would remain concentrated in its present area (North-West of CAEN).

Phase II was planned to start at 1400 hours D plus 1. At this hour the armoured divisions were to pass through the infantry and go straight for the final objectives, i.e.:—

4 Cdn Armd Div

Position itself facing West and South on the high ground Point 180–Point 195–Point 206 and keep contact with the enemy within the arc formed by the roads FONTAINE LE PIN–MESLAY and FALAISE–ARGENTAN.

1 Polish Armd Div

Position itself facing East and South on the high ground Point 170–Point 159 and keep contact with the enemy within the arc formed by the roads FALAISE–ARGENTAN and MONTBOINT–CONDE SUR IFS.

During this phase, 2 Cdn and 51 (H) Divs were to secure the Right and Left flanks at BRETTEVILLE SUR LAIZE and the woods South-East of ROBERTMESNIL respectively. 3 Cdn Div was to be ready to move forward on orders of the Corps Commander and take over the area HAUT-MESNIL–BRETTEVILLE LE RABET and the high ground Point 140.

Fire Support

With the details of the ground plan completed, the fire plan could be put into final form. It was decided that no preliminary bombardment would take place, although the active counter battery policy of the past few days would be continued up to H Hour.

Phase I

For this phase a barrage was to move on a frontage of 4,000 yards and to a depth of 6,000 yards. This was timed to start fifteen minutes after zero hour and during this time the leading troops had to advance fifteen hundred yards in order to be close to the opening line. The barrage lifted 200 yards every two minutes, with the mediums superimposed 400 yards in front of the field guns. The following guns were employed in firing the barrage:—

> 2 Cdn Inf Div Artillery
> 4 Cdn Armd Div Artillery
> 51 (H) Div Artillery
> 2 Cdn AGRA
> 9 AGRA
> Two medium regiments 4 AGRA.

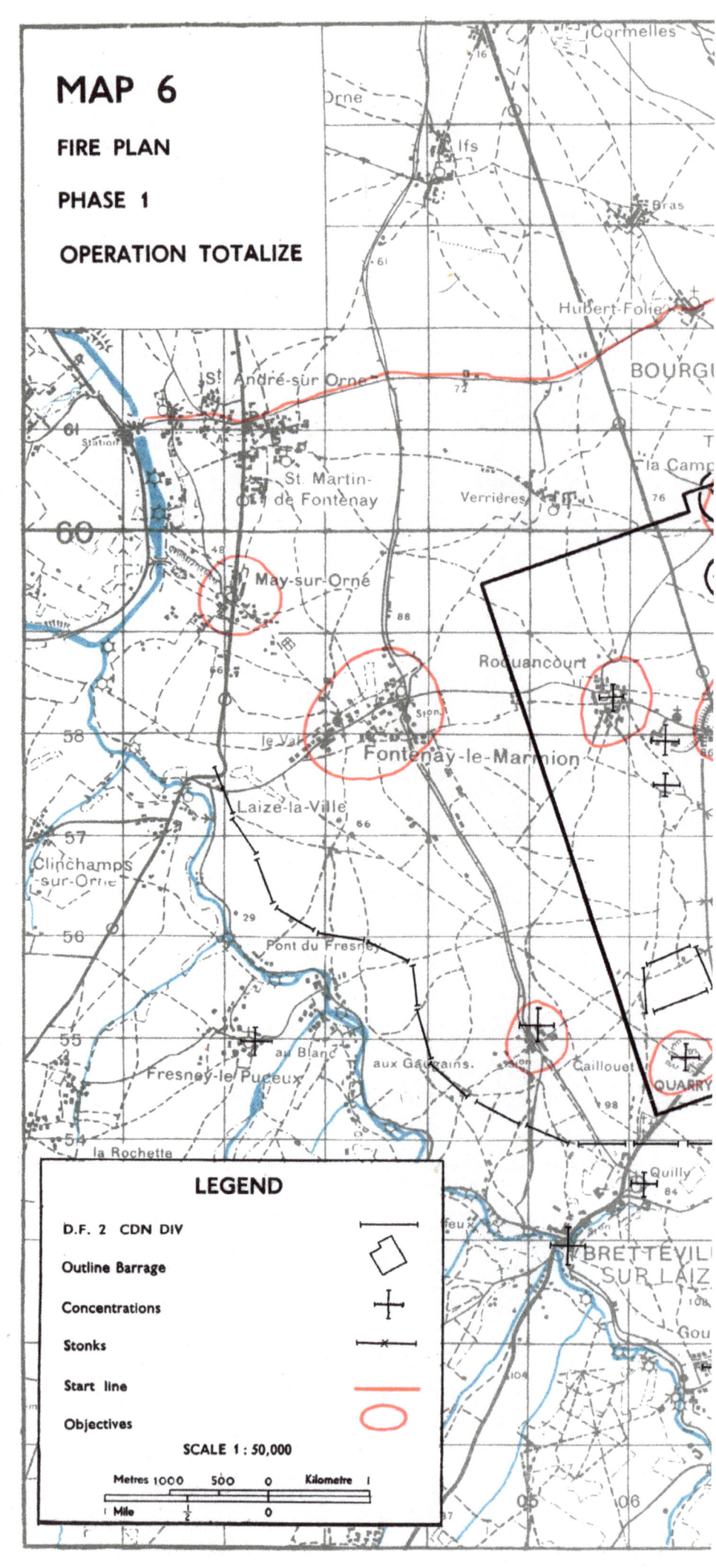

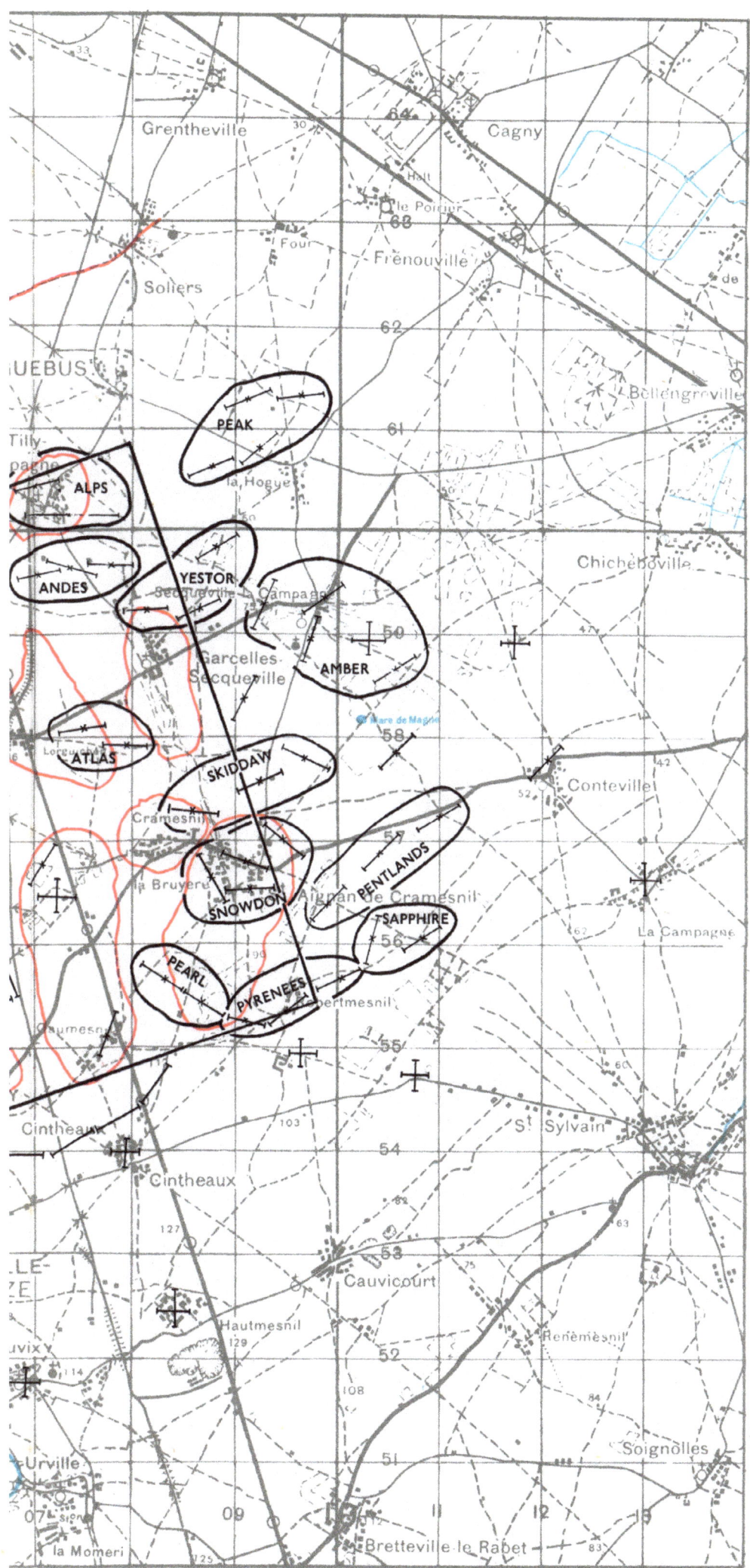

In the event of a check, the assaulting divisions could remove their own field guns from the barrage on the Divisional Commander's authority, the medium guns remaining on the barrage throughout.

Targets and areas requiring special treatment were selected by 2 Cdn and 51 (H) Divs and were to be dealt with by flanking AGsRA or Heavy Anti-Aircraft Regiments. Both assault divisions had an AGRA in support from the time the barrage finished until the completion of Phase I, together with fire support from flanking formations if available at the time. Pre-arranged Defensive Fire tasks had been fixed.

As mentioned above, normal counter battery was to be carried out throughout the twelve hours prior to the attack. Further, two intensive bombardments on known hostile batteries were to be fired : one shortly after the barrage had finished, the other in the early morning of 8 August.

To supplement the anti-tank weapons available in the attacking infantry divisions, two batteries of the Corps anti-tank regiment were placed under command of each division. A total of seven flights Air OP had been allotted to 2 Cdn Corps.

A counter flak programme was laid on in support of the heavy bombers. All known hostile anti-aircraft batteries were to be dealt with shortly before the bombing opened.

To assist in keeping direction during the night advance, arrangements were made for the Navigator's tank in each column to be fixed by Survey. In addition, each division was to have Bofors firing tracer on the thrust lines and, after completion of the bombing, green marker shells fired on Point 122 near the inter-divisional boundary. Finally there was to be diffused lighting by searchlights on the corps front under the control of the CCRA.

Phase II

4 Cdn and 1 Polish Armd Divs each prepared lists of concentrations to be fired on call as they advanced South to their objectives. Each division would have its own divisional artillery and one medium regiment under command and, in addition, one AGRA in support.

In all, 720 guns supported Operation TOTALIZE. Planning in earnest started on 4 August and was completed with the issue of task tables and traces by 1200 hours on 7 August. Within this short time, moves, the dumping of 200,000 rounds of ammunition and the production of all necessary data had been done.

D. THE AIR PLAN

This required that the flanks of the Corps armoured-infantry thrusts on the night of 7/8 August should be protected by a heavy bombing attack just before the ground troops began to move forward. Heavy aircraft of Bomber Command would attack MAY SUR ORNE, FONTENAY LE MARMION, LA HOGUE and SECQUEVILLE LA CAMPAGNE and the woods to the South. This bombing was intended to destroy the enemy defences and tank harbours by blast and fragmentation in forty five minutes. Although the forward troops would be moving ahead while the latter part of this bombing was actually going on, their advance to the initial objectives on either side of the FALAISE highway would not bring them within the danger zone of 2,000 yards from the bombers' targets.

The support for the daylight attack on 8 August was more comprehensive. Again the flanks of the advance were to be struck, the bombers being requested to attack BRETTEVILLE SUR LAIZE and GOUVIX on the Right and ST SYLVAIN on the Left, as from 1400 hours, simultaneously with the advance of 4 Cdn and 1 Polish Armd Divs down the highway. The tanks would be preceded by bombing on targets at CINTHEAUX and the woods South-East of ROBERTMESNIL, thence Southward to cover HAUTMESNIL and CAUVICOURT and the farther woods and copses. This carpet bombing was to be concentrated into thirty minutes, when the air attack would be moved South for forty-five minutes' further bombing to neutralize the enemy's guns at the time when the armoured advance should be gaining momentum. The targets at this stage were BRETTEVILLE LE RABET and GRAINVILLE LANGANNERIE on the FALAISE road, the LAIZE valley to the West and South from URVILLE, and ESTREES LA CAMPAGNE and the QUESNAY woods to the East.

On 5 August, at an Army/Royal Air Force conference in ENGLAND, the original plan for the night bombing was approved, though the Royal Air Force noted that wind or dust might prevent the targets being engaged in the order requested. Because of the dangers of noise and blast, the Royal Air Force insisted that the troops advancing behind the bombing must wear ear plugs. The daylight plan underwent revision. As the dust and smoke was likely to render the accurate bombing of successive targets as requested impossible, the Royal Air Forces declined to bomb as far North as CINTHEAUX. The alternative plan was to attack BRETTEVILLE SUR LAIZE and ST SYLVAIN during the morning of 8 August. These attacks were to be completed in sufficient time to allow the dust to clear away before other flights arrived to bomb astride the FALAISE road from GOUVIX through HAUTMESNIL to CAUVICOURT. Cratering here would be avoided and the area would not be carpeted, but the air forces promised a considerable spread of fragmentation bombs. Owing to the absence of precise targets in the vicinity of BRETTEVILLE LE RABET, QUESNAY woods and ESTREES LA CAMPAGNE, it was suggested that this area might be better dealt with by fighter-bombers.

But if the plan for using the heavy bombers by night escaped serious amendment at the hands of the joint Army/Air Force conference, it ran into unexpected difficulties the following day at HQ Bomber Command. There, the Chief of Staff, First Canadian Army, was informed that the technique required that the Master Bomber check the accuracy of the marker dropped by pathfinders visually, in order to ensure that the aim of the subsequent waves might be corrected. Thus it would be necessary either to carry out the bombing by twilight, or to prove that the coloured markers to be used to indicate the targets could be clearly identified at night. General CRERAR was immediately consulted by telephone across the Channel, and it was arranged to experiment that night by firing 25 pounder marker shells over the sector held by 1 Corps, for bombers overhead to locate. Should the experiment not be successful, the hour for the assault would require to be brought forward to enable the Royal Air Force to begin their bombing at 2130 hours. This course was most undesirable from the Corps Commander's point of view, as his plan depended on the advance being made simultaneously with the bombing in order to enable his troops to close with the defenders while they were still under its effects. General SIMONDS agreed that if necessary he must accept the earlier timing.

Fortunately the change was not necessary; the tests carried out that evening proved successful. As a result the final orders for the bombing, issued on 7 August, remained substantially the same as the original requests. The villages of MAY SUR ORNE and FONTENAY LE MARMION were to be marked by green shells: red markers were to indicate the targets lying East of the Highway. It was also understood that the Army would not fire flare shells for any other purpose while the bombers were overhead. A further difficulty was resolved when Bomber Command announced that it had no objection to the use of searchlights for illumination while the bombing was in progress, provided that the beams were directed at a low elevation and pointed only in a Southerly direction. To assist the aircraft in carrying out their task, a counter-flak programme was arranged, with a special allotment of field and medium ammunition: but to avoid confusion no fire was to be directed at batteries within 1,000 yards of the bombers' aiming points.

Details of the daylight bombing for the second phase were also confirmed, though the timing for the end of the attacks, set at 1345 hours in the final instructions, soon led to complications when, on the evening of 7 August, weather forecasts for the following day indicated that the visual bombing by Fortresses would have to take place at 1300 hours, if at all.

In addition to the bombing programme, 83 Group Royal Air Force, plus the resources of IX United States Army Air Force, agreed to carry out armed reconnaissance from first light D plus 1 over the general area South of the line URVILLE–BRETTEVILLE LE RABET–ESTREES LA CAMPAGNE, with the object of attacking all enemy movement from or to the battle area.

Close support as under was provided by two Visual Control Posts in 2 Cdn Corps area, positioned by 2000 hours D day.

(a) One Visual Control Post to maintain listening watch on 2 Cdn Div and 51 (H) Div ASSU net.
(b) One Visual Control Post to maintain listening watch on 4 Cdn Armd Div and 1 Polish Armd Div ASSU net.

E. DIVISIONAL OUTLINE PLANS

2 Cdn Div

2 Cdn Div planned to carry out the night attack on CAILLOUET–THE QUARRY–GAUMESNIL and Point 122, with an armoured and an infantry brigade advancing on two axes. 2 Cdn Armd Bde had 4 Cdn Inf Bde in armoured troop carriers under its command, and was to move with three columns on the Right axis and one on the Left. The composition and organisation of the columns were as follows:—

	Left Axis	*Right Axis* (Each of the three columns)
Gapping Force	Two troops 10th Canadian Armoured Regiment (The Fort Garry Horse) (10 Cdn Armd Regt)	Two troops 27th Canadian Armoured Regiment (The Sherbrooke Fusiliers) (27 Cdn Armd Regt)
	Two troops 1st Lothian and Border Yeomanry (1 LOTHIANS) (Flails) One troop 79th Assault Squadron RE (AVRE)	Two troops 1 LOTHIANS (Flails) One troop 79 Aslt Sqn RE (AVRE)
Assault Force	8th Canadian Reconnaissance Regiment (14th Canadian Hussars) (8 Cdn Recce Regt)	One infantry battalion—4 Cdn Inf Bde
	One squadron less two troops 10 Cdn Armd Regt	One squadron less two troops 27 Cdn Armd Regt
	Two troops 6th Canadian Anti-Tank Regiment (6 Cdn A Tk Regt)	Two troops 6 Cdn A Tk Regt
	One platoon The Toronto Scottish Regiment (TOR SCOT R) (MG)	One platoon TOR SCOT R (MG)
	One section Royal Canadian Engineers (RCE)	One section RCE
Fortress Force	10 Cdn Armd Regt less one squadron.	

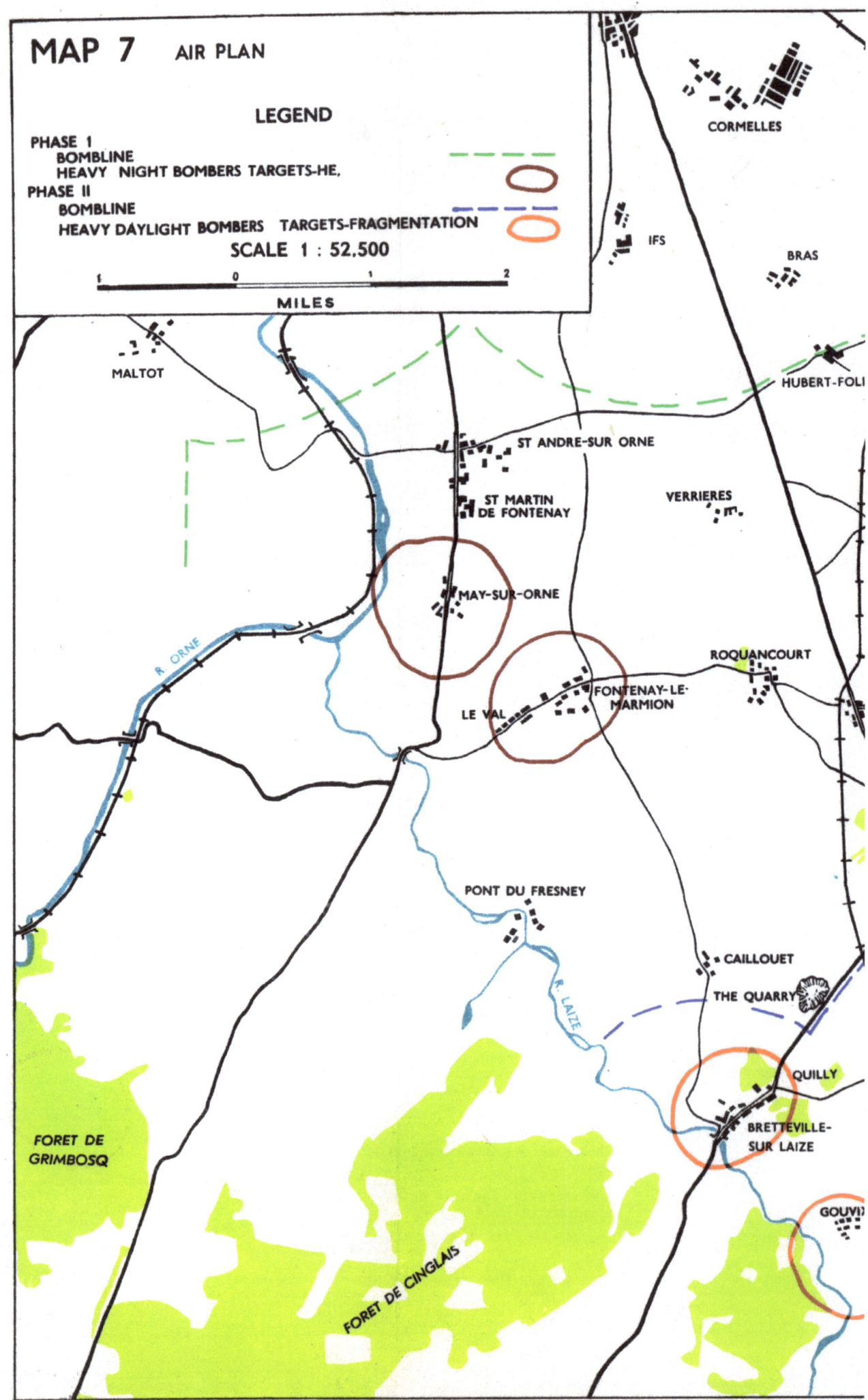

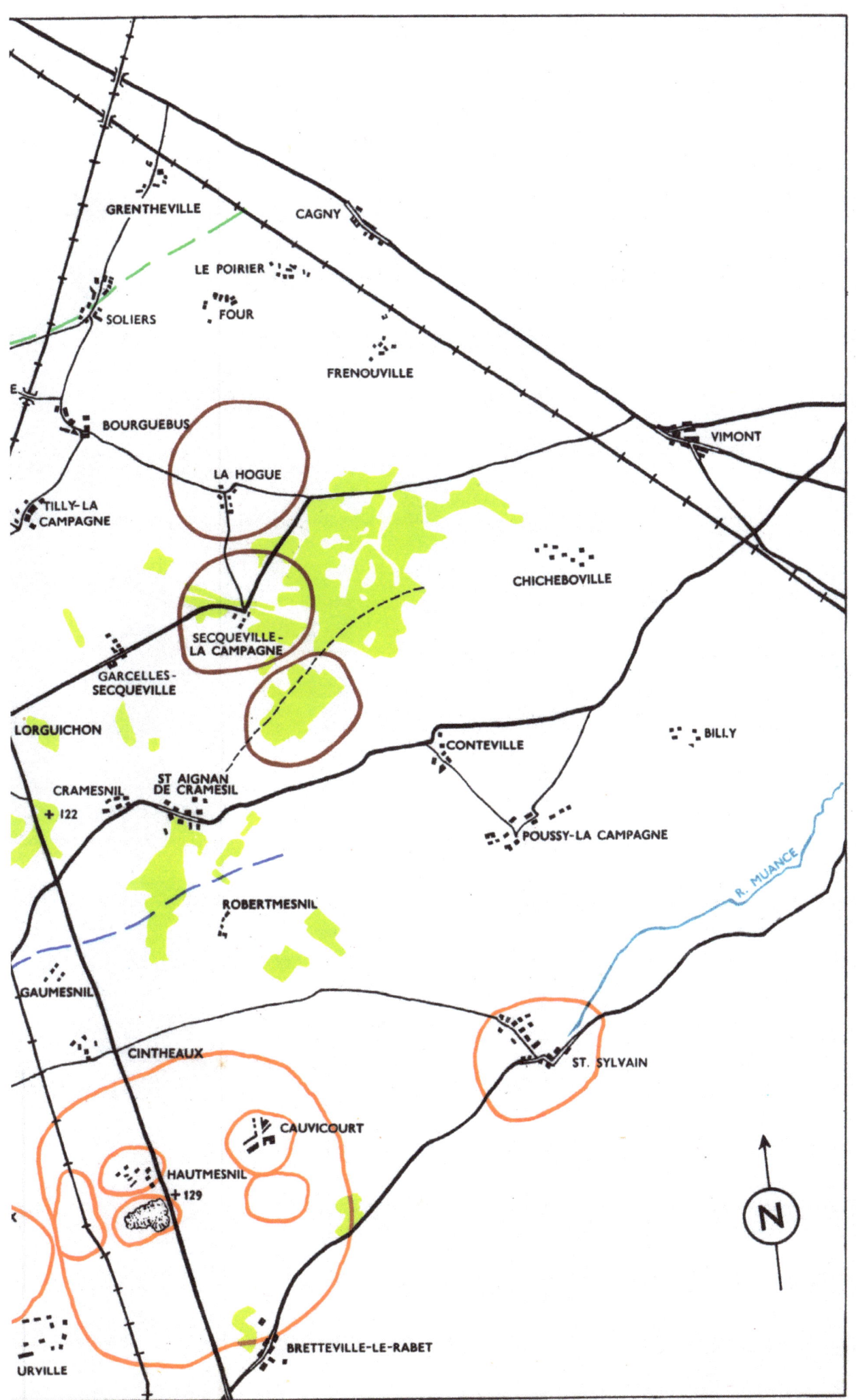

The Left axis ran very close to the FALAISE road, whilst the Right by-passed ROQUANCOURT to the West. The gapping force in all columns was under command OC 27 Cdn Armd Regt which, besides navigating and mine clearing, taped and lighted the routes for the columns. It was also responsible for the defence of the debussing area. Once debussing had been completed the assault force was to form up and attack the four objectives. As soon as these objectives had been secured their defence was co-ordinated by the Commander 4 Cdn Inf Bde. The fortress force was a reserve for the Commander 2 Cdn Armd Bde, who controlled the battle at this stage.

6 Cdn Inf Bde's task of mopping up the areas by-passed by the armoured columns had been greatly increased by the change of plan. It was now to include MAY SUR ORNE and FONTENAY LE MARMION—as well as ROQUANCOURT. Further, the barrage did not include the two former villages and only very limited fire support could be provided there until the barrage was completed. With the support of 4.2" mortars and one squadron of Crocodiles, it was decided to take advantage of the effects of the bombing and commit all three battalions of the brigade at H hour. The battalion objectives were MAY SUR ORNE, FONTENAY LE MARMION and ROQUANCOURT.

5 Cdn Inf Bde with 6 Cdn Armd Regt was in reserve. Its task was to be prepared to restore the momentum of the attack if lost. Secondly, in Phase II of the 2 Cdn Div plan, whilst the other formations were mopping up and reorganising, 5 Cdn Inf Bde supported by 2 Cdn Armd Bde was to capture BRETTEVILLE SUR LAIZE after the daylight bombing had been completed.

51 (H) Div

The operation was to be carried out as follows. In the first phase, 154 (H) Bde with 33 Armd Bde in support, was to capture and hold the area GARCELLES SECQUEVILLE–ST AIGNAN DE CRAMESNIL—the woods to the South of that village and CRAMESNIL. This attack was to be undertaken by two columns, each consisting of an armoured regiment and a battalion of infantry carried in defrocked Priests, half tracks and carriers. Enough of these vehicles, to lift the whole of 154 (H) Bde on to its objective, were provided under corps arrangements.

The start line for the two columns was to be the road HUBERT FOLIE–SOLIERS. The routes were to run roughly parallel with the main road CAEN–FALAISE and the columns were to by-pass the village of TILLY LA CAMPAGNE on either flank. H hour was fixed for 2330 hours on 7 August. Each column was to be under the command of the armoured regimental commander concerned. These officers were responsible for the navigation of their column, and for getting the infantry on to the objective.

The composition of columns was as follows :—

Left Route	*Right Route*
1st Northamptonshire Yeomanry (1 NYEO) with Flails and one troop AVsRE	144th Regiment Royal Armoured Corps (144 RAC) with Flails and one troop AVsRE
1st Battalion The Black Watch (Royal Highland Regiment) (1 BW)	7th Battalion The Argyll and Sutherland Highlanders (7 A & SH)
	148th Regiment Royal Armoured Corps (148 RAC)
	7th Battalion The Black Watch (Royal Highland Regiment) (7 BW)

When the objectives were reached, command was to pass to the infantry battalion commanders and the armoured regiments were to come into support of the infantry, with the task of repelling any enemy armoured counter-attacks that might take place on the following day.

At the same time as 154 (H) Bde advanced, one battalion from 152 (H) Bde was to leave its position at HUBERT FOLIE and capture TILLY LA CAMPAGNE. Another battalion, following behind 154 (H) Bde was to attack LORGUICHON village and wood, and the railway cutting to the North of the village. 152 (H) Bde was also to be prepared to find one battalion to help 154 (H) Bde, as well as to clear and occupy SECQUEVILLE LA CAMPAGNE and the woods just North and South East of that village. Finally 153 (H) Bde was to hold the area of BOURGUEBUS–FOUR-GRENTHEVILLE as a firm base, until relieved later in the battle. Then, helped if necessary by tanks and Crocodiles, it was to clear the woods to the West of CHICHEBOVILLE.

The divisional machine gun battalion, less one machine gun company under command of 154 (H) Bde, and the 4.2" mortar company in support of 152 (H) Bde, was to cover the Left flank during the advance to the first objective from positions just East of BOURGUEBUS, and thereafter to be used as required. The Reconnaissance Regiment was to remain North of CAEN, and the squadron of Crocodiles, which had been placed under command of the division, was to concentrate at CORMELLES and stay there until called forward. The regiment of Flails and the squadron of AVsRE were placed under command of 33 Armd Bde.

For Divisional Operation Orders see Appendices F, G, H and J.

SECTION V

TRAINING

The Corps Commander had wanted a full week in which to prepare for the attack, but, in the end, a bare forty-eight hours were available.

2 Cdn Armd Bde and 4 Cdn Inf Bde concentrated at LOUVIGNY on 5 August, although 1 LOTHIANS (Flails) and 79 Aslt Sqn RE did not arrive until the next day and one anti tank battery joined in the assembly area a few hours before the attack. This meant rehearsals and training were seriously handicapped. As already mentioned, there were to be two separate axes of advance with three columns on the Right and one on the Left and each column was composed of a gapping force, assault force and fortress force. The infantry companies practised embussing and debussing and runs were made to an imaginary dispersal area where the assault force debussed and attacked an objective, leaving the fortress force to secure the dispersal area.

Meanwhile 51 (H) Div, which was resting North of CAEN, began to prepare for the operation on similar lines. A sand table of the area of the forthcoming battle was built and the proposed plans of attack were studied in detail by all commanders down to Commanding Officers. Air photographs were carefully scrutinised and the information obtained from them played a big part in shaping the actual details of the plan as finally adopted. A great deal of work had to be carried out in the short time available, but the successes attained by this division in the early part of the battle were undoubtedly due to careful preliminary preparation. 154 (H) Bde selected a local area for training and 33 Armd Bde joined it there on 3 August. The armoured transport for the infantry arrived next day, and was organised so that each battalion had one mixed platoon of thirty Priests, half tracks and carriers. Conferences and practice runs took up all available time, day and night, between 4 and 6 August, and last minute adjustments such as fitting dimmed tail-lights and reorganising the stowage so that crews would be below the level of the armoured sides of the half tracks had to be completed. Great attention to detail was paid in the precautions against straying and in the instructions to commanders and drivers of vehicles. A very close liaison was established and the various practices carried out were most successful. The squadron and company commanders, who were to work together once the objective was reached got to know each other and there was one instance at least where the Jocks entertained all the tank commanders of one squadron in the CORMELLES factory : in fact, armour and infantry became great friends.

In addition to the above, the two armoured brigades carried out experiments with radio directional equipment. This consisted of a transmitting station sending out two separate signals on two beams. When advancing on the correct axis the 19 set in the navigating tanks would pick up dots and dashes of equal strength. When too far to the West, loud dots would be heard and when too far to the East, loud dashes. The accuracy of this was approximately 200 yards either side of the axis at 6 miles from the transmitter site. 33 Armd Bde decided that sufficient practice had not been possible to rely on this method. Furthermore, the navigator was required to listen-in the whole time and concentrate on picking up the signals to the exclusion of everything else. As a result, compasses, fitted to the turrets of the directing tanks, and air photographs for map reading, were the main aids to navigation, with Bofor tracer, searchlight beams, night marker shell and the wireless beam assisting the columns.

SECTION VI

FINAL ASSEMBLY

On 5 August, the Germans in ST MARTIN DE FONTENAY withdrew to MAY SUR ORNE. To determine whether a withdrawal on 2 Cdn Corps front was being carried out, in view of 12 Corps progress down the West bank of the ORNE, 5 Cdn Inf Bde attacked MAY SUR ORNE. The Black Watch (Royal Highland Regiment) of Canada (RHC) moved forward late in the afternoon and was allowed to approach close to the village, before being halted by heavy mortar and machine gun fire. Further attacks during the evening and following morning by Le Regiment de Maisonneuve (R de MAIS), made little further progress. Patrols could advance without drawing fire, but an attacking force produced a most violent reaction.

Further East, 4 Cdn Armd Div tested the defences of TILLY LA CAMPAGNE and LA HOGUE. The former village had always been stubbornly defended by SS troops, and 1055 GR, which was taking over at this time, proved no exception to this rule. Both attacks were repulsed with losses in infantry and tanks and proved beyond doubt there had been no withdrawal in this sector.

On 6 August 154 (H) Bde and 33 Armd Bde moved to their assembly area at CORMELLES without incident. During the night the remainder of 51 (H) Div took over the front East of the FALAISE road, with 152 (H) Bde at HUBERT FOLIE and BRAS, and 153 (H) Bde occupying BOURGUEBUS–SOLIERS–GRENTHEVILLE.

The following afternoon and evening, 2 Cdn Div was assembling between FLEURY SUR ORNE and IFS. The weather was fine, and although the area was secure from direct observation, the vehicles raised clouds of dust which must have been visible from the enemy OPs. However, no air action or shelling by artillery resulted. The columns were formed up exactly as they intended to cross the start line. Each column of the Canadian armoured force had four vehicles abreast with a frontage of sixteen yards, the width of the gap four flails could clear in a minefield, with only two yards separating each vehicle from the one behind it.

East of the road there were approximately two hundred vehicles in each assault column, which were also to move in four files on a frontage of approximately fifteen yards. The detailed order of march varied for each column, and, in the case of the Left column, was as follows :—

Two navigating tanks one behind the other.

Two troops A sqn 1 N YEO with reserve navigator.

Flails in four columns each of five flails.

Two troops A sqn 1 N YEO.

HQ A sqn 1 N YEO, RHQ less 2IC with FOO and Flail squadron commander.

HQ C sqn 1 N YEO with six AVsRE.

C sqn 1 N YEO.

1 BW (2IC 1 N YEO with OC battalion).

B sqn 1 N YEO less one troop.

Supporting weapons 1 BW.

Armoured revovery vehicles, half track ambulances, bulldozer.

One troop B sqn 1 N YEO.

In the case of 33 Armd Bde, the routes for both columns from the Start Line were to pass to the West of BOURGUEBUS. The Left hand column was forbidden by the Divisional Commander to by-pass BOURGUEBUS to the East, because it would then come too close to the bombing at LA HOGUE, On the morning 6 August, therefore, the navigating officer of the Left column, with an RE officer, reconnoitred a route skirting BOURGUEBUS to the West. Any such route would have to pass very close to TILLY LA CAMPAGNE, held by the Germans in some strength. Reconnaissance was consequently difficult, and any undue movement brought down fire from the enemy.

Nevertheless, the reconnaissance was carried out thoroughly, and two sunken roads were discovered right across the line of advance. These sunken roads were pronounced obstacles to half-track vehicles but probably not to tanks. The CRE 51 (H) Div agreed to send a party of sappers during the night 6/7 August, with instructions to make gaps in the banks of both these roads. The task was successfully accomplished, and when, on the morning 7 August, the navigating officer carried out a further reconnaissance, he reported that he thought that the half-tracks would now be able to negotiate the crossings.

As H hour approached, the area between CORMELLES and the bomb line became a mass of troops and vehicles. Guns in action waiting to fire the barrage, tanks, Flails, the Priests, half-tracks and the infantry brigades which were to attack on foot were all packed tightly together waiting for the bombers to arrive. To ensure safety from bombing, ST ANDRE SUR ORNE and VERRIERES were evacuated by 6 Cdn Inf Bde and BOURGUEBUS by the troops of 153 (H) Bde.

PART II
Account of the Battle

SECTION I

ACCOUNT OF THE NIGHT ATTACK 7/8 AUGUST

Armoured Columns

Punctually at 2300 hours the bombing started on targets marked by the flare shells. Half an hour later the solidly packed armoured columns and marching infantry crossed their start lines on either side of the FALAISE road and picked up the barrage without difficulty. The hundreds of vehicles added their dust to the dense clouds raised by the barrage. It was blinding to drivers, already struggling with the general obscurity and contrasted glare of the searchlights, and who were only able to see the nearest tail-lights ahead of them. This procession crawled in lowest gear at 100 yards a minute towards their objectives 6,000 yards away. It was not surprising that collisions occurred, that vehicles strayed from the column, even that some of the stragglers came to be fired on by their friends, much less that others were knocked out by the enemy's guns. The columns were guided by the Bofor tracer and in the Canadian columns, by the tapes and lights which the Royal Engineers of the gapping force laid, and from which the maximum benefit was derived during the early stages of the advance. The moon came up about midnight and did much to brighten the night.

The enemy appeared at first to be overcome with confusion, but recovered sufficiently to put down defensive fire with artillery and mortars. He was clever enough to add to the difficulties of a rising ground mist by thickening it up with smoke. Calls came back over the wireless to increase the intensity of searchlights and to restart and speed up the fire of the Bofors which had stopped at H plus 45. Though the leading tanks reported the Bofors effective, the searchlights were unable to pierce the dust cloud.

In the Canadian columns the problem of keeping direction became increasingly difficult and they went astray at ROQUANCOURT. Instead of passing West of the village, the Right hand columns took wrong routes. Although The Essex Scottish (ESSEX SCOT) kept to the West as intended, it completely lost its bearings. The Royal Hamilton Light Infantry (Wentworth Regiment) (RHLI) drove through the village after several attempts to get round it, and the Royal Regiment of Canada (R REGT C) by-passed it to the East. These delays meant the loss of protection and effect of the barrage, and the gapping force did not reach the debussing area till 0210 hours, over an hour after the barrage had finished.

Having lost touch with its navigating party at ROQUANCOURT, the ESSEX SCOT column halted close to the enemy defences. With the help of flares, the enemy succeeded in knocking out a number of its tanks and armoured troop carriers. Reports received at divisional HQ at 0340 hours stated that the column was still in difficulties in the same area, which was thought to be five hundred yards short of CAILLOUET. No contact could be made with its commander, one company was cut off, and it was still suffering casualties from enemy attacks. The second in command found the CO, who had been wounded in ROQUANCOURT and from the South Saskatchewan Regiment (S SASK R) obtained the unit's location. However, it took till 0800 hours to re-sort the column for its advance to CAILLOUET.

The RHLI, in the centre, managed to get most of its column through the middle of ROQUANCOURT and reached the debussing area. It advanced on foot towards the QUARRY, but was held up five hundred yards short of it where it consolidated. R REGT C attacked the Point 122 feature from the West and by 0700 hours had three companies firmly established there, with a squadron of tanks and supporting arms in position. 8 Cdn Recce Regt on the Left had also run into trouble at ROQUANCOURT. Its column was forced to halt, whilst enemy machine gun posts were subdued. Opposition proved stronger than was expected and little further progress was made beyond the railway bridge East of ROQUANCOURT.

East of the main road 33 Armd Bde and 154 (H) Bde advanced with 144 RAC and 7 A & SH leading on the Right axis directed on CRAMESNIL. Behind them were 148 RAC and 7 BW, which were to capture GARCELLES SECQUEVILLE. ST AIGNAN DE CRAMESNIL was the objective of 1 N YEO and 1 BW on the Left. The two columns formed up around CORMELLES at about 2200 hours, and started off at 2215 hours. The routes forward to the start line were lit by the RE. Both columns crossed the start line punctually at 2330 hours.

On the Right route the column had an early delay when the navigating party ditched their tanks in bomb craters about one mile from the start line. From this point there was considerable confusion in the column. Elements of the leading two squadrons and HQ became intermingled and split up into individual parties each led by an officer. Ultimately the leading tanks reached the railway crossing and as they crossed it were fired on by a party of enemy armed with bazookas. Two tanks were hit and in the fighting that followed a number of enemy were killed and one anti-tank gun destroyed. Further crossings were made to the North and the column was collected on the East side of the railway.

The problem now was one of control. The tanks had become very mixed up and no one knew where his troop or squadron leader was. The only practicable method was to give tank commanders a visible signal to follow. This was achieved by putting up an occasional Verey light to assist those in rear. At the same time leading tanks fired their machine guns into hedgerows and ditches, where enemy armed with bazookas might be hidden. At about 0330 hours the debussing area was reached. In fact, the leading vehicles had gone too far and were on the enemy position. One tank was destroyed and the remainder withdrew on to the middle of the field. Finally, 7 A & SH debussed five hundred yards from CRAMESNIL and attacked the village; by first light it had been secured and contact was being made with the units on either flank.

Following in the Right column, 148 RAC and 7 BW crossed the railway and moved without opposition to their dispersal area. By 0400 hours they had debussed and an hour and a half later GARCELLES SECQUEVILLE was captured.

In the meantime, the Left column had had a certain amount of difficulty in negotiating the sunken roads near BOURGUEBUS. First the Flails had found the banks a considerable obstacle, and then some of the half tracks got stuck. As a result of these hold-ups, the column did not catch up the barrage. However, after an eventful journey, the navigator brought the column to within fifty yards of his mark in the thick hedge, previously selected as the debussing point. Only two Priests had been shot up on the way, by an enemy SP gun which had followed the column for a short distance, and no enemy defensive fire was encountered.

At this hedge, the navigating officer, in company with the commanding officers of 1 N YEO and 1 BW, carried out a short reconnaissance. A number of gaps were discovered, probably made by German tanks. It was therefore decided not to debus there but to continue the advance through the hedge nearer to the objective, the village of ST AIGNAN DE CRAMESNIL. Having collected the infantry vehicles and re-sorted the companies, the advance over the last eight hundred yards was continued under cover of a pre-arranged artillery concentration lasting twenty minutes. The two leading squadrons of 1 N YEO pushed through the gaps in the hedge and shot up the forward edge of the village and the wood to the West. The third squadron continued to protect the rear of the column, as well as taking on the protection of the Left flank. The Germans were mortaring the area, but they did not appear to know the exact location of the column.

The fire support made motoring right up to the objective entirely successful. At 0345 hours the firing ceased, 1 BW debussed, and the two leading companies advanced into the village. There was a certain amount of opposition, but the enemy were withdrawing and some 40 prisoners only were taken. About an hour later, guides were sent back by 1 BW to bring forward the tanks to join up with their respective companies as planned. By first light the objective had been mopped up and the tanks were in position and ready for an enemy armoured counter-attack, which did not materialize until later in the day. The woods immediately to the South of ST AIGNAN DE CRAMESNIL were cleared during the morning.

The attack had been extremely successful, prisoners numbered 130 whilst the Brigade Group suffered only forty casualties. It was too misty at first light for any operations, which gave the attacking forces more time for reorganisation.

SECTION II

ATTACK ON AREAS BY-PASSED BY ARMOURED COLUMNS

The battalions of 6 Cdn Inf Bde moved up to the start line just before H hour. Les Fusiliers Mont-Royal (FUS MR), which was to capture MAY SUR ORNE, had an unfortunate start. As the battalion left the forming up area and again when it was moving through ST ANDRE SUR ORNE, it was subjected to heavy mortaring and shelling. The casualties sustained made it necessary to reorganise before advancing South from ST ANDRE. Supported by fire from the 4.2" mortars, the companies reached the outskirts of MAY SUR ORNE and one company got into the village, but was out of touch with the remainder of the battalion. At about 0150 hours, artillery support was called for and concentrations were fired, but the battalion was not able to make any headway against the accurate enemy fire.

The Queen's Own Cameron Highlanders of Canada (CAMERONS OF C) had a three thousand yard advance down the North-South road to FONTENAY LE MARMION. In the first three quarters of a mile, machine gun posts on the Left flank and a minefield on its main axis held up the advance. The sappers were brought forward to clear the mines and the infantry went on through it. Further enemy posts were encountered and by 0630 hours the capture of the Northern part of the town (up to the church) had been completed. It is pointed out that both FUS MR and CAMERONS OF C had had to rely on the accuracy of the bombing and the speed with which it could be followed up, so that the enemy positions should be reached whilst the defenders were still suffering from its effects.

At the same time, S SASK R advanced on ROQUANCOURT between the two armoured axes. Keeping close behind the barrage, the battalion entered the village about the same time as the RHLI column drove through it. It captured it without difficulty, and by 0330 hours the battalion was reorganising and preparing to meet the expected counter attack at first light.

Meanwhile, to the East of the FALAISE road, 152 (H) Bde was attacking TILLY LA CAMPAGNE, which the Germans had stoutly and successfully defended against all previous efforts to take it. Like S SASK R, 2nd Battalion The Seaforth Highlanders (2 SEAFORTH) advanced between two armoured columns, whose penetration on either side of, and beyond the village, was thought likely to have some effect on its defenders. TILLY LA CAMPAGNE had not been bombed, and was only just inside the area covered by the barrage. Additional support from 4.2" mortars and one machine gun platoon was provided, with artillery concentrations on call after the completion of the barrage.

As the leading companies approached the village, they were greeted with heavy small arms and machine gun fire. The artificial moonlight and the rising moon made visibility too good: it was possible to see men moving at about 200 yards, and as a result heavy casualties were suffered. Little definite news was heard until 0045 hours, when the Left company was reported to be in the orchard on the outskirts of the village, and engaging the enemy in close fighting. The reserve company was committed on this flank but no progress was made. The enemy fought stubbornly, bringing down heavy automatic fire, and had at least one SP gun in action on the North-East side of the village. 5th Battalion The Seaforth Highlanders (5 SEAFORTH) was holding part of the Divisional firm base at HUBERT FOLIE, and D coy from this battalion, which had been brought up to replace the reserve company, was now ordered to attack from the West. At this time, from reports received, the position of the two Right 2 SEAFORTH companies was thought to be close to their respective objectives, and it was intended that D coy 5 SEAFORTH should attack between them. In fact, the company which should have reached the South-West end of TILLY LA CAMPAGNE, had got lost and was North-West of the village. As a result the attack by D coy 5 SEAFORTH was made by one platoon only, the remainder of the company providing fire support on the open Right flank. This platoon was held up on the Western outskirts of TILLY LA CAMPAGNE near the level crossing, having suffered heavy casualties.

The situation deteriorated as the casualties mounted, and the two Left companies 2 SEAFORTH were down to a total of between forty and fifty men. At 0445 hours the Brigade Commander obtained permission to use the remainder of 5 SEAFORTH, as it was important that the village should be captured by first light. The two Left companies 2 SEAFORTH were placed under command 5 SEAFORTH, and pulled back five hundred yards to the North, so that artillery and machine gun fire could be brought down on the Eastern edge of TILLY. The new attack was timed for 0610 hours but was delayed by the mist—the Commanding Officer being unable to carry out a reconnaissance of the ground over which he was to attack.

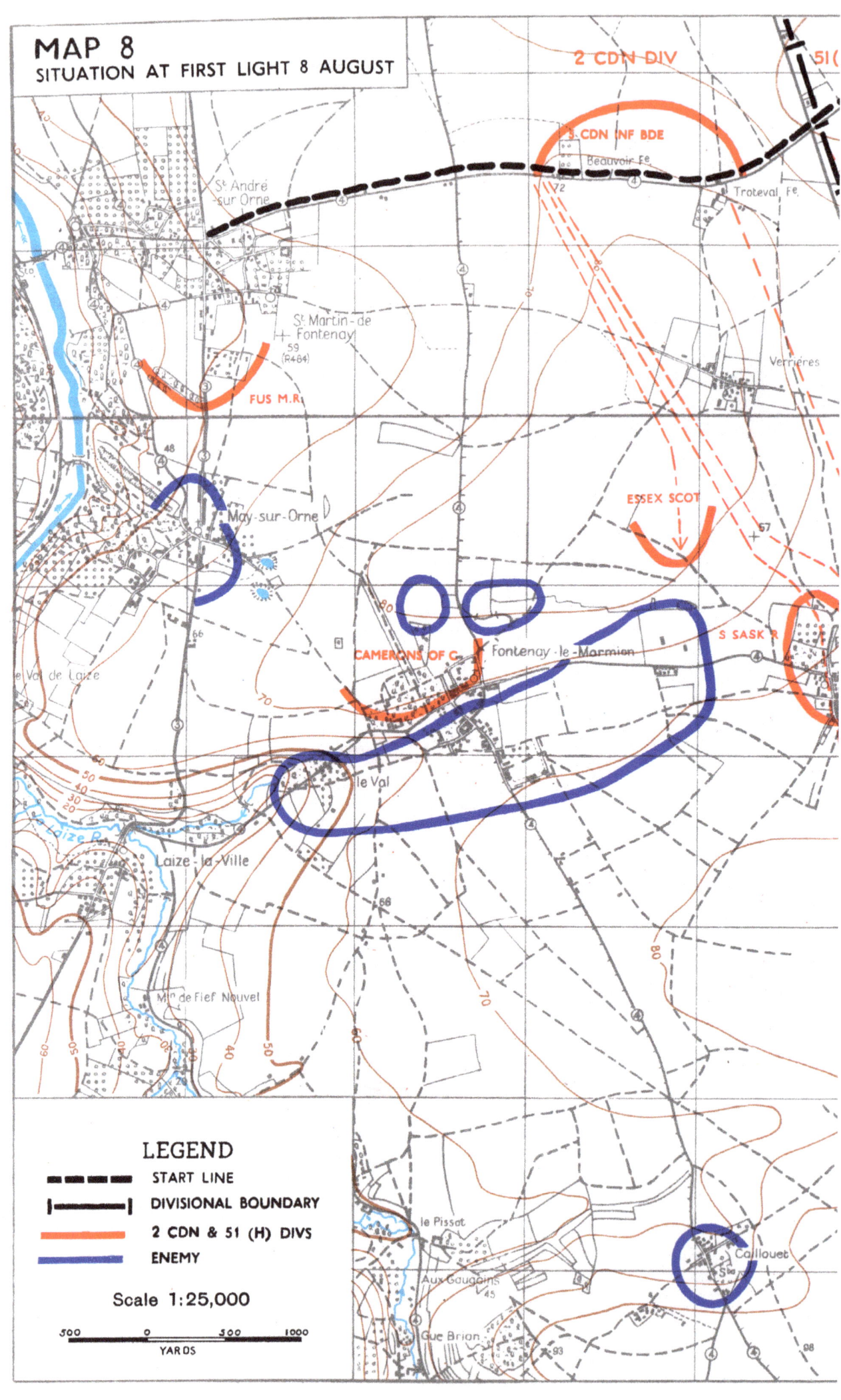

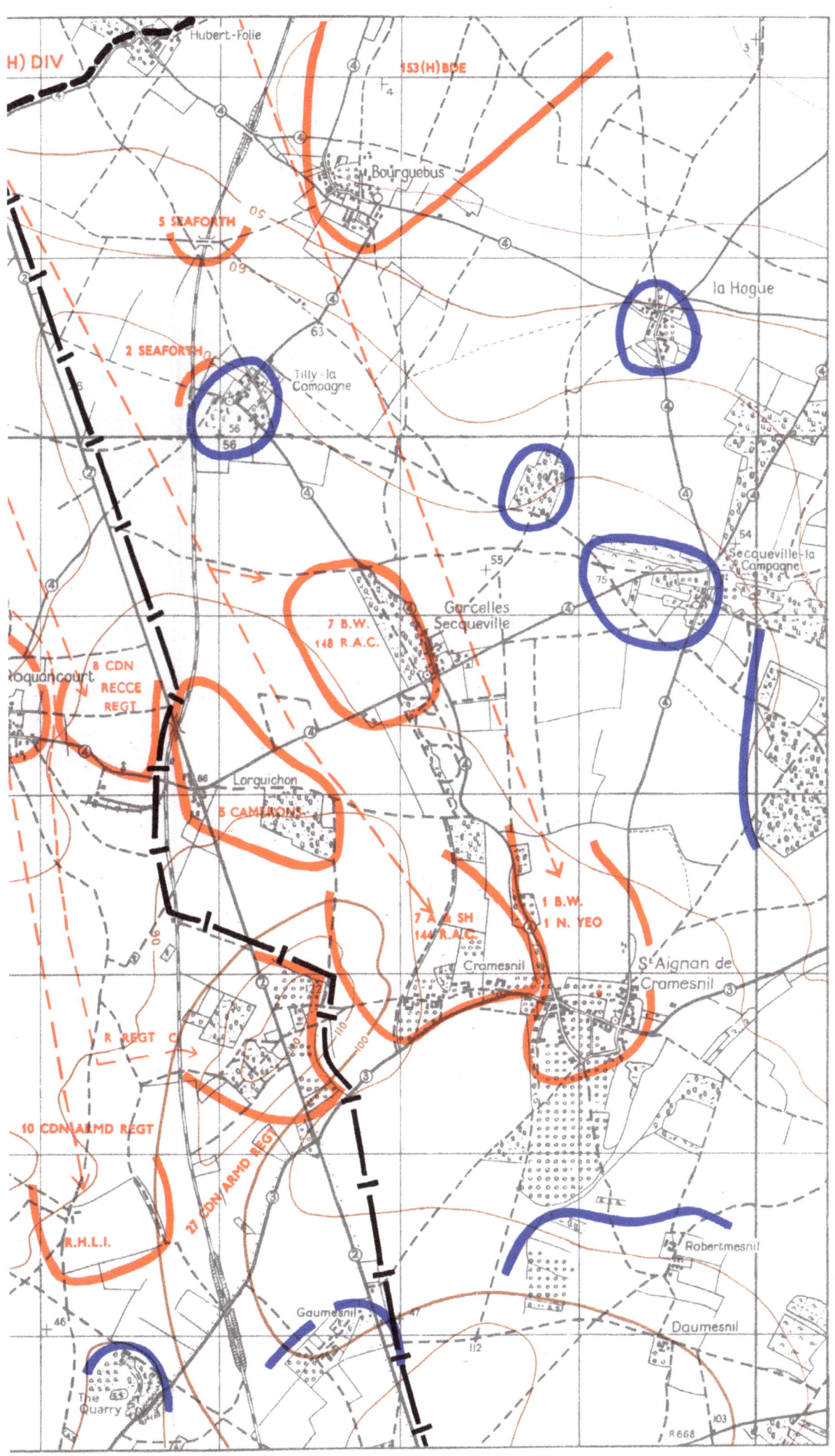

5th Battalion The Queens Own Cameron Highlanders (5 CAMERONS), which was advancing in rear of 7 BW was delayed owing to the hold ups at the head of the column. At 0130 hours it was ordered forward on the Right of the armoured column and advanced towards LORGUICHON. By 0445 hours the village and the level crossing on the FALAISE road had been captured. An hour later LORGUICHON Wood had been cleared and the battalion was consolidating in its new position.

The situation at first light was :—

On 2 Cdn Inf Div front, CAILLOUET, THE QUARRY and GAUMESNIL were still in enemy hands, but the debussing area and South to within five hundred yards of the QUARRY and the Point 122 feature were firmly held. The Northern half of FONTENAY LE MARMION. and ROQUANCOURT had been taken by the Canadians, but MAY SUR ORNE had not fallen,

On 51 (H) Div front, 154 (H) Bde and 33 Armd Bde had captured CRAMESNIL, ST AIGNAN DE CRAMESNIL and GARCELLES SECQUEVILLE, with the woods to the South of ST AIGNAN still to be cleared. LORGUICHON was held by 152 (H) Bde but the enemy was still firmly in TILLY LA CAMPAGNE.

SECTION III

DAYLIGHT OPERATIONS 8 AUGUST

The mist did not lift until 0830 hours, which gave the battalion and regimental groups time to investigate their newly won objectives and prepare for the counter attacks to come. The slow process of house to house search in the villages was still to be completed, and the ground between the battalion objectives had not been cleared. The enemy had by now realised the extent to which his defences had been penetrated, and as the visibility improved, the shelling and mortaring increased.

2 Cdn Div Front

At FONTENAY LE MARMION the situation was confused. The weakened CAMERONS OF C was being heavily shelled, was unable to clear the Southern part of the village and had had its main axis cut. Battalion HQ was hit, and for the second time in twelve hours the battalion lost its commanding officer. Artillery support was the only assistance possible until such time as S SASK R had completed its task and a company could be spared.

ESSEX SCOT, supported by 8 Cdn Recce Regt, was now ordered to advance to CAILLOUET. After considerable delays, due to 8 Cdn Recce Regt's difficulty in moving across ground still held by the enemy, the columns started. The mist cleared and tanks were observed near the village. Conflicting reports as to their identity caused another hold up and eventually, with artillery concentrations and a squadron of 27 Cdn Armd Regt in support, CAILLOUET was captured at midday.

With the better observation, reports of enemy activity increased, and information from ground and air OPs produced targets for fighter bombers and rocket firing aircraft. Throughout the day successful attacks were made on enemy tank concentrations. At 0930 hours S SASK R was being heavily shelled, and sniped from posts to the North, but the suspected counter attack did not materialize. RHLI and R REGT C were both attacked about this time. Enemy infantry supported by tanks had closed up to the Point 122 feature but were driven off with losses on both sides. From the QUARRY the enemy with the help of fire from anti-tank guns tried to dislodge RHLI but was unsuccessful.

At 1200 hours a squadron of 6 Cdn Armd Regt was made available to help mop up in the 6 Cdn Inf Bde area. A pincer movement was planned with FUS MR supported by a squadron of Crocodiles advancing on MAY SUR ORNE from the North, whilst two companies of S SASK R with the squadron of tanks advanced West along the ridge from ROQUANCOURT and then South into FONTENAY LE MARMION to help CAMERONS OF C. Owing to the late arrival of the Crocodiles, the two attacks did not go in simultaneously as intended, but both were successful. The two companies of S SASK R captured two hundred and fifty prisoners and opened up the axis to FONTENAY LE MARMION. By 1800 hours FUS MR had cleared MAY SUR ORNE.

Throughout the morning 5 Cdn Inf Bde was moving its battalions South from IFS in preparation for the attack on BRETTEVILLE SUR LAIZE.

51 (H) Div Front

At this time, 5 SEAFORTH was completing preparations for its attack on TILLY LA CAMPAGNE, which was to start as soon as visibility allowed a quick reconnaissance to be made. At 0700 hours one squadron of 148 RAC had been ordered back to support the battalion. It drove through the village and reported the opposition to be only a few snipers and some Spandau fire. As the mist cleared more enemy appeared. The squadron swept the village from East to West and took a number of prisoners. One officer offered to surrender the garrison. As a result the 5 SEAFORTH attack was cancelled and the tanks, escorted by 2 SEAFORTH, returned to the village where four officers and seventy prisoners were taken. Three SP guns were captured.

At GARCELLES SECQUEVILLE 7 BW had been subjected to some very heavy shelling and mortaring and had suffered many more casualties in the first two hours of the morning than it did during the night operation. Snipers were active and it was not until tanks had removed the nearby haycocks, disclosing enemy weapon pits underneath, that the situation improved. A counter attack on ST AIGNAN of about company strength supported by two tanks was beaten off, but further reports of enemy movement and tank concentrations South of the village suggested that another attack was likely. At 1220 hours the shelling and mortaring increased in intensity and twenty Panthers were reported moving North-East from CINTHEAUX, where they had been located earlier. 1 N YEO moved out in front of 1 BW FDLs and engaged the enemy tanks, knocking out three. During the next two hours the enemy made two more attempts to break into the ST AIGNAN position. Infantry supported by artillery and mortar concentrations, and both Panther and Tiger tanks, advanced from the South and South-East but each time were repulsed. Eleven enemy tanks were knocked out for the loss of twenty Shermans.

Advance of 4 Cdn Armd Div

By first light 4 Cdn Armd Div was moving up behind the start line and was ready to advance down the 2 Cdn Armd Bde axis of the previous night. 4 Cdn Armd Div field regiments were the first to move forward and deployed in the still uncleared area North of FONTENAY LE MARMION. The leading armoured regiment was held up near ROQUANCOURT till 1200 hours where a tremendous traffic jam occured. Little progress was made, owing to the fact that the columns could not cross the bombline until the daylight bombers had completed their task at about 1400 hours. The advance was further delayed until the capture of GAUMESNIL was completed by R REGT C at 1530 hours.

Once clear of GAUMESNIL, the enemy defences at CINTHEAUX had to be overcome. An attempt to by-pass the village resulted in some tanks being destroyed by 88 mms, but in spite of these losses, 22 Canadian Armoured Regiment (The Canadian Grenadier Guards) (22 Cdn Armd Regt) moved on to the East of CINTHEAUX. The Argyll and Sutherland Highlanders of Canada (A & SH of C) captured the village at 1800 hours taking seventy prisoners, five 88 mm and three SP guns. Having completed this task A & SH of C advanced and captured HAUTMESNIL supported by 22 Cdn Armd Regt on its Left. At last light the armoured reconnaissance regiment was advancing on BRETTEVILLE LE RABET whilst an armoured regiment battalion group was directed on Point 195.

While 4 Cdn Armd Div operations had been taking place, 2 Cdn Inf Bde had completed the capture of BRETTEVILLE SUR LAIZE. 5 Cdn Inf Bde with 6 Cdn Armd Regt in support had intended to begin this attack immediately after the bombing, but the artillery, which was required to fire a smoke screen protecting the Right flank, was engaged in supporting 6 Cdn Inf Bde. The attack started at 1600 hours with one battalion directed on BRETTEVILLE, whilst another dealt with QUILLY and the surrounding orchards.

The tanks and infantry made a spectacular advance through blazing wheat and the rifle companies reached their objectives opposed by spasmodic mortar and machine gun fire. The Commanding Officer, The Calgary Highlanders (CALG HIGHRS) having cleared BRETTEVILLE SUR LAIZE, decided to hold it from the high ground to the North and having obtained permission from Brigade HQ, withdrew the battalion. Unfortunately it was caught by enemy shell fire as it withdrew up the slopes and suffered heavy casualties. R de MAIS was at this time at QUILLY, with RHC the third battalion of 5 Cdn Inf Bde on its Left.

Advance of 1 Polish Armd Div

1 Polish Armd Div, after an approach march during the previous night, had advanced slowly during the morning down the 51 (H) Div axis and by 1400 hours had reached 154 (H) Bde positions. The enemy counter-attacks previously mentioned, halted its advance. For the remainder of the day, 1 Polish Armd Div engaged these enemy tanks which had withdrawn some two thousand yards to the South-East of ST AIGNAN. Six enemy tanks were knocked out but little further advance had been made by last light.

Meanwhile 153 (H) Bde had been relieved by 146 Inf Bde of 49 Div and 1st Battalion The Gordon Highlanders (1 GORDONS) was moved up in Priests to a dispersal area East of ROQUANCOURT, preparatory to attacking SECQUEVILLE LA CAMPAGNE. To support this attack one squadron 148 RAC, two troops 141 RAC (Crocodiles), and one platoon 4.2" mortars were made available. In the planning for Operation TOTALIZE, a barrage had been laid on to support this attack, but at the time only one field regiment could be made available. Further, tanks of 1 Polish Armd Div, whose exact location was not known, were reported in the area between GARCELLES SECQUEVILLE and the objective. Timed concentrations were therefore fired from H hour onwards on SECQUEVILLE LA CAMPAGNE.

The enemy was known to be holding the village and was also dug-in between the latter and GARCELLES SECQUEVILLE. Reports during the morning had shown considerable enemy movement in the vicinity of SECQUEVILLE and the woods to the East, and stiff opposition was expected. Time was very limited and no detailed reconnaissance was possible except by the Commanding Officer. 1 GORDONS moved on foot to an assembly area at LORGUICHON Wood, and joined up with the tanks and Crocodiles on the start line at GARCELLES SECQUEVILLE as the attack started. Luckily the heavy enemy shelling of GARCELLES slackened as the battalion formed up, and only sporadic fire and one particularly accurate defensive fire concentration were met during the advance.

The support from the artillery concentrations, mortar fire and Crocodiles was very effective, and although the enemy in the village fought hard, all objectives had been captured by 1800 hours, an hour after the attack started. Sixty-five prisoners from 1055 GR were captured and many more had been killed during the action. Patrols pushed out along the tracks through the woods to the East, but few enemy were seen.

In the meantime, the other two battalions of the brigade had moved up in armoured troop-carriers and as one was committed, the next took its place. 5th Battalion The Black Watch (Royal Highland Regiment) (5 BW) passed through 1 GORDONS and cleared the small wood to the North-East of SECQUEVILLE LA CAMPAGNE and occupied LA HOGUE. 5/7th Battalion The Gordon Highlanders (5/7 GORDONS) advanced into the wood from the South-East of the village and by 2100 hours had reached the track which runs from South-West to North-East through the wood.

At the conclusion of daylight operations on 8 August, Phase II of Operation TOTALIZE was well under way. On the Canadian front only searching remained to be completed North of BRETTEVILLE SUR LAIZE. East of the FALAISE road the large wood to the West of CHICHEBOVILLE and those to the South-East of ST AIGNAN had still to be cleared.

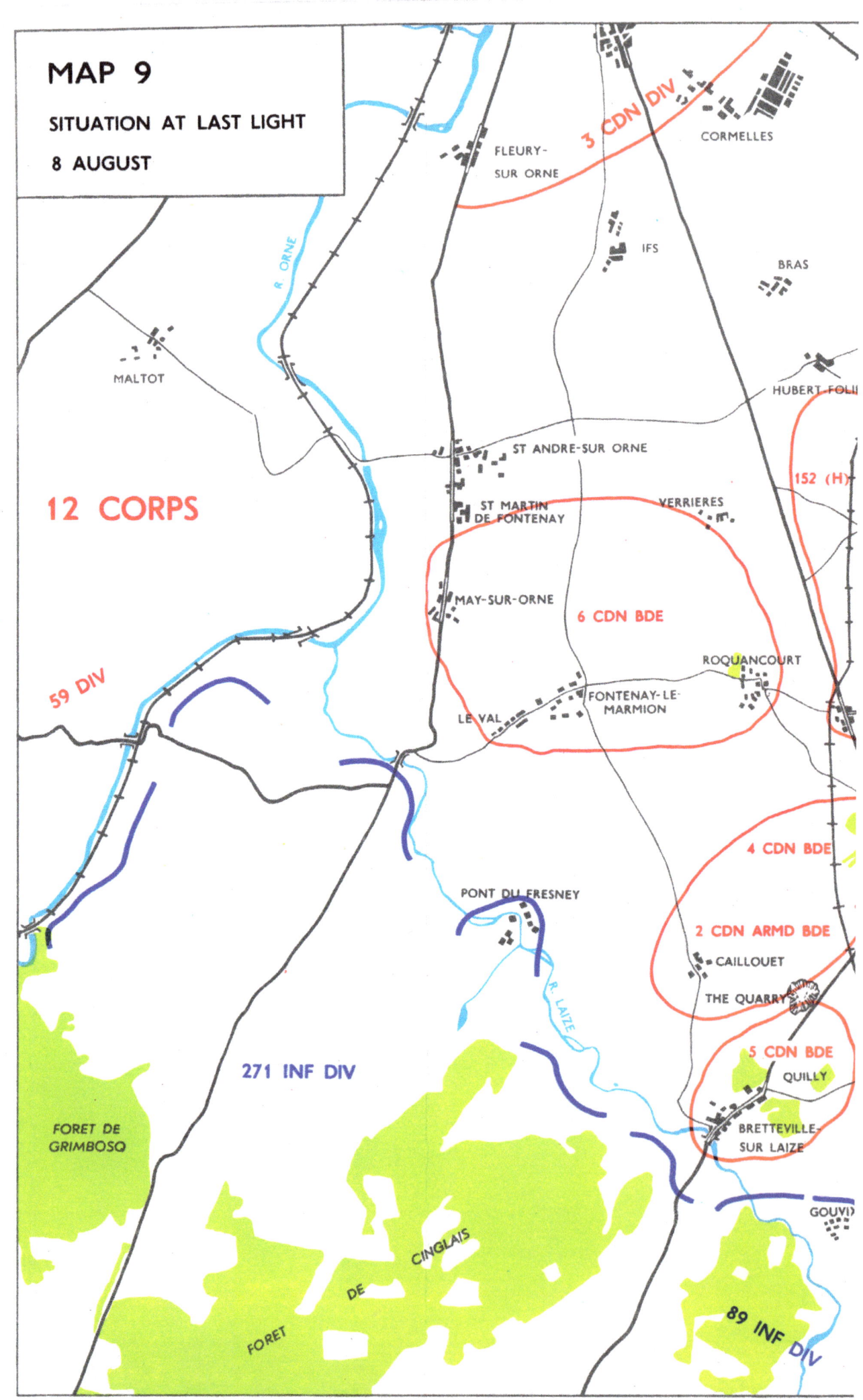

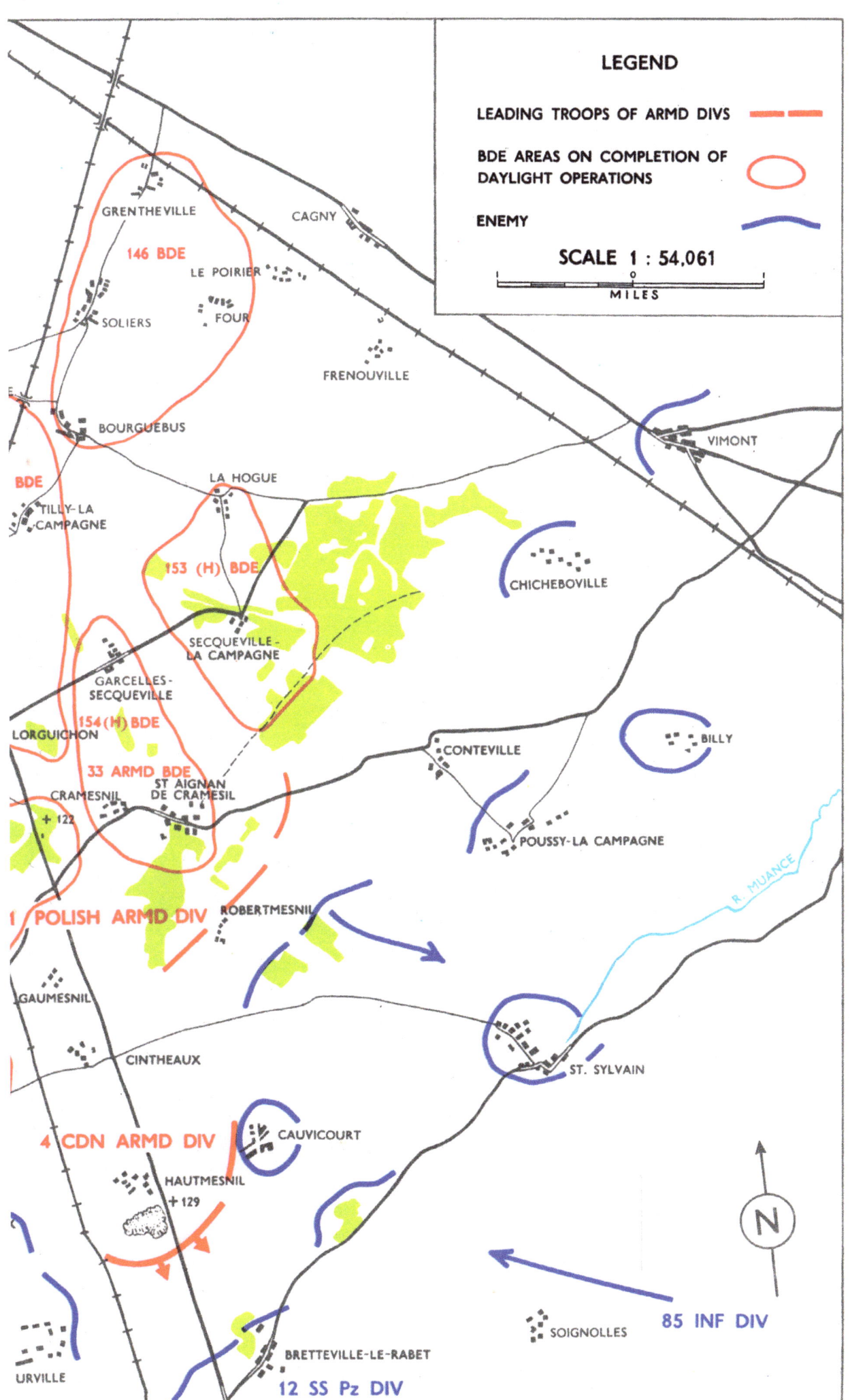

SECTION IV

A SHORT ACCOUNT OF PHASE II

(Note : This is included in order to show what happened in Phase II of the operation and is not intended to form a part of the Tour. Reference should be made to the pocket map.)

Throughout the night 8/9 August, 2 Cdn and 51 (H) Divs were engaged in patrolling and clearing up the objectives captured during the previous afternoon and evening. Although the roads and bridges at BRETTEVILLE SUR LAIZE were impassable, parties of Germans were withdrawing through the town from the FORET DE CINGLAIS between the Rivers ORNE and LAIZE. 1 Polish Armd Div was in the woods immediately South of ST AIGNAN DE CRAMESNIL. Meanwhile 28 Canadian Armoured Regiment (The British Columbia Regiment) (28 Cdn Armd Regt) and The Algonquin Regiment (ALQ R) were advancing on Pt 195. By 0600 hours 28 Cdn Armd Regt reported it was half a mile South of BRETTEVILLE LE RABET, but no more was heard from either regiment for some time.

During 9 August, GRAINVILLE LANGANNERIE and BRETTEVILLE LE RABET were occupied by 10 Cdn Lorried Inf Bde supported by 22 Cdn Armd Regt. 3 Cdn Div took over the CINTHEAUX HAUTMESNIL area and later in the day GOUVIX, GRAINVILLE LANGANNERIE and BRETTEVILLE LE RABET. 1 Polish Armd Div captured ST SYLVAIN and was in contact with the enemy at ST MARTIN DES BOIS. Further West SOIGNELLES and ESTREES LA CAMPAGNE were being cleared late in the evening. 51 (H) Div searched the big woods to the East of SECQUEVILLE LA CAMPAGNE, captured CONTEVILLE and POUSSY LA CAMPAGNE and took over ST SYLVAIN from 1 Polish Armd Div. At midnight 51 (H) Div reverted to command 1 Corps.

Throughout the day the information received from 28 Cdn Armd Regt and ALQ R had been very confusing. They reported that they were on Pt 195 and had suffered considerable casualties from the 88 mm's of a flak regiment and from counter attacks by tanks of 12 SS Pz Div. Efforts by 4 Cdn Armd Bde to send help to them had resulted in 21 Canadian Armoured Regiment (The Governor General's Foot Guards) (21 Cdn Armd Regt) being halted just South of GRAINVILLE LANGANNERIE by heavy anti-tank fire from the QUESNAY Woods. Further, there were no signs of tanks on Pt 195 nor could any firing be heard from that direction. There was a battle going on to the East of the main road, but 4 Cdn Armd Div thought it was a 1 Polish Armd Div action and it was some time before it was established that the leading Polish tanks were not so far South. Eventually it was discovered that 28 Cdn Armd Regt had lost direction during the night advance and was on the high ground due East of ESTREES LA CAMPAGNE, between Pts 88 and 111 (1449). 28 Cdn Armd Regt and ALQ R were withdrawn during the night having fought a very gallant action on their own and suffered very heavy casualties.

Pts 180 and 195 were occupied during the night and early morning 9/10 August by 4 Cdn Armd Div and the next night an attack was made by 3 Cdn Div on QUESNAY, with AISY and SOUMONT ST QUENTIN as second phase objectives. This attack was not successful. At the same time 51 (H) Div captured the woods 2000 yards South-East of ST SYLVAIN but was counter attacked four times next day by 12 SS Pz Div.

Enemy opposition had hardened and further attempts to advance on either flank were proving costly and difficult. It was clear that a strong anti-tank screen had been formed from FONTAINE-LE-PIN to QUESNAY and along the high ground protecting the LAISON valley. It was estimated that there were fifty 88 mm's deployed here and 12 SS Pz Div had 85 Inf Div and the remnants of 89 Inf Div to help hold the front from FONTAINE-LE-PIN to CONDE SUR IFS. 271 Inf Div was further West. To break through this position 2 Cdn Corps Operation TRACTABLE was planned for 1200 hours 14 August. Regrouping for this attack occupied the time up to the 14 August except in the case of 2 Cdn Div which continued to advance on either side of the LAIZE valley and had reached LA CRESSONNIERE and HAMEL by the morning 14 August.

PART III

(Directing Staff Edition)

Personal Accounts of Actions for Study

SECTION I

INTRODUCTORY LECTURE

Extracts taken from a lecture given by
Lieutenant General G. G. SIMONDS, CB, CBE, DSO
(Commander 2nd Canadian Corps in July, 1944)
at CABOURG (NORMANDY) on 23 June 1947

General SIMONDS stated that the details of planning operation TOTALIZE were set out in Part I of the book and that he did not propose to do more than speak about the following major points :—

(a) The importance of the CAEN hinge.

(b) Armoured Personnel Carriers.

(c) Training.

(d) The Air Support for the Operation.

(e) Phase II of TOTALIZE.

The CAEN hinge

General SIMONDS explained that from the time the bridgehead had been established, it was obvious that sooner or later an attack to break through the German defences round CAEN would have to be made. It was the intention to capture CAEN itself on D Day if possible, because it was foreseen that as the build up in the bridgehead progressed, the use of the lateral roads radiating from CAEN to the West would be of the greatest importance. The portion of the town that lies North of the River ORNE was not captured until 9 July—and by then the need for more room in the bridgehead, particularly East of the ORNE where operations were likely to develop, had become apparent. The 8 Corps attack on 18 July 1944 in which 2 Cdn Corps took part, resulted in considerable gains in ground to the East and South of CAEN and the capture of VAUCELLES, the Southern portion of the town. Bridges could now be built over the River ORNE at CAEN.

It was the general opinion of all commanders that the Germans intended to make a planned withdrawal to the SEINE should this be necessary. To do this, as long as they fought West of, or on the line of the River ORNE, they must hold the CAEN area as a pivot. That they had every intention of holding this sector is borne out by the fact that this front was manned, for as long as it was possible, by as good troops as the German Army possessed—the SS Pz Divisions. Further a series of defence lines in depth was being prepared which would develop to the full the advantages that the combination of the ground and the characteristics of the German weapons offered.

The next Allied action, and possibly the most important of all from an Army Group point of view, was the attack made here in conjunction with the break out in the West on 25 July 1944. Field Marshal MONTGOMERY'S instructions were that a limited attack should be made by 2 Cdn Corps with the object of retaining the German armour in its position East of the ORNE. General SIMONDS said that he was also warned that it was probable that his Corps would be required to effect the break through the German defences South of CAEN at a later date. This holding attack was therefore planned to capture the VERRIERES ridge and TILLY LA CAMPAGNE, the use of which would be of the greatest value for the break-through battle to come.

The fact that the ground favoured the defence has been explained in the book, but he emphasised that the German positions here were particularly strong. Both Panther and Tiger tanks as well as SP guns had alternative dug in positions. Large concentrations of mortars whose fire was accurate, well directed and well timed caused casualties. During this holding attack the VERRIERES ridge was captured and held and TILLY LA CAMPAGNE was entered, but we were driven out. In a subsequent attack just prior to TOTALIZE we again got a foothold in the village but once more we were driven out.

APCs

Before the war there was a school of thought which considered that infantry were not really necessary and that given reasonable going, tanks could motor along by themselves at 25 mph and capture an objective. Events soon proved this conception to be false, and that the infantry soldier was required as much as ever when it came to taking and holding ground. Various methods had been tried of moving the infantry forward with the tanks and at tank speed, but none had been really successful. General SIMONDS stated that he had given this subject a good deal of thought and efforts had been made to get a special vehicle, but the trouble was to find a suitable one, as no one at that stage of the war was inclined to produce a new one.

Just at this period when he was studying the problem, the field regiments which had taken part in the assault landing had started to exchange their American Priest 105 mm SP guns for either SP or tractor drawn 25 pounders. The former were on loan from the Americans and, by previous agreement, were to be handed back as soon as the Corps was settled in the bridgehead. General SIMONDS continued:—

"I was one day watching some of these vehicles and it occurred to me that, if the equipment was stripped, they would be sufficiently roomy and have adequate protection to provide the sort of vehicle I had in mind. I therefore asked General CRERAR if he would intervene with the Americans to allow us to strip the equipments and use them for this particular operation."

Time was getting short and it was not until about a week before the operation that American authorisation was received; workshops had, however, already been warned and the work was rushed ahead. Having got the equipments, the next problem was to sell the idea to the troops. General SIMONDS explained:—

"It was obviously going to be quite useless to mount the infantry if they felt like a lot of sardines in a tin and had no confidence in the likelihood of the operation succeeding. So I quickly suggested to 2 Cdn Div that we might be able to produce some form of Armoured Personnel Carrier in order to get them thinking about its possibilities. As soon as the operation began to harden and I had received definite orders, I at once asked that my second infantry division should be detailed. The Highland Division was nominated and I was a bit worried as to how the Scots would like it, because they had the reputation of being rather canny and having their own ideas about things. General RENNIE, who was unfortunately later killed at the Rhine crossing, came over to see me as soon as they had been nominated and I had a talk with him. He was very taken with the idea and I knew from that first talk that I had his support one hundred per cent and subsequently 51 (H) Div took to it with great enthusiasm."

When originally considering the problem, General SIMONDS had visualised that the troops concerned would have something like a month's training because a great deal of work was needed to rule out the likelihood of very serious hitches. In the event, many units only received two days' training and the last Kangaroos, as they were subsequently called, were delivered to units only twenty four hours before the attack. He continued:—

"We should have liked a great deal more time, but whether or not that was a disadvantage only long term history can judge. I think that in many respects we lost in finesse, we probably suffered more casualties and things did not go as well as they might: but, on the other hand, the Germans were at this time reacting very quickly to our various thrusts and the long term judgment may well be that, by allowing them little respite, we benefited in the long run."

It was clearly apparent that the main difficulty in getting the infantry forward would be from the German concentrated artillery, mortar and small arms fire, all well directed and well timed. The problem for the tank was the long range, hardhitting 88 mm and 128 mm guns which were mounted in the German tank; these could usually kill our tanks whilst standing out of range, and, although this did not always apply to the 17 pounder, the gun advantage was certainly with the enemy. The German infantry defence was on an area and zonal fire basis, whilst the anti-tank defence depended on aimed shooting. General SIMONDS considered that if we could therefore get our tanks to operate at night or through a really thick smoke screen we should eliminate the aimed shot and nothing could stop them. He continued:—

"So I planned therefore that, in addition to carrying out the advance at tank pace and with the infantry in armoured carriers, the attack should be made at night. Again, I had no illusions as to the risks involved and, in particular, the difficulties of keeping direction at night. I was quite certain in my own mind that we should succeed, provided that the armoured columns could keep direction and there the features on the ground did offer some assistance: there was the main FALAISE road, the railway which would provide a guiding line on the 2 Cdn Div front in the later stages of the advance and the LORGUICHON works; in addition, the villages stood out clearly in the open country. But against this it was mid-summer and there was the problem of the dust from the bombing and artillery bombardment; in fact, there was no certainty that any of these landmarks would be seen for more than a few yards at night. So we devised every possible means to assist the columns to keep direction, including Bofors firing over the columns and an improvised wireless direction - finding apparatus; we did not expect any of these things to work by themselves, but hoped that a combination of them all would enable direction to be maintained. I had heard that the Americans had some luminous discs on posts which AVRE crews could stick in the ground as they went along and we got hold of some of them and equipped the route signing parties. I believe that during the actual operation the most useful aid was the guide parties of 79 Armd Div, whose work was outstanding."

Training

General SIMONDS next discussed the question of training and explained that, although most of the troops had not been in action before arriving in NORMANDY, they had had about three years training in ENGLAND and that it was true to say that this was the first time in the history of the British Empire that a fully trained army had been put in the field. He continued:—

"I have had probably as much experience as anybody in putting in new formations. I put in every Canadian division that went into action during the war except 3 Cdn Div, the Polish Armd Div, an American division and 52 (L) Div and there is one lesson which impressed me. A well trained division comes into the field in top form but is very inclined to start by saying "This is war now, all the things we have been learning about can be thrown over the fence - away we go". They tend, when they first go into action, to discard a lot of the minor lessons of training and they get one or two sharp lessons. Later, they come back to it and, when they reach that stage, they really reach the top of their form because the conviction has been forced on them that their training has been sound, and that all the little points of detail which need looking after when mounting an operation are not just the fantasy of somebody's mind."

Air Support for the Operation

With regard to air support, General SIMONDS pointed out that the planning was full of complications. He felt that at the time there was a school of thought which considered that it was quite wrong to use heavy bombers for tactical operations, that they were being diverted from their primary strategical tasks and that to employ them in that role was mis-using their characteristics. This, as he said, might well have been true at the time, but it was vital to remember that the greatest asset of the air arm is flexibility, and that when mounting future operations of this kind we shall forfeit this greatest asset if the air power is not so designed that it can throw its whole weight into the scale. When planning TOTALIZE, General SIMONDS had been promised full air support, but the required organisation to ensure quick decisions did not exist. HQ Bomber Command was in England and the officers who visited NORMANDY had not the authority to give definite answers; this led to long delays while matters were argued across the Channel.

The air plan is fully covered in the book, but General SIMONDS stressed the following points :—

"What I had in mind for this operation was to use the air mainly in Phase II, when artillery support would be getting to a minimum. This was essential because in an attempt to break through and penetrate to a depth of some four to five thousand yards, an attack is liable to fade out when it runs out of full artillery support. But also I wanted it in Phase I, to seal off the flanks of the very narrow corridor through which the armoured columns were to pass and, in particular, from enemy armour. I thought I could time the attack so as to use the heavy bombers at night, and then get a second lift about noon the following day. The air staff said that this was possible but, in the event, decided that our own heavy bombers from Bomber Command would only do the night lift and that the bombing the following day would be done by VIII USAAF. This led to further complications as VIII USAAF was not equipped with the same aids for precision bombing and would have to depend largely on visual identification of targets."

PHASE II

In his remarks with regard to Phase II of the attack General SIMONDS drew attention to the very narrow gap between CINTHEAUX and ROBERTSMESNIL. He had originally planned to go through with one armoured division up and then feed the other through behind it. When however it appeared that the layback position was held in greater strength, he decided, in order to save time, to launch the two divisions together with their tails organised behind them and ready to fan out as they came through the gap. He went on to say :—

"Phase II did not go off with the bang we had hoped and there were, I think, three or four contributory factors. I had stressed very strongly to the two armoured divisional commanders that, when the time came for them to pass through, they were to take up the battle regardless of the position reached by the infantry divisions. In other words, there was to be no quibbling about whether they should wait until one of the infantry divisions had taken some part of their final objective. At that stage we had two AGsRA each of five medium regiments, one in support of each armoured division. All likely targets on the flanks and front had been carefully registered and given code names. In order to keep the tempo going, I again stressed to the armoured divisional commanders that they must not get involved in probing out the position before they called down fire or the fighter bombers. Neither did so and this was one of the reasons why the pass through was rather sticky. In the case of the Polish Armd Div, this was largely a question of language difficulty and we hadn't the understanding that we built up later on."

General SIMONDS next mentioned that, on the day prior to the attack, a German flak 88 mm regiment had deployed in the area. These guns were sited so as to be effective in an anti-tank role and they caused very heavy casualties among the leading regiment in 4 Cdn Armd Div.

The last factor was "roadboundness" and General SIMONDS continued :—

"This was an inevitable failure of training in England, where it is very difficult to get away from the roads. There were cases where there was all the room in the world to deploy across country but nevertheless the armour kept to the road and, in due course met the anti-tank gun sited to cover it. It must be borne in mind that both these divisions were in action for the first time and my remarks have not been made in any sense of reflection. They both did extremely well, but had they been in the form they reached two weeks later they would have gone straight through."

In conclusion General SIMONDS mentioned that there is a school of thought which claims that future wars can be won by strategic action alone. This, he said might be true, but the history of warfare had so far shown that victory can only be confirmed by the infantryman on his feet delivering a coup de grace in one form or another. He ended :—

"I feel most strongly that it behoves any of us who are concerned with the future of an army to do everything we can and to work our brains so as to ease the tasks of the infantry man. It must always be the toughest job of all and we must devise every means to lighten his task, minimise his casualties and ensure that the rewards of success are as great as possible."

SECTION II

ITINERARY

(Time has been allowed at each stand for debussing and embussing)

Time	Event/Account	Speaker
0915	Arrive STAND 1. (MR 05806185)	
	A. Description of ground, enemy positions, FDLs, fire plan, air support and concentration	Conducting Officer
	B. Task of 144 RAC—7 A & SH column, plan for the advance, Order of March, aids to navigation	CO 144 RAC
	C. Loading of 7 A & SH in APCs, Order of March	CO 7 A & SH
	D. Forming up and advance to the Start Line	CO 144 RAC
	Questions	
0955	Depart STAND 1	
1000	Arrive STAND 2. (MR 06775935)	
	A. Description of ground and general situation	Conducting Officer
	B. Description of 144 RAC's advance and action at the railway crossing	CO 144 RAC
	C. Account of 7 A & SH progress in rear of the column	CO 7 A & SH
	Questions	
1050	Depart STAND 2	
1055	Arrive STAND 3. (MR 08205727)	
	A. Description of the ground and general situation	Conducting Officer
	B. Account of the advance to the Debussing Area and deployment of 144 RAC in support of 7 A & SH	CO 144 RAC
	C. Plan for and an account of the capture of CRAMESNIL	CO 7 A & SH
	Questions	
1145	Depart STAND 3	
1155	Arrive STAND 4. (MR 07155543)	
	A. Description of the ground	Conducting Officer
	B. Account of the night attack by 2 Cdn Div, and their actions during daylight 8 Aug	
	Questions	
1240	Depart STAND 4	
1250	Arrive STAND 5. (MR 08105909)	
	A. Description of the ground and general situation	Conducting Officer
	B. Detailed information available to CO 1 GORDONS concerning the following:—	
	(a) Enemy Dispositions	CO 1 GORDONS
	(b) Own Troops Dispositions	
	(c) Supporting arms available for the attack on SECQUEVILLE LA CAMPAGNE	
	Issue Problem	
	Consider Problem. Lunch	
	Move to STAND at (MR 08685863)	
	C. Discuss Problem. Account of the capture of SECQUEVILLE LA CAMPAGNE by 1 GORDONS	CO 1 GORDONS

Time	Event/Accounts	Speaker
1445	Depart STAND 5	
1500	Arrive STAND 6. (MR 06286193)	
	A. Description of the ground and general situation	Conducting Officer
	B. Planning the capture of TILLY LA CAMPAGNE	Comd 152 (H) Bde
	C. 2 SEAFORTH plan	OC C Coy 2 SEAFORTH
	Questions	
1540	Depart STAND 6	
1550	Arrive STAND 7. (MR 06946044)	
	A. Description of the enemy defences and account of the action at TILLY LA CAMPAGNE	OC C Coy 2 SEAFORTH
	B. Lessons from the action	Comd 152 (H) Bde
	Questions	
	Summing up	
1630	Depart STAND 7	

SECTION III

PERSONAL ACCOUNTS

(Note : Officers, ranks and decorations are shown as they were in June 1947. Appointments shown are those held in August 1944)

STAND 1. (MR 05806185)
(Spectators stand facing North)

Object of Stand

(a) A brief introduction to Operation TOTALIZE.

(b) To study the plan, forming up and advance of 144 RAC—7 A & SH column.

A. CONDUCTING OFFICER

Description of the ground

You are now standing beside the Corps Start Line for Operation TOTALIZE—the lateral road which is just behind you. On your Right in the belt of dark trees is the village of HUBERT FOLIE. To the Left of it is BRAS some 1200 yards to your front. Looking at the Left end of BRAS, you will see a chimney and water tower side by side. That is the CORMELLES factory.

Immediately on your Left flank, 200 yards away beside the main road is a house. Further down the main road towards CAEN is another group of buildings. In between the latter and the house, across the other side of the main road is the village of IFS and beyond it the black tower and the church spire of FLEURY SUR ORNE can be seen. Reference house and the first telegraph pole to the Left of it—to the Left of the telegraph pole you can see some grey roofed houses and a barn sticking up over the intermediate crest and below the skyline (Grid Bearing 275). That is MALTOT on the far bank of the River ORNE ; the hill to the Left of MALTOT on the skyline is Pt 112. Moving Left handed from Pt 112 and in front of us on the nearest crest is BEAUVOIR FARM, which is on the Corps Start Line. Nearer still and on the far side of the cross roads to your Left front is TROTEVAL FARM, with MONT PINCON sticking up behind it.

The village to the Left of TROTEVAL FARM is VERRIERES. From VERRIERES look Left along the crest until you come to a battered grey church tower and the mine shaft buildings of ROQUANCOURT. To the Left of the mine shaft building and on this side of the main road on the skyline is a clump of trees, through which runs the power-line, that is Pt 122. The dark wood to the Left of Pt 122 is LORGUICHON Wood. The village to your Left front with the red roofed barn is TILLY LA CAMPAGNE and the belt of dark trees to the Right of TILLY hide GARCELLES SECQUEVILLE and CRAMESNIL.

Between TILLY LA CAMPAGNE and HUBERT FOLIE, the church tower of BOURGUEBUS is just visible, (Grid Bearing 104°). A railway runs across the front from Left to Right, passing this side of TILLY LA CAMPAGNE, crosses the main road opposite ROQUANCOURT and then runs South towards FALAISE.

The Enemy

(a) FDLs

On the Right of the main road the enemy FDLs are out of sight beyond the crest. ROQUANCOURT was held by the enemy and from there the line crossed the main road approximately at Pt 76, 062603 (describe by reference to a suitable object on the ground). It included TILLY LA CAMPAGNE and stretched away to the East to LA HOGUE, which is out of sight from here between BOURGUEBUS and TILLY LA CAMPAGNE.

(b) Formations in the Line

89 Inf Div had recently taken over this front from the ORNE to LA HOGUE from 1 SS Pz Div. 89 Div came from NORWAY direct here except for a short stay at AMIENS. It was a pocket division, which is smaller than the normal infantry division, having only two infantry regiments instead of the normal three. The artillery regiment had three battalions instead of four and the anti-tank battalion two companies instead of four.

89 Div was deployed with 1056 GR Right and 1055 Left with ROQUANCOURT inclusive to 1055 GR. Each regiment had two battalions up and in the case of 1055, III Battalion held the front from inclusive ROQUANCOURT to inclusive TILLY LA CAMPAGNE. II Battalion was from exclusive TILLY to inclusive LA HOGUE with I Battalion in reserve about Pt 122 and GARCELLES SECQUEVILLE and protecting the gun areas further back.

12 SS Pz Div was nine miles South of here on the River LAISON. Moving up to this front, as fast as it was able, was 85 Inf Div, but it did not go into action before 10 August.

Own Troops

2 Cdn Corps FDLs ran from the River ORNE about ST MARTIN DE FONTENAY–VERRIERES–HUBERT FOLIE–BOURGUEBUS–FOUR (2000 yards North East of BOURGUEBUS). They were held by two divisions 2 Cdn Div Right and 51 (H) Div Left, the latter replacing 4 Cdn Armd Div the night before the attack. Each division had two brigades up with the divisional boundary the FALAISE road.

The plan for this attack was similar in both divisions. Briefly, in each case, an armoured brigade with an infantry brigade in Armoured Personnel Carriers advanced on two axes to objectives some 6000 yards away, which on this side of the main road, are on the skyline in front. At the same time an infantry brigade from each division, using a battalion for each objective, dealt with strong points such as TILLY LA CAMPAGNE and ROQUANCOURT by-passed by the armour.

On 2 Cdn Div front, the armoured column on the Right axis crossed the start line at BEAUVOIR FARM passed West of VERRIERES and ROQUANCOURT to attack Pt 122 and objectives West of it. The column on the Left axis started at TROTEVAL FARM and passed East of VERRIERES and ROQUANCOURT and was also to capture Pt 122.

Support

To support this attack 640 heavy bombers attacked LA HOGUE, SECQUEVILLE LA CAMPAGNE, the woods to the South of SECQUEVILLE and two targets on the Right flank during the half hour before H hour. A barrage was fired by nine field and nine medium regiments and advanced at 100 yards in 1 minute. Its opening line was some 400 yards South of VERRIERES and extended from approximately 1000 yards to the Right of that village to TILLY LA CAMPAGNE which was just included.

Assembly

The assembly area for this operation was the area CAEN–FLEURY SUR ORNE–IFS–BRAS and CORMELLES. There were already eleven field regiments and two AGRAs deployed in this area, together with 4 Cdn Armd Div in VAUCELLES and 51 (H) Div and 2 Cdn Div astride the main road. 2 Cdn Armd and 4 Cdn Inf Bdes moved in on the afternoon and evening of 7 August. In spite of the dust clouds raised by the vehicles, the enemy made no attempt to interfere by shelling or air attack.

We are now going to deal briefly with the 51 (H) Div plan and in particular with the leading Armoured Regiment-Battalion group on the Right axis.

B. COLONEL A. JOLLY, DSO, MC, CO, 144 RAC

144 RAC Plan

The axis of the column whose fortunes we are going to follow in detail passed through this point where we are standing. This was the Right of the 51 (H) Div's two axes. We therefore had the Canadians on our Right (on the other side of the CAEN–FALAISE road) and another armoured column of 51 (H) Div on our Left.

These Highland Division columns were found by 154 (H) Bde supported by 33 Armd Bde—an independent armoured brigade equipped with Sherman tanks. Each infantry battalion was carried in improvised APCs and supported by a regiment of tanks.

The column on this axis consisted of 144 RAC which I was commanding and the 7 A & SH commanded by Col MEIKLEJOHN. Also under my command was one squadron of Flails (22 DRAGOONS), in case we met an unexpected minefield, one troop of AVsRE (80 Aslt Sqn RE), a detachment of the divisional RE and two armoured bulldozers.

On the night 7/8 August, my regiment's task was to escort 7 A & SH, to cross this road which was our start line at 2330 hours, by-pass TILLY to the West, deal with any opposition on the centre line, and put the infantry down three miles from here outside the village of CRAMESNIL, which was their objective. The infantry was then to dismount and capture the village by night attack. At first light the tanks were to occupy battle positions previously selected from air photographs as the enemy was expected to react with an armoured counter-attack, which he did.

On our Left, a similar column consisting of 1 N YEO with 1 BW, was to by-pass TILLY to the East and occupy ST AIGNAN.

148 RAC with 7 BW was to follow us on this Right hand axis until they reached the railway and then turn off Left, occupying the village and woods of GARCELLES SECQUEVILLE. This would place them to our Left rear, protecting the Left flank of the position. The Canadians were doing the same sort of thing on our Right.

Simultaneously, a battalion of 152 (H) Bde was to attack TILLY under cover of the barrage and another battalion of that brigade was to follow up the advance on this axis and occupy LORGUICHON village and wood.

Each of the armoured columns was to be commanded by the armoured regimental commander as far as the debussing point and he was to decide when the infantry was to dismount, should this become necessary before reaching the objective. After the infantry had debussed, their commanding officer was to be in command in the normal way with the tanks acting in support.

It was appreciated that the main problem was likely to be in maintaining control and keeping direction in the dark. But, whereas in daylight the advantages were with the enemy, as he could knock out our tanks at long range if they attempted to move over this very open country, at night, provided we could keep direction, the advantages would be with us. The enemy anti-tank gunners would, we hoped, be taken by surprise and would not have enough light for accurate shooting until we were right on top of them.

The open nature of the country was an advantage by night as there were few obstacles to movement by armour. As far as this column was concerned the only serious obstacle might be the line of the railway as parts of it run through a cutting and it was thought that the other parts might be mined. However, no mines had been definitely reported.

So much for my task and the problem as it appeared to me from the regimental commander's point of view.

On 3 August we concentrated on the other side of CAEN with 51 (H) Div. On the morning of 4 August we heard the divisional plan from General RENNIE and started our own planning. The next day there was a further divisional conference and we heard that the attack which was to have taken place on the night of 8/9 August, had been advanced 24 hours to the 7/8. We carried out a daylight rehearsal that afternoon (5 August) and a night rehearsal that night—LEBISEY wood representing our objective. There was no time for more and the next day, 6 August, we moved across the ORNE to our Assembly Area in the CORMELLES factory, the chimneys of which you can see behind you. There was a certain amount of shelling that night and the Flail squadron had some casualties.

The next morning I gave out detailed orders and issued a diagram showing the exact position of each vehicle in the column. The plan, which was similar for each column in 33 Armd Bde, was to advance in a solid phalanx, four vehicles abreast with about two yards between vehicles, making a column approximately 16 yards wide by 350 yards long.

My column was to be led by the Officer Commanding Recce Troop acting as regimental navigator followed by two troops of A Sqn in line. Behind these two troops came four troops of Flails each troop in line ahead, then the RE party, AVsRE and bulldozers, then the remaining two troops of A Sqn. The whole of this block was under command of the Officer Commanding A Sqn during the advance.

The next block was the Regimental HQ party consisting of myself, my second-in-command and LO, the Flail squadron leader, with some light tanks as chargers and for liaison, and a Bren carrier loaded with spare ammunition.

B Sqn came next, again four abreast, with each of the four troops in line ahead.

This was followed by the whole of 7 A & SH in its APCs. C Sqn brought up the rear in the same formation.

We had the normal wireless communications and, in addition, my regimental LO was with Col MEIKLEJOHN in his command vehicle with an additional No 19 Set on my regimental net. Each infantry company had with it a squadron liaison officer in a tank.

The column was all armoured and all tracked. There were no administrative vehicles with the exception of the Bren carrier loaded with spare ammunition.

Navigational aids were of particular importance to this Right hand column. From the air photographs it looked as though the cutting through which the railway runs was likely to be an obstacle except for a stretch of about 500 yards South of TILLY—that is on the other side of TILLY as we look at it from here. As TILLY itself was strongly held I wanted to give it as wide a berth as possible and this therefore reduced the area for crossing the railway to the immediate neighbourhood of a certain railway hut which is the next stand and which lies about 1000 yards to the other side of TILLY.

From here, which was our Start Point, to this railway hut, was a magnetic bearing of 162 degrees and a prolongation of this bearing took us on through a very distinctive square field surrounded by tall trees, past the corner of LORGUICHON Wood to the debussing point. It was therefore of some importance for us to keep on this bearing.

We had one regimental navigator with two reserve nagivators immediately behind him. They each had a P 8 compass and were also trying to use a wireless beam method whereby they heard a series of dots if they went too far to the Right and dashes if they went too far to the Left.

Bofors tracer was also used as a navigational aid, one burst being fired along the axis every five minutes.

Movement light was also provided, the searchlights pointing in the general direction of, and above, the objective.

There was a fairly generous allotment of air photographs and all officers knew what landmarks to look for. This was found to be the only reliable navigational aid, although the Bofors tracer and movement light were of very great assistance.

Finally, in order to keep control and maintain direction, it was impressed on everyone that there must be no gaps in the column; the leaders would go at the speed of the barrage—approximately 3½ mph—and every vehicle was to keep closed right up to the one in front. No attempt was even to be made to leave any gaps between Squadron blocks. Tail lights were to be kept on but were blacked out except for a small chink of light.

Before I deal with the forming up and move to the Start Line I will ask Col MEIKLEJOHN to tell you how he organised his APCs.

C. LIEUTENANT COLONEL J. C. MEIKLEJOHN, DSO, CO 7 A & SH

Loading of the battalion into APCs

No written orders were issued for this show; everything was given out at a series of O Groups and conferences, so that I can only speak from my own memory and from what I have got from other officers.

Owing to weakness of numbers, particularly in officers and NCOs, all battalions in the Brigade were for this operation reduced to three companies, as it was considered preferable to attack with three strong companies with sections of 1 and 6, rather than with four weak ones.

Thirty APCs were received, Priests and half tracks, and they were allotted three to Battalion HQ and eight or nine to each company, depending on the number of Priests they got. Not all the companies loaded their vehicles in the same way but the following is an example.

Company HQ less stretcher bearers in one half track. Each platoon was loaded either in two Priests or one Priest and two half tracks. A half track took 8—10 men depending on their load and carried one section comfortably. A Priest took 12—14 men and carried two sections or one section and platoon headquarters. Although they looked very big, the Priests did not hold as many men as you would think because of the number of bits and pieces that were sticking out inside them.

Each sub-unit formed a separate block in the column, with two or more rows of four vehicles each. We realised that this was not the best formation from the point of view of guiding and control; for this, it would have been better to have all the company vehicles following the company commanders in one long snake, but this did not fit in with the rest of the column and it would have made deployment after debussing difficult.

B Coy led in the first block with 8 or 9 vehicles. Battalion HQ followed, consisting of three half tracks, a White scout car containing wireless sets, the gunner's half track, the RAP in a captured German half track and a detachment of RE in two scout cars—total 8. A and D Coys followed each consisting of 9 vehicles. An FOO moved with A Coy in a tank and each company had a liaison officer from 144 RAC. Last of all came F Echelon, consisting of my own S Coy and a troop of Canadian M 10s. S Coy, including the two carriers of each rifle company and S Coy's carriers with the battalion reserve ammunition, consisted of about thirty carriers and six 4×4 15 cwt trucks towing the anti-tank guns. There were about 40 vehicles in F Echelon, so that the total number in the whole battalion was about 80.

D. COLONEL A. JOLLY, DSO, MC, CO 144 RAC

Advance to the Start Line

While I was giving out orders on the morning of 7 August my Second-in-Command had made very detailed arrangements for forming up the column and marking the route. At ten minutes past nine that evening we moved out of the CORMELLES factory through the narrow streets on the outskirts of CAEN. An hour later the tightly packed column of over 150 vehicles was drawn up in the FUP looking more as though the occasion was a review than a battle. 148 RAC and 7 BW followed behind us and formed up on our Left as there was no room for them between the tail of our column and the built-up area behind. 1 N YEO and 1 BW were forming up in a similar manner the other side of BRAS. The head of our column was about a mile North of here which, as you can see, was the nearest point at which we could form up and still be in dead ground from the enemy. Between there and the Start Line, where we are standing, the route was marked by a double line of green and amber directional lights.

It was a perfect, still Summer's evening, and everyone was very quiet while we waited until it was time to move off. At ten minutes to eleven, as the light was just beginning to fail, the silence was broken by the engines starting up and we began to move slowly up to the Start Line. The speed for this first mile was 1½ mph as we did not want to forfeit surprise with a lot of dust and noise before reaching the Start Line. We also wanted to make certain that we started off with the column well closed up.

The air bombardment was in progress while we were moving up to the Start Line but the noise of the tanks was so great that we hardly realised it was on and certainly did not require the ear plugs with which we had been ordered to provide ourselves. So far there was no enemy reaction and at H hour—half past eleven—by which time it was dark, we crossed this road and speeded up to 5 mph. This was in order to be close up to the barrage when it opened fifteen minutes later on a line just over a mile from here. This part of the advance was also without incident and we were up to time when the barrage opened up on the line I have mentioned, just this side of TILLY.

QUESTIONS

STAND 2 (MR 06775935)

Object of Stand

To study the progress of the night advance by the 144 RAC—7 A & SH column.

A. CONDUCTING OFFICER

Description of the Ground and General Situation

To your Right front is the level crossing over which the 144 RAC—7 A & SH Group was to pass (MR 06865932). To the Right of the ruined hut you can see GARCELLES SECQUEVILLE amongst the trees and to the Right again you get a closer view of LORGUICHON Wood and Pt 122.

In the Left foreground is TILLY LA CAMPAGNE and to the Left the belt of trees at HUBERT FOLIE which we have just left. The village behind you is ROQUANCOURT.

It was about 0130 hours when the leading tanks reached the crossing and the general situation was as follows.

ROQUANCOURT village had been captured but the Canadian armoured columns as they by-passed the village were meeting opposition. Most of the leading group of vehicles in each column were by now beyond the village, but the main bodies were still this side. An 88 mm firing at short range at the columns on the Right axis was causing the delay there and this side of the village machine gun posts had to be eliminated.

TILLY LA CAMPAGNE was still held by the enemy. 2 SEAFORTH was held up to the North of the village.

1 N YEO and 1 BW on the Left, after delays at the start, were making slow but steady progress and were somewhere in the area of 080595 (describe with reference to some object on the ground).

B. COLONEL A. JOLLY, DSO, MC, CO 144 RAC

144 RAC's Advance to the Railway Crossing

We left the column just short of the opening line of the barrage about 1000 yards North of here—just the other side of TILLY. As soon as the barrage started the column was immediately enveloped in a dense cloud of dust which reduced visibility literally to a few yards.

The Regimental Navigator, leading the column, had so far not heard a sound from his beam wireless, either dots or dashes, but his compass had been working fairly well. But when the barrage started, the needle immediately swung wildly to all points of the compass and became useless. He could see nothing in the dense dust cloud and his light tank almost immediately fell into a bomb crater about ten feet deep. The two reserve navigators, following behind him, tried to avoid this crater and went into another. These three tanks were only pulled out with some difficulty the next day and my Technical Adjutant and two other ranks were killed by shell fire during the recovery operation. About this time my regimental LO reported that the infantry battalion Commander's vehicle had broken down. This would mean that Col MEIKLEJOHN would have to transfer to another vehicle and I should have no communication with him. Not long afterwards the cheerful voice of the LO came on the air to say that the Command Vehicle was now going again and so all was well. But at the time I felt it was not a very good start to lose all three navigators and to be out of effective touch with our infantry so early in the proceedings.

It is difficult, standing here in daylight, to imagine the complete and utter disintegration of the column which occurred in the thousand yards between the opening line of the barrage and here. The confusion was indescribable. Everyone had been told to keep closed up and follow the tank in front but it was soon obvious that it was the blind leading the blind. Great shapes of tanks loomed up out of the fog and asked you who you were: Flails seemed to be everywhere, and their great jibs barging about in the dust seemed to add to the confusion.

A number of officers by now had dismounted and were leading groups of tanks on foot. After what seemed like a lifetime, OC A Sqn, my leading Squadron Leader, reported to me that he had reached the railway hut here, the selected crossing place. He put up a Verey light as a guide and when I arrived at this point he was just beginning to lead the way across, followed by a 17 pr tank of his leading troop—the one you see in front of you (MR 06865932). Suddenly there were two flashes in quick succession accompanied by showers of molten sparks as the enemy Bazookas, fired from behind the hut, hit the tanks. The leading one did not brew up and everyone baled out without serious injuries including the Squadron Leader and the regimental navigator who had climbed on board the Squadron Leader's tank when his own went into the bomb crater. The Squadron Leader had both eardrums broken, and I took him into my tank, where he amused himself clearing stoppages to the machine gun later in the action.

The second tank brewed immediately. The wireless operator was wounded but the other three members of the crew were killed. The tank commander could be seen trying to free himself, but then collapsed and was engulfed in flames. A good deal of rather indiscriminate shooting followed, of more or less equal danger to both sides, and a dismounted tank party threw a number of hand grenades into the hut area. The action was not entirely one-sided, as you will see from the three German graves on the track behind you.

Meanwhile, my Second-in-Command had been having a look at the railway to our Left, and reported that it appeared to be clear and not mined. I therefore told him to collect as many as possible of the confused elements in this area and take them across about a hundred yards further North. I still did not quite realise the extent of the confusion in the column. As A Sqn, the Flails and RHQ were in this area, I imagined that B Sqn, next in order of march, would be coming along in a more or less orderly manner behind. I therefore got on the air to my B Sqn Leader and told him to make for the burning tank and take over the lead, which would give A Sqn time to sort themselves out. B Sqn Leader heard this order with some surprise as his squadron was equally disorganised and he himself was over near the road trying to disentangle some of his tanks from a Canadian column which had come over our side of the road. However, he obediently made for the burning tank and crossed the railway. But getting other tanks to follow was a slow business. I have never realised before how dependent one is, when controlling tanks by wireless, on sub-units and individual tanks knowing where they are in relation to each other. In this situation different squadrons and troops were all mixed up. An order might be given to Baker 3: "Move straight to your front and halt when you get to the other side of the railway." But Baker 3 was probably over on the FALAISE road and the order did not make sense to him. Able 3, who was the chap who was really being spoken to, only heard a call for Baker 3, so did not take any notice—so nothing happened, or only very slowly.

Eventually the bulk of the leading two squadrons, still hopelessly intermingled, was collected in the field on the other side of the hedge to your front. I managed to get hold of OC B Sqn and the Second-in-Command of A Sqn, whom I told to take over the squadron. His was the Squadron Leader in my tank with burst ear drums. OC B Sqn I sent back to the railway crossing to find out whether the infantry part of the column was still intact and was coming across the railway. Meanwhile, an enthusiastic young second lieutenant asked whether he could take an AVRE to blow up the railway hut just in case there were still any Bosche left in it. This I allowed him to do, which accounts for its condition.

During this time, my Second-in-Command having tried to collect a party and get them across the railway, had led the way himself and had then gone on alone a good way towards the objective accompanied by a very gallant bulldozer. When he realised how long it was taking to collect everyone together he came back and personally collected a few more tanks, all commanded by officers.

The time must have now been about two o'clock in the morning. The dust had cleared, as the barrage had long since left us, and the moon had come up. OC B Sqn had meanwhile come back and reported to me that the infantry column was coming across the railway in good order so I called for a concentration on LORGUICHON Wood, which we suspected was held, and ordered all tanks in front of the infantry to spread out and advance in line, "brassing up" hedges and other places where they might be other bazooka parties as they went along.

Control was now the problem. It was still impossible to know who was who and the only thing to do was to move forward by bounds and fire Verey lights. I called up all tanks on the air and told them to follow the lights. The excellent gridded oblique air photographs with which we had been issued and our study of various land marks were invaluable.

Our progress over the next few fields was slow but steady, with tracer filling the air and certainly frightening the leading tanks even if it didn't frighten the enemy. The first bound was just the other side of the square shaped field I mentioned, where I fired a large number of Verey lights and was joined by the bulk of the regiment.

C. LIEUTENANT COLONEL J. C. MEIKLEJOHN, DSO, CO 7 A & SH

The Tail of the Column

In giving our story of the night advance, I want to emphasise that we were merely passengers until the debussing point was reached and consequently did not have much real idea what was going on.

The forming up was carried out successfully at last light and the column moved off at about 2250 hours to cross the Start Line by 2330 hours. Battalion HQ was rather put out of its stride by my own half track very soon breaking down, and after breaking two tow ropes we had to transfer all the men we could and their vital WT sets to the Second-in-Command's truck which was following us, and by the time we had finished this, the whole column including 7 BW and 148 RAC had passed us and we were alone. However, when we had sorted ourselves out, we went like the bats of hell and fairly soon rejoined our proper place.

The barrage started at 2343 hours and the bombing on the flanks some time before. I believe the noise was terrific, but we never heard a sound. The bombing was most accurate and there were no shorts.

All went well for about the first mile but then the column began to get rather spread out and vehicles were no longer in station. About half way to the objective three of the leading tanks disappeared into a large bomb crater and as you have heard these were the navigating tanks. It was here that the first enemy was encountered and B Coy came under Spandau fire and several hand grenades were thrown at the company HQ troop carrier; one which landed inside was promptly picked up and thrown back by one of the Signallers. The post was soon dealt with, two Germans being killed and three wounded, but in leading the men to it, the company Second-in-Command was shot through the stomach and had to be left behind in charge of a stretcher bearer, an elderly man called Cameron. When the column had moved on and left them, three Germans appeared out of the darkness and made for them. But Cameron ran at them with his Sten, killing one, wounding another and putting the third to flight.

The railway then had to be crossed and this further disrupted the column. From here to the Debussing Point things were pretty confused with a few tanks burning here and there and Besa fire and white tracer flying about on all sides. The column had now completely lost the nice neat formation it had started off in and was just a porridge of vehicles, with tanks and APCs and everything mixed up anyhow. Also, I could not for the life of me see what the tanks were firing at and did not like to ask over the air, so that when I had word from Col JOLLY that it was getting on for time for us to debus, I was not very clear where we were or what the position was.

QUESTIONS

D. CONDUCTING OFFICER

We now move to CRAMESNIL, driving over Pt 122 which will give you an idea of how this feature dominated the front over which the attack was made.

STAND 3 (MR 08205727)

Object of Stand

To study the completion of the night advance and the capture of CRAMESNIL by 144 RAC—7 A & SH Group.

A. CONDUCTING OFFICER

Description of ground and General Situation

On your Right is the village of CRAMESNIL and to its Left through the trees and adjoining it is ST AIGNAN. Behind you is Pt 122 and on your Left flank LORGUICHON Wood.

The leading tanks of 144 RAC reached here about 0300 hours. 148 RAC and 7 BW which were following this column were closing up to GARCELLES SECQUEVILLE, which is through the belt of trees to your Left front. On 144 RAC's Right the Canadians had reached their debussing area which is opposite Pt 122 on the other side of the main road from here, but had not yet secured the high ground. 1 N YEO and 1 BW had arrived at their debussing area (MR 08845779) which is 800 yards to your front the other side of the copse.

B. COLONEL A. JOLLY, DSO, CO 144 RAC

The Advance to the Debussing Area

During this last thousand yards the bulk of the Regiment kept fairly well together and I fired the last series of Verey lights just the other side of the hedge which you can see in front of you. LORGUICHON Wood gave us no trouble, though we passed it with some trepidation. We realised that we were nearing our objective when we were asked by 1 N YEO—1 BW to desist from "brassing up" any more hedges as they were getting most of the benefit of it. Their Centre Line took them the other side of that line of woods you see to your Right, and they were now fairly close to us on our Left. I had been counting the hedges from my gridded air photographs and reckoned that we were now in the field where the infantry were due to debus. My Second-in-Command however, with the small party of about half a dozen tanks which he had collected, had taken a different route further to our Left and was now a little ahead of us and announced on the wireless that he was just entering the last field before the objective. In fact, he had gone one field too far and almost immediately one of the tanks with him came up on the air and reported "Able 16 has just been blown to bits". His tank had been hit by a Bazooka at close range and "brewed up" immediately. He and the Regimental Signal Officer, who was also in the tank, were killed, and two other ranks were wounded, only the driver escaping unhurt. Almost immediately there followed a heavy "stonk" from some heavy weapon which we thought afterwards might be a Nebelwerfer fired at close range.

I ordered the tanks which had gone into the next field with my Second-in-Command to pull back into this field where the remainder of us were. I then got on to my Liaison Officer with the Infantry Battalion Commander and told him that the infantry should now dismount. I thought they must still be about a thousand yards from the debussing point but in fact they were close up and only about 200 yards short of it. Within a matter of a few minutes, or so it seemed, the infantry had sorted themselves out and were going through us to assault the village. It was now about 0330 hours and there was about another hour to go before it would begin to get light so we formed ourselves into a rough Close Leaguer until we could sort ourselves out later. While this was being done there was another of those now all-too-familiar showers of sparks from one of the tanks in the Leaguer. The shot had come from behind us and we concluded that it was from an anti-tank gun by-passed in the LORGUICHON Wood area. The tank "brewed up" at once and all except one member of the crew were killed. We were in a very vulnerable position and it was an unpleasant situation waiting in the dark for the next tank to go up. However, the rest of the night was uneventful and we never solved the problem of who fired that last shot as no anti-tank gun was found the next day.

As it grew light, it was possible to sort tanks out into their proper squadrons, C Sqn being told to go over to the Right, B Sqn to the Left and A Sqn to the rear. We took stock, and felt a little surprised to find ourselves still more or less intact after such a nightmarish performance. Word also came back that the infantry had made short work of the village and by daylight it was practically cleared. Another infantry battalion from 152 (H) Bde had followed up the tanks very closely and had occupied LORGUICHON Wood by the time it was daylight. About 8 o'clock a thick ground mist, which had come down about 4 o'clock in the morning, began to clear and we moved into the previously selected positions that is with one squadron supporting the infantry on the high ground behind you and the other two squadrons and RHQ in reserve on the high ground to your Left. If you will turn round you can see the positions more clearly, that is, we had a tight lodgement area based on this high ground. The Canadians were on our Right, inclusive of the FALAISE road; then came ourselves with one of my squadrons supporting 7 A & SH. On our Left were 1 N YEO with the 1 BW occupying the village of ST AIGNAN and the woods to the South of it. 148 RAC with 7 BW formed a refused Left flank by occupying the village and woods of GARCELLES SECQUEVILLE. Those are the woods you can see to your Left rear.

Meanwhile, another infantry battalion, supported by a squadron of 148 RAC, had attacked TILLY from the rear and had brought it under control by about 8 o'clock. It had been by-passed during the night advance and was still holding out in the morning in spite of the night attack which had been launched against it.

The Canadians repulsed a small attack during the morning but the main armoured counter attack on our positions here did not materialize until the afternoon. The brunt of this fell on 1 N YEO on our Left but it held its own and destroyed about fifteen of the enemy's tanks for a loss of about the same number of its own. My squadron destroyed one Tiger and one Mark IV and also lost two tanks.

The casualties during the night operation were officers two killed and two wounded, other ranks seven killed and four wounded, and four tanks had been destroyed.

During the day 8 August we had approximately the same number of casualties but only lost two tanks, the remaining casualties being from shelling.

LESSONS

I would like to conclude by mentioning the main lessons which came out of this operation as far as the armour was concerned. I will not deal with the question of the first use of Kangaroos as the fundamental importance of this innovation is, I think, accepted by everyone and the lessons are of course only as they appear to us, again from the regimental level.

(i) The effect of night operations by armour on the enemy

An intercepted message, I believe, proved the consternation which was felt by the enemy commanders at armoured columns motoring through their lines in the dark. This consternation was equally marked on a subsequent occasion during the advance to ST PIERRE SUR DIVES when my regiment carried out a similar night "swan" but without any infantry.

(ii) The use of darkness to force the enemy to fight you on your own ground

Before this operation, the enemy had the advantage of being in concealed positions, from which he could inflict heavy casualties on us when we attempted to move our tanks over the very open country South of CAEN to attack him in daylight. As a result of this night attack however, the tables were turned. With comparatively few casualties we were able to occupy this commanding ground and he was forced to try to get us off it by attacking over the open with his tanks. This enabled us to destroy a number of them while still retaining the important ground.

(iii) The difficulties of tactical control in bad visibility

On this particular occasion I think we would have done better without a barrage but conditions may be such that one cannot avoid a barrage with its dust and smoke. Navigational and station keeping aids must therefore be developed which will enable control to be maintained under these conditions. We are doing a good deal of work with this end in view at the Specialised Armour Establishment.

(iv) The need for a shooting light

As counter measures are developed, the moral effect of tanks at night will decrease unless they can produce aimed fire. Technical developments in the future, I am sure, must aim at enabling the tank gunner to see his target at night and this is a problem on which we are also working at SAE. Whether the final answer will be infra-red or some form of searchlight it is too early to say. Technical improvements of this sort may, in the future, enable us to make deeper penetrations at night than were possible in the recent war. In this operation, for instance, we only penetrated the enemy's FDLs and then came up against a lay-back position. A deeper penetration would have taken us through this and might have avoided the stiff fighting of the next few days.

(v) Tactics

As regards tactics, tanks must undoubtedly keep closer together at night than by day. Tactical formations and control must be more of a drill and the plan adopted must be extremely simple. Suitable conditions of ground and enemy must also be present. But it seems open to question whether it is sound to commit the whole of a column of over 150 vehicles at the beginning as we did in this case unless there is no other method of keeping control. In this particular instance I think the method adopted was probably the only feasible one but, in future, and given the necessary technical aids, I feel that one should use an advanced guard consisting of say a tank squadron and a company of infantry to secure successive bounds before the main body is committed. Had we met a minefield along the line of the railway the situation might have been very sticky.

Anyway, we achieved our object and that was to enable the infantry to capture their objective CRAMESNIL.

C. LIEUTENANT COLONEL J. C. MEIKLEJOHN, DSO, CO 7 A & SH

(Spectators should move fifty yards into the field the other side of the track at 08305724 and face towards CRAMESNIL.)

The Plan for and Capture of CRAMESNIL

The Brigadier's orders to me were
1. To capture CRAMESNIL.
2. To prevent interference from LORGUICHON Wood until 5 CAMERONS captured it.
3. To make firm contact with the Canadians on Pt 122.

In our planning, we had assumed that we would be up to time and would move into the village under the barrage, but if this did not happen, prearranged artillery concentrations could be called for. The debussing point was picked off the air photograph and it was the hedge junction here. The companies were to debus here, collect themselves together and then move straight to their objectives.

All the company objectives and the positions of anti-tank guns, were chosen from the air photographs, and, where necessary, tied up with the battalions on the flanks.

B Coy, then the leading company, was to get off first and it was to get the centre of the village as far as the first lateral road, which runs just behind the big chateau straight in front of you. It was to get the fir wood on the Right and the orchard on the Left. By taking the centre and rear part of the village, I reckoned that it would split the defence in two and form a firm base if necessary for a deliberate attack on the rest of the village.

A Coy's objective was the line of houses to your Right and the triangular shaped orchard beyond them right up to the second lateral road.

D Coy on the Left was to get the big square farm of which you can see the wedge shaped roof through the trees to your Left and the orchard to the Left of it again as far as the edge of the ST AIGNAN orchards. It also was to go as far as the second lateral road.

The carrier platoon was to contain LORGUICHON Wood by fire until 5 CAMERONS came up.

The remainder of S Coy and the troop M 10s were to leaguer in the big field which we have just left and mop up the hedges for snipers and bazooka men. As soon as they received the success signal, the M 10s and the battalion anti-tank guns were to move straight to their consolidation positions.

The code word for debussing was LILY and at about 0300 hours, I had word from Col JOLLY to be ready to debus. I warned companies accordingly and shortly afterwards B Coy came on the air and asked "Shall I be a Lily now"?

It was very difficult to see just where we were. In addition to the dust of the barrage and the tanks, there was a very heavy ground mist which was aggravated by the smoke from burning haystacks. I reckoned we were pretty close to the village for I had seen the loom of LORGUICHON Wood to the Right and I thought I had recognised from the air photographs the line of tall elm trees at the beginning of the debussing field. The column seemed to be pointing in the right direction. Odd Germans were appearing out of the corn and giving themselves up.

I ordered all companies to debus and as B Coy was pretty well together, I told it to attack at once so as not to lose the moral effect of the tanks, and at the same time I called for a 15-minute artillery concentration on the far edge of the village, with the idea of preventing interference with B Coy and softening A and D Coy's objectives.

OC B Coy asked me for a direction but all I could tell him was to go on the axis of the tanks. This he did and he had only passed the head of the column by a few yards when he hit the debussing point here dead—a tribute to the accuracy of the tank's navigator. The Company advanced two platoons up and one back and had to pass through the Bosche DF, which hadn't so far slackened off. They were ordered not to use their rifles and Brens as the tanks had been told to fire at any rifle and LMG fire. In spite of these various handicaps however, the company pushed on and the thick visibility enabled it to surprise the Germans out of their holes. Over to your Left front where you can see a cross, the leading troops came upon twelve Germans including a CSM, in the open. They killed five and took the rest prisoner. In a short time, the Company had got on and mopped up all its objective.

Both A and D Coys were so scattered and mixed up that it took a lot of time to collect all their men. OC A Coy indeed only had one section and his company HQ with him, but his senior platoon commander had done a good job in bringing up the rest of the company and it was able to get going with its attack only a few minutes after the artillery concentration finished. It advanced two platoons up, 7 on the Right and 9 on the Left. 7 Platoon went down the line of the hedge you are standing against and immediately ran into strong opposition from an enemy position of about platoon strength dug in in front of the line of houses. The slits were in the field but bolt holes had been dug through to the houses so that it was easy for the Germans to escape at the last minute. They used their PIAT and mortar against the walls of the house and the blast was very effective. They then assaulted through the orchard and suffered a number of casualties from small grenades slung between trees. In the close fighting they killed a few Germans and took 15 prisoners but their platoon commander, who had led them very gallantly, was mortally wounded and died later in the RAP.

The success of the platoon paved the way for the Left platoon which came in on the flank of the houses and it captured and mopped up all of them. The third platoon then advanced through the others and secured the orchard beyond, right up to the second road.

D Coy on the Left had a very easy passage and captured its whole objective with negligible opposition. It also captured about six nebelwerfers, all loaded and ready to fire.

4 Platoon had not long to contain LORGUICHON before 5 CAMERONS came up and took it over from them and then it beat the hedges and ditches of the S Coy field and got quite a few Bosches out of them.

Soon after B Coy reported its objectives captured, Battalion HQ moved in to its area and a short time later, both the flank companies reported themselves firmly in position, so the anti-tank guns moved up. Incidentally, the troop commander of the M 10s was a pleasure to deal with; I had thought he would want an infantry escort to get his guns up to their positions, but so far from wanting an escort, his idea was to lead my companies on to their objectives with his vehicles.

By 0500 hours, the village was firmly in our hands and it only remained to contact the flank battalions. I went first to A Coy and there the company commander and I had some difficulty in deciding just what was Pt 122. The map showed a sharply defined ridge sticking out like a thumb and practically overhanging the village and all we could see was a gentle rise. However, the tracks on the map and ground agreed, so he sent off a patrol in his carrier and they found the Canadians well in position.

When I visited D Coy next, I found it already in touch with 1 BW in ST AIGNAN.

Enemy casualties were about 8 killed and 40 captured, excluding wounded. They were all from 89 Div and seemed quite glad to be captured. They said they had only moved up the night before and had not had time to settle in. Their officers had left them about a quarter of an hour before the attack went in, telling them to stay put. They were very bitter about this.

Our own casualties, including those in the night advance, were one officer and two other ranks killed, and one officer and eighteen other ranks wounded.

QUESTIONS

D. CONDUCTING OFFICER

The route to Stand 4 takes us back over Pt 122 to the main road and as you approach the main road a very good view of the ground over which 2 Cdn Div attacked is obtained.

STAND 4. (MR 07155543)

Object of Stand

To give a description of the actions fought by 2 Cdn Div during the night attack and daylight 8 August.

A. CONDUCTING OFFICER

Description of the Ground

At this stand we deal with the operations carried out by 2 Cdn Div. First a brief description of the ground. To your Right rear is Pt 122, and to the Left of it, the mine shaft buildings and village of ROQUANCOURT. In the foreground to your Right front is a field surrounded by a thick hedge; that is the debussing area used by the Canadian columns (MR 06705552). The village which can be seen through the Right edge of the debussing area is FONTENAY LE MARMION, with MAY SUR ORNE just out of sight behind the crest beyond FONTENAY LE MARMION. To the Left of the debussing area is the village of CAILLOUET. Across the other side of the field to your Left front is a light green grass bank with some bushes on it and damaged trees behind it. This is the QUARRY (MR 06605470). To your Left flank is another mine shaft building, and the hill beyond and to the Left of it is Pt 195, part of the final objective. To your Left rear the buildings of GAUMESNIL can be seen among the trees.

B. ACCOUNT OF 2 CDN DIV OPERATIONS

(This account is compiled from Personal Accounts and the Canadian Army Historical Section's August Report. It deals with the armoured columns first and refers to each by the name of the regiment or battalion which formed the major part of it.)

It had been planned that the three columns on the Western axis were to advance, passing to the Left of ROQUANCOURT, to the debussing area, which was to be secured initially by the gapping force. Following behind was the assault force of each column and on reaching the debussing area ESSEX SCOT was to capture CAILLOUET, RHLI the QUARRY and R REGT C Pt 122 and the area of the cross roads where we turned off the FALAISE road. Subsequently R REGT C was to capture GAUMESNIL. On the other axis 8 Cdn Recce Regt, passing to the Right of ROQUANCOURT was to go direct to Pt 122.

The columns started at 2330 hours guided by the tapes and lights laid by the gapping force and by the Bofors tracer. Progress was good during the first half hour but the columns then encountered the same trouble as the 51 (H) Div columns. As well as the dust, a rising ground mist, to which the Germans were clever enough to add smoke, made visibility nil. As it approached ROQUANCOURT ESSEX SCOT, which had lost touch with its gapping party, strayed too far to the West. Shelling and mortaring, which up till now had not been as heavy as anticipated, was on the increase. The FOOs with the leading companies in the assault force reported that they were unable to see the tanks immediately in front of them and asked for their location. There were frequent halts whilst the stragglers were collected and the advance was now very slow with everyone trying to recognise landmarks. At about 0115 hours, A Coy reported that it had joined up with the squadron of 27 Cdn Armd Regt again and that they were in front of the objective and about to attack it. Almost immediately an 88 mm opened up on the column at a range of two hundred yards, setting fire to some half tracks. This split the column into two and threw it into a state of great confusion. Some of the leading vehicles went on, whilst others in the scramble to move out of the line of fire of the 88 mm, reversed into each other. Difficulties were increased by the number of stragglers from other columns who had previously joined on and who now thought it was not such a healthy spot to be. No contact could be made with the Commanding Officer nor with A Coy. The Second-in-Command collected the remaining company commanders and a troop leader from 1 LOTHIANS, the only tank commander who could be found. A short conference was held. No one knew in what direction CAILLOUET or the debussing area lay, but all agreed that they were beyond both. In fact, they were not yet level with ROQUANCOURT. A platoon was despatched to deal with the crew of the 88 mm but was driven off by machine gun fire. As visibility was improving, the infantry were ordered to debus and dig slit trenches and efforts were made to sort out the column away from the 88 mm. At about 0430 hours a message was received from the Commanding Officer stating that all was now clear and the column was to continue the advance. There was still the 88 mm and some LMG posts to be dealt with in front of the column, and before this information could be passed to the Commanding Officer the wireless failed.

Whilst the column was being re-sorted, the Second-in-Command went to the nearest village, found it to be ROQUANCOURT and that his Commanding Officer was there and had been wounded. On returning to the battalion the Second-in-Command found that fourteen half-tracks had been knocked out or were missing, two M 10s had been brewed up and the squadron of 27 Cdn Armd Regt was no longer there, having gone on when the column split.

In the centre, RHLI fared better. The column ran into the same 88 mm gun and immediately turned East. Unsuccessful attempts were made to get round the village and eventually the vehicles drove through it and reached the debussing area about 0330 hours. From there the infantry advanced to the thick hedge in front of the debussing area and dug in.

R REGT C also turned East outside ROQUANCOURT and after some difficulty managed to force its way through the gap between the village and the mine buildings and reached the debussing area about 0300 hours. One company had become detached in the confusion round ROQUANCOURT, and did not rejoin the regiment until the following afternoon. Minus one company, and having overshot the selected railway crossing over which the tanks were to go to reach Pt 122, a further delay occurred while a new plan was made. However, two companies were on the objective by 0430 hours and the remaining company and the supporting arms were all in position by first light.

8 Cdn Recce Regt also made good progress at the start and by 0100 hours the regiment thought it was very close to Pt 122. Reports of heavy machine gun fire and more opposition than was expected and the fact that it had been stationary for some time were next received. Finally the location of their leading troops on the railway bridge North East of the mine buildings put them much further away from Pt 122 than the original estimate. The regiment was not able to make any headway during the remainder of the night.

At the same time as the armoured advance, 6 Cdn Inf Bde was to attack three objectives each with a battalion. MAY SUR ORNE, FONTENAY LE MARMION and ROQUANCOURT were the three objectives. The two former villages were outside the area covered by the barrage and little support was available for the two attacking battalions until it had been completed.

FUS MR was heavily shelled in the forming up area. A platoon of the leading company got into the outskirts of MAY SUR ORNE, but was unable to retain its position. The companies were withdrawn and about 0430 hours another attack was made which was also unsuccessful.

CAMERONS OF C had, by 0630 hours, cleared FONTENAY LE MARMION up to the church. During its advance straight over the hill down into the village it had run into a minefield and had left uncleared many enemy posts on the ridge North of the village. As the mist cleared the enemy holding these posts became very active and the 88 mm gun, which had caused so much trouble to the armoured columns, now controlled CAMERONS of C axis.

S SASK R had the advantage of advancing between the two armoured axes and with the support of the barrage. The regiment was determined to get to ROQUANCOURT as close behind the barrage as possible. In spite of darkness, the standing crops, shell holes, slit trenches and machine gun posts, some of which were manned and had to be dealt with, the leading company, according to the personal account of its Commander "hit the village right on the nose close behind the barrage. In the orchard there, we captured six mortars, their detachments and ammunition complete. The other companies passed through and by 0100 hours the village had been taken. By first light its defence and the digging-in was completed. A slight flurry occurred then, when tanks were heard approaching in the mist, but they turned out to be ours which were coming back for repositioning."

The position therefore at first light was as follows. MAY SUR ORNE on the Left was still held by the enemy. CAMERONS OF C had cleared the Northern portion of FONTENAY LE MARMION, but its axis was cut and no one could get to it nor could any wounded be evacuated.

ESSEX SCOT was between FONTENAY LE MARMION and ROQUANCOURT about 047593.

ROQUANCOURT was in our hands and to the East of it was 8 Cdn Recce Regt.

R REGT C was on Pt 122.

RHLI was just in front of us here.

CAILLOUET, THE QUARRY and GAUMESNIL had not been captured.

10 Cdn Armd Regt was holding the debussing area.

It is worth mentioning that the gapping force consisting of tanks of 27 Cdn Armd Regt, including those of the ESSEX SCOT column, Flails, AV'sRE, etc, reached the debussing area without the loss of a vehicle.

The mist began to clear at 0800 hours and the ESSEX SCOT and 8 Cdn Recce Regt were ordered to make a joint attack on CAILLOUET. ESSEX SCOT was still without its squadron of tanks and 8 Cdn Recce Regt had difficulty in overcoming opposition in the first few hundred yards of the advance. At 1015 hours ESSEX SCOT reported four tanks on the objective. It took nearly an hour to establish their identity by which time the tanks had withdrawn. The battalion drove up to the outskirts of the village and occupied it, the enemy being hastened in their withdrawal by HE from 6 pounders. About 0900 hours enemy infantry supported by SP guns counter attacked the RHLI position, but after a short engagement the enemy withdrew. A patrol sent to the QUARRY later on reported it to be clear of the enemy.

At the same time a small force of enemy tanks and infantry had closed up to Pt 122. R REGT C repelled this attack but not before a Panther had got within 70 yards of Battalion HQ and had brewed up five carriers, two Shermans and an M 10.

At FONTENAY LE MARMION, CAMERONS OF C, whose companies were now down to forty or less, was being engaged by enemy holding the Southern part of the village and also by those occupying the positions on the ridge to the North. Battalion HQ was hit and there were a number of officer casualties including the acting CO and the FOO. Supported by artillery concentrations, the battalion held on to its position all the morning. A pincer movement was planned to clear up MAY SUR ORNE, FONTENAY LE MARMION and the area up to ROQUANCOURT. A battalion with Crocodiles in support attacked MAY SUR ORNE whilst two companies of S SASK R from ROQUANCOURT, with tanks to assist them, cleared the ground towards FONTENAY LE MARMION. These operations were carried out during the afternoon and were most successful, 250 prisoners being captured. GAUMESNIL was taken by R REGT C at 1530 hours, by which time 4 Cdn Armd Div had crossed the Start Line for Phase II (road BRETTEVILLE SUR LAIZE-ST AIGNAN) and had advanced beyond the village.

QUESTIONS

STAND 5. (MR 08105905)

Object of Stand

To study the plan for and capture of SECQUEVILLE LA CAMPAGNE.

A. CONDUCTING OFFICER

Description of the ground and General Situation

The village to your Right is GARCELLES SECQUEVILLE. In front of you is a Nissen hut and beyond it is a belt of trees stretching to the Left and ending in a number of dead ones. To the Right of the dead trees you will be able to pick out the ruined house and church tower of SECQUEVILLE LA CAMPAGNE.

To your Left front is a triangular shaped bushy wood which will be referred to as Wood (MR 08785970). Beyond this Wood and just out of sight except for one roof is LA HOGUE.

In between the Wood and SECQUEVILLE is another large patch of scrub which will be called Scrub (MR 09305933).

To your Left rear is TILLY LA CAMPAGNE.

The situation here at approximately 1430 hours on 8 August was as follows.

144 RAC and 7 A & SH were holding CRAMESNIL and 1 N YEO and 1 BW ST AIGNAN, both of which are out of sight to the Right of this village and about a mile distant.

About this time Battle Groups of 12 SS Pz Div were counter attacking 1 N YEO—1 BW position and the shelling here was heavy.

148 RAC and 7 BW were in GARCELLES and 5 CAMERONS was behind in the area of LORGUICHON.

TILLY LA CAMPAGNE had been captured this morning.

1 Polish Armd Div was moving up to ST AIGNAN for Phase II on the axes used last night and its leading regiments were in this area.

B. LIEUTENANT COLONEL THE HON. H.C.H.T. CUMMING-BRUCE, DSO, CO 1 GORDONS

The Capture of SECQUEVILLE LA CAMPAGNE

After receiving orders from Commander 153 (H) Bde to attack SECQUEVILLE LA CAMPAGNE on 8 August, I left in my carrier for GARCELLES SECQUEVILLE where I arrived at 1430 hours. My orders were to attack through 7 BW not later than 1630 hours. I ordered the Second-in-Command to bring the battalion to an area East of LORGUICHON, and later notified subordinate commanders and supporting arms to RV at house 078585 at 1530 hours for orders. On arrival at GARCELLES I started to reconnoitre possible FUPs and axes.

This was exceedingly difficult owing to the thickness of the country and on account of the heavy shelling which forced me to take cover every few minutes. I was not able to find any officer of 7 BW and time was too short for a prolonged search. I quickly realised that the only threats to the axis were from the woods East and North East of SECQUEVILLE. Two fields South East of the GARCELLES crossroads appeared to make good FUPs, concealed from front and flanks with room for tanks to marry up and a hedge as an inter-company boundary.

To take advantage of all possible cover, I chose an axis 200 yards South of the road GARCELLES–SECQUEVILLE LA CAMPAGNE and parallel to it.

Only one field regiment was available in support, plus a 4.2 inch mortar platoon.

These preliminaries took exactly an hour and I met company commanders at the RV. Commanders of supporting arms arrived at varying periods and extended the time taken over orders. (Issue of these verbal orders was much facilitated by a copy of SOS headings for verbal orders, which were so thorough that no details were omitted).

The plan was to attack two companies up, supported by tanks, followed by Tac HQ followed by two companies, the Left rear one supported by Crocodiles. The Left rear company was to turn off the axis and deal with the scrub West of SECQUEVILLE. Artillery concentrations were fired on the village from H hour, timed to lift on arrival of the leading companies at SECQUEVILLE. The mortars were to keep sustained fire on the wood North East of the village. The carrier platoon was in reserve for immediate exploitation.

The GOC postponed H hour to 1700 hours, but even so company commanders could only give out short orders and all companies and supporting arms arrived in the FUP at H hour exactly, marrying up taking place on the move. Fortunately, the enemy shelling had stopped.

The Right forward company found heavy enemy DF in front, so swerved to the South and entered SECQUEVILLE from that flank. Battalion HQ (CO, IO and three signallers) walked in to an enemy position half way between GARCELLES and SECQUEVILLE and took 20—30 prisoners. Just beyond were two troops of Polish tanks. As they were firing enthusiastically into the backs of the leading companies, I endeavoured to stop them, ultimately with success.

The objectives were soon taken and little fighting took place in SECQUEVILLE, but heavy mortaring caused casualties. The Crocodiles passed through the Left rear company and fired the edge of the scrub. One petrified German was found by the gunners three days later, still cowering in a slit trench which had been just out of range of the flames. Subsequent investigation of the wood disclosed a large number of Germans dead in their trenches as a result of the 4.2" mortar fire.

Immediately after the capture of SECQUEVILLE, I sent carrier patrols half a mile down each track in the wood East of SECQUEVILLE, which engaged small parties of enemy till dark. Another patrol was sent to LA HOGUE and captured it, returning with a number of prisoners.

The following morning I took the carrier platoon and cleared the whole wood, which saved a further attack by 5 SEAFORTH, scheduled for that afternoon.

QUESTIONS

STAND 6. (MR 06286193)

Object of Stand

To consider the factors affecting and the plan for the capture of TILLY LA CAMPAGNE.

A. CONDUCTING OFFICER

Description of the ground and General Situation

We are back on familiar ground again and here we deal with the plan for the capture of TILLY LA CAMPAGNE. Just to remind you of the names of the villages. On your Left is HUBERT FOLIE. In front of you is BOURGUEBUS and to the Right and beyond its church tower is LA HOGUE. Further Right still, the ruined house of SECQUEVILLE stands out very clearly. The red roofed barn provides the landmark for TILLY LA CAMPAGNE and to the Left of it amongst the trees is GARCELLES SECQUEVILLE which we have just left.

We are back again now to 2330 hours on the night 7/8 August with the 33 Armd Bde—154 (H) Bde columns advancing on either side of us. We have already dealt with the column on the Right axis and on the Left 1 N YEO—1 BW advanced between the railway and BOURGUEBUS and between GARCELLES SECQUEVILLE and SECQUEVILLE LA CAMPAGNE, giving TILLY as wide a berth as possible. Both LA HOGUE and SECQUEVILLE were bomber targets and were being bombed at this time.

B. BRIGADIER A.J.H. CASSELS, CBE, DSO, Comd 152 (H) Bde

Planning the Capture of TILLY LA CAMPAGNE

Background

It was thought by the Divisional Commander (and I entirely supported his opinion) that, in this particular battle, TILLY would not be a very tough nut to crack because of the two armoured thrusts on each flank and the consequent disorganisation of the enemy in the rear. We thought that the rumble of armour from each side and behind would make the TILLY garrison look eagerly over its shoulder and "pack in" comparatively easily.

For these reasons it was accepted that :—

(a) One battalion could do the trick though we knew that two strong attacks by the Canadians had failed previously.

(b) The weight of artillery on TILLY and its speed of advance need not be as heavy or as slow as normally required for an infantry attack.

(c) The other two battalions of the brigade would be given other tasks quite apart from TILLY.

It will be seen that these factors seriously affected the plan and nearly caused its failure; because our main premise was entirely false as, in the general din, the enemy in TILLY had no idea that armoured thrusts were encircling them and merely regarded the whole performance as yet another attack which must be defeated.

The Plan

You will have seen from 51 (H) Div OO No. 6 of 6 August 1944 that 152 (H) Bde was given the following tasks :—

(a) To capture TILLY with one battalion (2 SEAFORTH).

(b) To capture area LORGUICHON with one battalion (5 CAMERONS).

(c) To be prepared to assist 154 (H) Bde in clearing its area. If necessary, the whole of 152 (H) Bde might be called for to do this after (a) and (b) above had been completed. In any case, one battalion (5 SEAFORTH) was to be earmarked for this.

(d) To capture area SECQUEVILLE LA CAMPAGNE and woods all round it.

(e) Be prepared to exploit to POUSSY LA CAMPAGNE–BILLY–CONTEVILLE.

It is clear that this was a very big commitment for one brigade, but in view of our original, but false, premise, I was reasonably happy about it. The only point that worried me was that I could not allot any reserve for the TILLY battle as 5 SEAFORTH had to be left untouched in case 154 (H) Bde wanted it. After discussion with the Divisional Commander I was allowed to allot one company of this battalion as reserve, if required, for 2 SEAFORTH.

Artillery

All the artillery was on a Corps plan, which naturally and correctly was designed to cover the advance of the armoured columns. The result was that TILLY was only just included and only three lifts worth of barrage actually hit the area. In fact the barrage was clear of TILLY in three minutes.

I did register a very strong complaint about this but for many adequate reasons I could get no change. I did, however, get the whole of the Divisional 4.2 inch mortars which were valuable, but, of course, are no use for actually leading infantry into a position.

In fact the armoured columns decided after the battle that they would have preferred little or no artillery on their fronts and would have liked concentrations each side and in the middle of the advance. This, of course, would have suited me admirably.

Timings

Again, a major snag arose here. H hour was at 2330 hours and nobody was theoretically allowed to cross the Start Line (South edge of HUBERT FOLIE) before H hour owing to the heavy bombing of LA HOGUE and SECQUEVILLE.

On the other hand the barrage was due to start at 2343 hours.

Thus the leading companies had to advance some 1500 yards in thirteen minutes to be on the heels of the barrage when it started. This was clearly impossible and I tried to gain permission to cross at H—15 and risk the bombing. Eventually a compromise was reached at H—5 which, as you will hear from Major GILMOUR, was not enough though we thought that it might be done.

Light

The armoured columns wanted as much light as possible. I wanted just enough for infantry to see where they were going. Naturally the armour won and the result was that there was far too much light for an infantry attack.

4.2 inch Mortars

I used these to plaster all areas in TILLY where we thought the enemy was but as you know these concentrations had to be lifted when we expected the infantry to be within 400 yards. As in fact the infantry were late for reasons explained above, the mortars actually lifted when most of the infantry were 600 yards away. On lifting I put the whole lot on the small wood in 0859 as this wood was not touched by the Left armoured column and was a likely trouble spot from the defence overprint. In fact this was a most successful shoot, as next day, as you have already heard, a lot of dead Bosches were found in the wood; also a brewed up Panther which was claimed by the mortar company.

Positions of Battalions before the attack

    5 SEAFORTH — HUBERT FOLIE
    2 SEAFORTH — Western outskirts of BRAS
    5 CAMERONS — Northern outskirts of BRAS

Strength of Battalions

We were short of men in all battalions as a result of three weeks in the BOIS DE BAVENT plus our share of Operation GOODWOOD (18–22 July), where casualties, although not heavy on any one day, were fairly severe over the whole period. Major GILMOUR will give you the form as far as 2 SEAFORTH was concerned and the other battalions were similar.

C. MAJOR A. M. GILMOUR, MC, OC C Coy 2 SEAFORTH

2 SEAFORTH Plan

Owing to the shortage of personnel, the battalion was organised for this action as follows :—

(a) Four companies each consisting of :
    Company HQ (normal).
    Two platoons (normal).
    One support group composed of seven or eight men armed with 2 inch mortars and automatic weapons, under the control of company HQ.

(b) Headquarter and Support Companies normal.

The planning and reconnaissance, on a battalion and company level for this action, started several days before the operation was due to start. All company commanders had the opportunity of seeing the ground from excellent viewpoints beforehand—the forward edge of the woods at HUBERT FOLIE, the church tower there and the railway bridge between HUBERT FOLIE and BOURGUEBUS. I particularly remember climbing up the church tower because every time one did this, it was almost impossible not to ring the church bell.

In general, various factors, all of them inherent in the Corps plan, seriously limited the choice of action open to the Commanding Officer. The chief of these was :—

(a) Timing—this has already been explained by Brigadier CASSELS.

(b) Distance and going from Start Line to enemy FDLs.

    In order to cover the 1500 yards in the eighteen minutes available, the companies were forced to advance in file down the only available track and deploy into formation for the attack at the level crossing (069611). The manoeuvre of deploying whilst on the move without a pause had been practised beforehand. To have advanced deployed all the way from the Start Line through the high standing crops could not have been done in the time available.

(c) The proximity of the axes of advance of the armoured columns meant that a frontal attack on TILLY was the only possible method of assault.

(d) The village was a mass of rubble and all streets appeared from air photographs and ground reconnaissance to be blocked. This and the time factor forced the Commanding Officer to choose company objectives on the outskirts of the village, so that they could be reached with the least possible delay and with the maximum advantage that the barrage would offer.

For these reasons the plan adopted was as follows.

Phase I

Attack with two companies up from the railway crossing at 069611.

    Right — D Coy — Objective Track and railway crossing (068602).

    Left — A Coy — Objective Orchard (073603).

Phase II

B Coy was to follow behind A and D as far as the level crossing and as soon as D Coy was reported on its objective, but without waiting for it to be mopped up, B Coy was to move by the Right flank to an objective on the Southern edge of TILLY (072598).

C Coy was to concentrate during this Phase just North of the level crossing (069611).

Phase III

C Coy to move round whichever flank was considered most hopeful and establish itself astride the road TILLY-GARCELLES SECQUEVILLE (075597).

The village would therefore be closely surrounded by infantry and further cut off by the advance of the armoured columns. The centre of the village was to be cleared at first light and companies had been given definite sectors for which they were responsible.

As already explained, the barrage only covered TILLY for a period of three minutes. To help neutralise the village, concentrations by 4.2 inch mortars and 3 inch mortars of 5 SEAFORTH were put down on known enemy positions in and around the village. Certain prearranged artillery targets were also fixed and company commanders could call for these on the 18 set net by mention of a code-word. Defensive Fire tasks had also been arranged.

The battalions supporting arms were kept fully mobile in BRAS ready to be called forward immediately. Positions for anti-tank guns had already been selected.

QUESTIONS

STAND 7. (MR 06946044)

Object of Stand

To study the action by 2 and 5 SEAFORTH at TILLY LA CAMPAGNE.

A. MAJOR A.M. GILMOUR, MC, OC C Coy 2 SEAFORTH
Account of 2 SEAFORTH Action

The enemy defences here consisted of a network of trenches dug along the hedgerow in front of you (MR 06886028 to 07076052) and stretching from the level crossing to the end of the hedge marked by the shattered tree to your Left. The hedge was not nearly as thick as it is now, but provided sufficient cover to hide the enemy positions that I have mentioned.

The Action

The leading companies made good progress as far as the level crossing but in crossing the railway and going up the hill on the other side soon found that they were well behind the barrage, particularly on the Left.

D Coy managed to reach its objective where it was engaged in confused fighting and mopping up for about an hour. Any attempt to approach near the village was met by heavy small arms fire at close range. A report finally reached Battalion HQ that it was secure by about 0130 hours.

A Coy was out of touch by wireless but a report soon came in by runner that it had met with heavy fire and suffered many casualties at a hedgerow about 400 yards over the railway and that it was pinned down there.

B Coy had started off to go through D Coy but wireless communication appeared to have broken down. C Coy was by this time waiting just short of the level crossing.

Personal Account of C Coy action

On reaching the level crossing my company met with fairly heavy mortar fire (about 0015 hours). As I did not expect an immediate move, I ordered platoons to dig shallow slits in the plough and went to find the Commanding Officer and get some orders. On finding him I learned that D Coy on the Right was on its objectives and engaged in close quarter fighting on the outskirts of the village. A few minutes later, A Coy's runner came in with news that A Coy was held up at the hedgerow.

B Coy's last report was that it was in touch with D Coy.

The Commanding Officer considered that things were going alright on the Right but that the hedgerow position must be captured before dawn as it commanded the approaches to TILLY in daylight. He therefore ordered me to go and assist A Coy take the position and proceed to my original objective afterwards. I got A Coy runner to guide me to its HQ, telling my platoon commanders on the way what was happening.

On reaching A Coy commander, I found that one platoon had walked right on to an enemy position which appeared to have recovered from the effects of the barrage and opened up on the platoon at point blank range and practically wiped it out. (This was confirmed the next day by finding the dead bodies, some of them almost in the German trenches.) The other platoon of A Coy was also depleted.

A Coy had therefore barely one effective platoon left and was very short of ammunition.

In consultation with each other we made a plan as follows:—

To get one platoon of C Coy in position alongside A Coy and distribute heavy fire along the enemy position to discover where the Left flank was. Having discovered this, under cover of similar covering fire, to get in behind the position with the other platoon of C Coy and take the position from the rear.

My platoon commanders had meantime come up. By the time orders were issued and A Coy's ammunition replenished, over an hour had elapsed before all was ready (about 0300 hours). The drawing of the enemy's fire was successful and showed the enemy's Left flank. I therefore ordered the other platoon round in a wide sweep giving it fifteen minutes before covering fire was opened. It was then to rush in from the Left behind the position.

The attack was not successful. The flanking platoon took too narrow a sweep and bumped the end of the position and was repulsed. The platoon withdrew after some difficulty, taking its wounded with it. The platoon commander's body along with five others was found next day almost on top of the enemy trenches.

By this time it was beginning to get light and we were in a hopeless position on a bare slope within a few yards of the enemy (within grenade range) and almost out of ammunition. In consultation with A Coy Commander I therefore decided to thin out and withdrew to the cover of the railway. We dug in there under cover of the mist.

We observed that 5 SEAFORTH was preparing for a further attack on the village and also heard that A and C Coys were to come under its command and act as a firm base for this attack.

At dawn we heard tanks in the direction of the enemy. They were firing with their machine guns apparently in our direction. At first I thought that it was a counter attack, but they appeared out of the mist and were seen to be Shermans which had come through TILLY from the South and also taken the hedgerow position from the rear. The Squadron Commander of 148 RAC reported that he had received an offer of surrender from the garrison. 5 SEAFORTH attack was called off and the remnants of A and C Coys of 2 SEAFORTH returned to TILLY with the tanks. The remainder of the garrison then surrendered.

It was only at this stage that I heard what had actually happened to B and D Coys during the night. D Coy had managed to keep close to the barrage and reached its objective, surprising and mopping up some enemy positions on the way. B Coy was slow to follow through and was held up by determined enemy before it even reached D Coy. These enemy had reoccupied positions already overrun by D Coy. B Coy remained here, that is on the railway behind D Coy, for the remainder of the battle. D Coy 5 SEAFORTH came under command 2 SEAFORTH at 0300 hours. It was ordered to put in an attack through D Coy 2 SEAFORTH. This attack failed with heavy losses.

B. BRIGADIER A.J.H. CASSELS, CBE, DSO, Comd 152 (H) Bde

The Capture of TILLY LA CAMPAGNE

Major GILMOUR has told you the doings of 2 SEAFORTH and has given you a description of the enemy defences. I will now give you the story as I remember it from the Brigade point of view. When it was clear that 2 SEAFORTH attack was stuck, I ordered the company of 5 SEAFORTH allotted as reserve to go forward under command 2 SEAFORTH. Owing to the incorrect information from B Coy 2 SEAFORTH, this company also got involved in the wrong place. It was held up alongside D Coy 2 SEAFORTH and suffered very heavy casualties.

It was clear that something drastic had to be done and at about 0330 hours I asked the Divisional Commander if I could use the whole of 5 SEAFORTH. He agreed. This of course was alright in theory, but not so hot in practice, as 5 SEAFORTH had made no study whatsoever of the problem, having been given two other tasks later in the battle. I saw the Commanding Officer at about 0400 hours and told him the situation and ordered him to take his battalion forward to capture TILLY LA CAMPAGNE in conjunction with 2 SEAFORTH from the West. Naturally, he was somewhat taken aback but, after a justifiable moan or two, he set off to reconnoitre and ordered his battalion to a RV. I warned the Commanding Officer 2 SEAFORTH of the form.

5 SEAFORTH attack was delayed owing to mist, which in the end was really a boon to us and saved a lot of lives. I was chasing 5 SEAFORTH to hurry and as it got light I asked Division if some tanks could be switched from the GARCELLES SECQUEVILLE area to move to TILLY from the South. This was done with excellent effect. The net result of all this effort was that the garrison finally surrendered at about 0800 hours.

Our casualties were heavy—sixty officers and other ranks were killed.

LESSONS

1. Never take the enemy lightly and rely on the effect of other operations to sap his morale. He will probably know nothing about them.

2. Infantry attacks by night must either have properly timed and heavy artillery support or the night must be dark enough to make a "winkling" attack possible.

3. There must be a reserve which is free to study its future possible roles and be used when and where required.

4. Question of four companies of two platoons or three strong companies. Which is the better?

QUESTIONS

SECTION IV

THE PROBLEM

A. SITUATION

OC 1 GORDONS received orders in BOURGUEBUS to move the battalion in APC's to ROQUANCOURT. It arrived at 1200 hours and had a good meal. At 1330 hours OC 1 GORDONS received orders from Commander 153 (H) Bde as follows :—

"You will attack and capture SECQUEVILLE LA CAMPAGNE with H hour not later than 1630 hours. APC's have been recalled and will not be available.

The enemy are holding SECQUEVILLE in some strength and are also in the fields between the village and GARCELLES SECQUEVILLE. A few tanks or SPs have been seen. 7 BW is in GARCELLES, 2 SEAFORTH is in TILLY LA CAMPAGNE. LA HOGUE is still held by the enemy.

You will have only one field regiment in support as our gun lines were bombed this morning. You will also have a 4.2 inch mortar platoon, one squadron tanks, and two troops Crocodiles. You had better get moving pretty fast."

Orders were sent to the battalion to be prepared to move to an Assembly Area West of GARCELLES by 1530 hours. Brigade sent orders to tank, Crocodile and mortar commanders to report to OC 1 GORDONS at GARCELLES at 1530 hours, which was the earliest time they could arrive and battalion O Group was ordered for that time. GARCELLES is being subjected to very heavy mortar fire on the line of this road every few minutes. This continued unabated for an hour, necessitating the Commanding Officer spending as much time on his face as on his feet. There are no signs of enemy but BLACK WATCH soldiers in the FDLs say the enemy are close, just beyond the second hedge on the Right of the road GARCELLES SECQUEVILLE–SECQUEVILLE LA CAMPAGNE

The time is 1430 hours 8 August. You have one hour to consider the problem which is the same time as OC 1 GORDONS had, and you have the added advantage of not having to prostrate yourselves every few minutes on the ground. Remember that the front line is the road running North and South through GARCELLES. You can order the battalion to move to any Assembly area you wish. The exact location, together with a suitable place for an O Group, was sent back by OC 1 GORDONS to his Second-in-Command soon after he arrived at GARCELLES SECQUEVILLE.

B. REQUIREMENT

As OC 1 GORDONS, outline your plan for the capture of SECQUEVILLE LA CAMPAGNE with particular reference to :—

(a) Axis of advance.

(b) Tasks allotted to the tanks.

(c) Use of Crocodiles.

(d) Artillery Support.

(e) Use of mortars.

(f) H hour.

On completion of the capture of the village, what would be your next action ?

SECTION V

MAJOR LESSONS FROM THE BATTLEFIELD TOUR

The following major lessons are brought out in the Battlefield Tour.

MORALE

The operations emphasised that morale, as always, is the most important factor in war. On occasions, the rapid mounting and concentration resulted in troops going into battle tired. Quicker results on the battlefield would probably have been achieved if the troops had been fresh. In all operations the great results produced by enterprising junior leadership are apparent.

The very high standard of training which the units and staffs of 21 Army Group had attained in ENGLAND before the North West European campaign was one of the most important contributory factors to its success. The mounting of the various operations was always done against time at every level, and the speed with which they were launched could NOT have been achieved without quick and accurate staff work combined with smooth and efficient execution by the formations and units concerned.

TANK AND INFANTRY CO-OPERATION

Close co-operation between tanks and infantry is vital. Tanks by themselves seldom achieve results. The more infantry and tanks have trained and operated together before a battle, the quicker and greater will be the results.

FIRE SUPPORT

In these operations, large supporting programmes with air and artillery were generally laid on and good progress was made up to the limit of that support. Thereafter, the attack, was liable to falter and lose momentum. The enemy defences are often deeper than expected, and supporting fire must, therefore, be in depth. The later part of this supporting fire may be out of range of artillery and have to be carried out by air bombardment.

AIR BOMBARDMENT

The bomb must be suited to the country. If the country is open and the enemy is in strong houses or deep field defences, fragmentation bombs are useless except for very fleeting neutralisation, and HE must be used. Cratering can be accepted in villages in open country, since they can be by-passed. In large towns, blocked roads should, in the future, be quickly cleared by mechanical equipment of improved design.

SURPRISE

The value of surprise is frequently brought out in these operations, and must be sought, in the future, through new methods and improved equipment. The use of night vision equipment will enable more fighting to be carried out at night, and the development of amphibious tanks will assist in gaining speed in crossing rivers.

DISPERSION AND CROSS COUNTRY MOBILITY

The degree of air supremacy attained in NORMANDY must NOT be expected during the early stages of future operations, though it may ultimately be achieved again. The increased threat from the air, coupled with the increased efficiency of weapons will enforce a greater degree of dispersion prior to battle. The ability to disperse for movement and concentrate quickly for battle will depend on cross country mobility. Further, the necessity for delaying concentration as late as possible will also demand a high degree of cross country mobility coupled with accurate staff work, strict march discipline and good traffic control.

ARMOURED PERSONNEL CARRIERS

Cross country mobility for infantry can, in the future, be achieved by mounting them in APCs. Infantry in these armoured carriers must advance whenever possible right on to the objective. A great part of the value of APCs is their ability to get the infantry over the last 300 yards. On arrival at the objective, however, the sub-unit commander must know exactly what to do when his sub-unit dismounts.

SECTION VI

NOTES FOR THE GUIDANCE OF CONDUCTING OFFICERS

Appended below are some notes on the preliminary work and administrative detail carried out by the Conducting Officer prior to the 1947 Tour. This took place in June and there were a hundred senior officer spectators.

1. **Preliminary Lecture**

    A large scale layered wall diagram was produced, based on Map 5 in the book.

2. **Use of Ground**

    Arrangements were made for a French Army Officer to be attached to the directing staff. The conducting officer took him round each stand and permission was obtained on the spot from the local mayor and land owners to use the ground, cut hedges and remove cattle where necessary.

3. **Provost**

    A detachment from the Corps of Royal Military Police was made available. A preliminary reconnaissance with a Provost representative was carried out to indicate the route for the day and what signing was required, and what signs were required at each stand.

4. **Signals**

    A detachment from the Royal Signals operated the loud speaker equipment. There were two jeeps, each a complete station, which leap-frogged from Stand to Stand. A reconnaissance is necessary to show the operators the route between stands and the exact positions for the loud speakers and microphone.

5. **Transport**

    Buses were used to convey spectators and again a reconnaissance is necessary with the transport officer or NCO to indicate the route, ensure that the buses can get down the lanes and to find turning places where necessary.

6. **Lunch**

    A buffet lunch was provided and the avenue of trees close to Stand 5 makes a convenient and pleasant place for it. A 3 ton lorry is required and a tent was carried in case of wet weather.

7. **Stands**

    (a) Although the countryside on the whole is open and the crops were not fully grown, it is often remarkably difficult to find an area at each stand from which a hundred spectators can see all the ground that the speakers mention. Therefore it is advisable to mark the limits of the selected site with posts or with tape so that some control over the spectators can be maintained.

    (b) The conducting officer should carry the following equipment in his car :—
    Megaphones
    Wire Cutters
    50 ft barbed wire for mending fences; or make arrangements for this to be done.

    (c) There are several alternative positions for Stand 4 which may prove better at different times of the year.

    (i) The Western slopes of Pt 122 about 07005645.

    (ii) The ridge between ROQUANCOURT and VERRIERES.

8. **Conduct of the Tour**

    It was arranged that the Conducting Officer was the first away from each stand and that the French LO followed immediately behind him to cope with traffic problems such as farm waggons which might be met in the narrow lanes.

Appendices

APPENDIX "A"

ORDER OF BATTLE

2 CDN CORPS
(Lieutenant General G. G. Simonds, CB, CBE, DSO)

4 CDN ARMD DIV   (Major General G. Kitching, DSO)

    4 CDN ARMD BDE   (Brigadier E. L. Booth, DSO)
        21 Cdn Armd Regt   — The Governor General's Foot Guards
        22 Cdn Armd Regt   — The Canadian Grenadier Guards
        28 Cdn Armd Regt   — The British Columbia Regiment
        LAKE SUP R (Mot)   — The Lake Superior Regiment (Motor)

    10 CDN INF BDE   (Brigadier J. C. Jefferson, DSO, ED)
        LINC & WELLD R   — The Lincoln and Welland Regiment
        ALQ R   — The Algonquin Regiment
        A & SH of C   — The Argyll and Sutherland Highlanders of Canada
                (Princess Louise's)

        10 Cdn Independent (MG Coy)
        29 Cdn Armd Recce Regt   — The South Alberta Regiment

    RCA   (Brigadier J. N. Lane, DSO)
        15 Cdn Fd Regt
        19 Cdn Fd Regt
        23 Cdn Fd Regt
        5 Cdn A Tk Regt
        8 Cdn LAA Regt

    RCE
        8 Cdn Fd Sqn
        9 Cdn Fd Sqn
        6 Cdn Fd Pk Sqn

    Under Command 4 CDN ARMD DIV
        18 Cdn Armd C Regt   — 12th Manitoba Dragoons

2 CDN DIV   (Major General C. Foulkes, CBE)

    4 CDN INF BDE   (Brigadier J. E. Ganong)
        R REGT C   — The Royal Regiment of Canada
        RHLI   — The Royal Hamilton Light Infantry
                (Wentworth Regiment)
        ESSEX SCOT   — The Essex Scottish

    5 CDN INF BDE   (Brigadier W. J. Megill)
        RHC   — The Black Watch (Royal Highland Regiment) of Canada
        R de MAIS   — Le Regiment de Maisonneuve
        CALG HIGHRS   — The Calgary Highlanders

    6 CDN INF BDE   (Brigadier H. A. Young)
        FUS MR   — Les Fusiliers Mont-Royal
        CAMERONS of C   — The Queen's Own Cameron Highlanders of Canada
        S SASK R   — The South Saskatchewan Regiment

        TOR SCOT (MG Bn)   — The Toronto Scottish Regiment
        8 Cdn Recce Regt   — 14th Canadian Hussars

RCA (Brigadier R. H. Keefler, ED)
    4 Cdn Fd Regt
    5 Cdn Fd Regt
    6 Cdn Fd Regt
    2 Cdn A Tk Regt
    3 Cdn LAA Regt

RCE
    2 Cdn Fd Coy
    7 Cdn Fd Coy
    11 Cdn Fd Coy
    1 Cdn Fd Pk Coy

Under Command 2 CDN DIV

2 CDN ARMD BDE (Brigadier R. A. Wyman, CBE, DSO, ED)
    6 Cdn Armd Regt — 1st Hussars
    10 Cdn Armd Regt — The Fort Garry Horse
    27 Cdn Armd Regt — The Sherbrooke Fusiliers Regiment

    1 LOTHIANS (Flails)
    56 Bty 6 Cdn A Tk Regt
    74 Bty 6 Cdn A Tk Regt
    A Sqn 141 RAC (Crocodiles)
    70 Aslt Sqn RE (AVRE)

3 CDN DIV (Major General R. F. L. Keller, CBE)

    7 CDN INF BDE (Brigadier A. W. Foster)
      R WPG RIF — The Royal Winnipeg Rifles
      REGINA RIF — The Regina Rifle Regiment
      1 C SCOT R — The Canadian Scottish Regiment (Highlanders)

    8 CDN INF BDE (Brigadier K. G. Blackader, DSO, MC, ED)
      QOR of C — The Queen's Own Rifles of Canada
      R de CHAUD — Le Regiment de la Chaudiere
      N SHORE R — The North Shore (New Brunswick) Regiment

    9 CDN INF BDE (Brigadier J. M. Rockingham)
      HLI of C — The Highland Light Infantry of Canada
      SD & G HIGHRS — The Stormont, Dundas and Glengarry Highlanders
      NTH NS HIGHRS — The North Nova Scotia Highlanders

    CH of O (MG Bn) — The Cameron Highlanders of Ottawa
    7 Cdn Recce Regt — 17th Duke of York's Royal Canadian Hussars

RCA (Brigadier P. A. S. Todd, OBE, ED)
    12 Cdn Fd Regt
    13 Cdn Fd Regt
    14 Cdn Fd Regt
    3 Cdn A Tk Regt
    4 Cdn LAA Regt

RCE
    6 Cdn Fd Coy
    16 Cdn Fd Coy
    18 Cdn Fd Coy
    3 Cdn Fd Pk Coy

1 POLISH ARM DIV (Major General S. Maczec, CB, DSO)

    10 POLISH ARMD BDE
      1 Polish Armd Regt
      2 Polish Armd Regt
      24 Polish Armd (L) Regt
      10 Polish (Mot) Bn — Dragoons

3 POLISH INF BDE
    1 Polish Inf Bn   — Highland Battalion
    8 Polish Inf Bn
    9 Polish Inf Bn

    1 Polish Armd Div MG Coy
    10 Polish Mtd Rifle Regt
       (Armd Recce Regt)

RA
    1 Polish Mot Fd Regt
    2 Polish Mot Fd Regt
    1 Polish A Tk Regt
    1 Polish LAA Regt

RE
    10 Polish Fd Sqn
    11 Polish Fd Sqn
    11 Polish Fd Pk Sqn

51 (H) DIV   (Major General T. G. Rennie, CB, DSO, MBE)

    152 (H) BDE   (Brigadier A. J. H. Cassels, CBE, DSO)
       2 SEAFORTH
       5 SEAFORTH
       5 CAMERONS

    153 (H) BDE   (Brigadier H. Murray, CB, DSO)
       5 BW
       1 GORDONS
       5/7 GORDONS

    154 (H) BDE   (Brigadier J. A. Oliver, DSO, MBE, TD)
       1 BW
       7 BW
       7 A & SH

       1/7 Mx (MG)
       2 DERBY YEO

    RA   (Brigadier W. A. Shiel, CBE, DSO, MC)
       126 Fd Regt
       127 Fd Regt
       128 Fd Regt
       61 A Tk Regt
       40 LAA Regt

    RE
       274 Fd Coy
       275 Fd Coy
       276 Fd Coy
       239 Fd Pk Coy

Under Command 51 (H) DIV

    33 ARMD BDE   (Brigadier H. B. Scott, DSO)
       1 N YEO
       144 RAC
       148 RAC

       22 DGNS (Flails)
       33 Bty 6 Cdn A Tk Regt
       103 Bty 6 Cdn A Tk Regt
       80 Assault Sqn RE (AVRE)
       D Sqn 141 RAC (Crocodiles)

RCA 2 CDN CORPS   (Brigadier A. B. Matthews, DSO)

    2 CDN AGRA
        3 Cdn Med Regt
        4 Cdn Med Regt
        7 Cdn Med Regt
        15 Cdn Med Regt
        1 Hy Regt

    In support RCA 2 CDN CORPS

    RA 49 DIV
        143 Fd Regt
        150 Fd Regt
        185 Fd Regt

    3 AGRA

    4 AGRA
        53 Med Regt
        65 Med Regt
        68 Med Regt
        79 Med Regt

    9 AGRA
        9 Med Regt
        11 Med Regt
        107 Med Regt

        108 HAA Regt
        51 Hy Regt
        2 Cdn HAA Regt
        109 HAA Regt

APPENDIX "B"

EQUIPMENT AND ORGANISATION

(Allied and German)

The following tables give the main details of the organisation of British and German formations at the time of Operation TOTALIZE, and the principal data about the tanks and special equipment in use at the time.

Table 1 — ALLIED TANKS

Type	Crew	Weight (tons)	Armament	Amn carried (rounds)	Max Speed (mph)	Radius of action (miles)
Cromwell V	5	27.5	1 × 75 mm 2 × 7.92 mm Besa MGs	64 4950	38	165
Cromwell VI	5	27.5	1 × 95 mm 2 × 7.92 mm Besa MGs	51 4950	38	165
Sherman III	5	31.2	1 × 75 mm 2 × .300 Browning MGs	99 6750	30	215
Sherman V	5	31.75	1 × 75 mm 2 × .300 Browning MGs	99 6750	22	125
Sherman Vc	4	34	1 × 17 pr 1 × .300 Browning MGs	78 5000	22	125
Churchill IV	5	38.5	1 × 6 pr 2 × 7.92 Besa MGs	84 6975	16.9	123
Churchill VII	5	39.5	1 × 75 mm 2 × 7.92 mm Besa MGs	83 6525	13.5	142

Table 2 — ALLIED SPECIAL EQUIPMENTS

1. **SHERMAN "FLAIL" (CRAB II).** (See Photograph No. 4 following page 103)

This was a mine clearing device, employing a rotating drum mounted in front of the tank: the drum was fitted with 43 chains, and rotated at 180 revolutions per minute, so that the chains beat the ground in front of the tank and exploded the mines. Speed, while flailing, was about 3 mph.

The Flail was mounted on a Sherman V (see Table 1). Its length was 27' 5½" and width 11' 6"; the weight was 34 tons and the radius of action 120 miles. There was a crew of five.

The 75 mm and .300 Browning in the turret could still be used as on the normal tank: 73 rounds and 4250 rounds respectively were carried for these weapons.

2. **CHURCHILL "CROCODILE" FLAME THROWER.** (See Photograph No. 3 following page 103)

The "Crocodile" consisted of the normal Churchill VII (see Table 1) with a flame thrower installed in place of the hull MG.

The tank towed a trailer which contained 400 gallons of special fuel: the maximum range of the flame-thrower was 110 yards. The length of the vehicle with trailer was 40' 6" and the weight 47.2 tons.

The 75 mm and the MG in the turret could be used in the normal way: 83 rounds and 3600 rounds respectively were carried for these weapons. The speed and radius of action were not appreciably affected.

3. **ASSAULT VEHICLE, ROYAL ENGINEERS (AVRE).** (See Photograph No. 2 following page 103)

The AVRE consisted of a normal Churchill IV (see Table 1) with a Petard mounted in the turret in place of the gun. The inside of the tank was modified for the storage of explosive charges, and it carried a crew of six. The AVRE was also equipped to carry a fascine or an assault bridge if required and, to perform many other engineer tasks.

The Petard was a large mortar which fired an explosive charge called a "Dustbin". 14 Dustbins were carried : each one weighed 30 lbs and contained 18 lbs of HE. The accurate range of the Petard was 80 yards, though a "dustbin" could be fired up to 180 yards. The rate of fire was 2—3 rounds per minute.

The AVRE also carried 18 Wade charges for placing by hand.

4. **ARMOURED PERSONNEL CARRIER** (See Photographs Nos. 5 and 6 following page 103)

This consisted of the Priest S.P. gun from which the 105 mm gun, ammunition bins and seats had been removed. Over the opening in the front left by the removal of the gun, steel plates were welded. Twelve to fourteen men could be carried and the vehicle had the normal performance of a Sherman. The only armament was one Browning mounted on a bracket on the off front side of the crew compartment. This vehicle was improvised for this operation and was the first APC used in action.

Table 3—GERMAN TANKS

Type	Crew	Weight (tons)	Armament	Amn carried (rounds)	Max Speed (mph)	Radius of action (miles)
Pz KW IV	5	23	1×75 mm 2×7.92 mm MGs	87 4500	30	125
Pz KW V "PANTHER"	5	45	1×75 mm 2×7.92 mm MGs	79 4500	34	125
Pz KW VI "TIGER"	5	56	1×88 mm 2×7.92 mm MGs	87 5700	23	73

Table 4—EQUIPMENT OF ALLIED and GERMAN DIVISIONS

ALLIED	Formation	Tanks in Armd Regt	Tanks in Armd Recce Regt
	4 Cdn Armd Div	Sherman III, V and Vc	Sherman III and Vc
	1 Polish Armd Div	Sherman III, and Vc	Cromwell V and VI
	2 Cdn Armd Bde	Sherman III, V and Vc	
	33 Armd Bde	Sherman III, V and Vc	
GERMAN	Formation	Type of Tank	
	12 SS Pz Div	Pz KW IV and V	
	101 Hy Tk Bn	Pz KW V and VI	

TABLE 5 — OUTLINE ORGANISATION OF

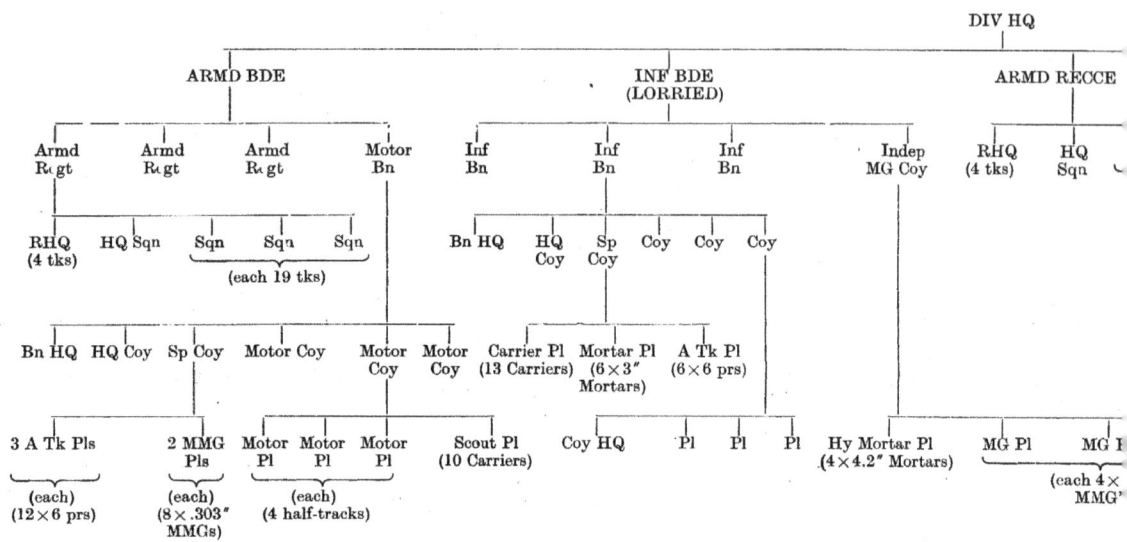

NOTES

1. Approx total strength (WE) of the Armd Div = 13,500 (incl Services)
2. Strength of fighting tanks in the Armd Div = 259
3. 20 TCVs were allotted to each Lorried Inf Bn from Div RASC.

TABLE 6 — OUTLINE ORGANISATION OF A B

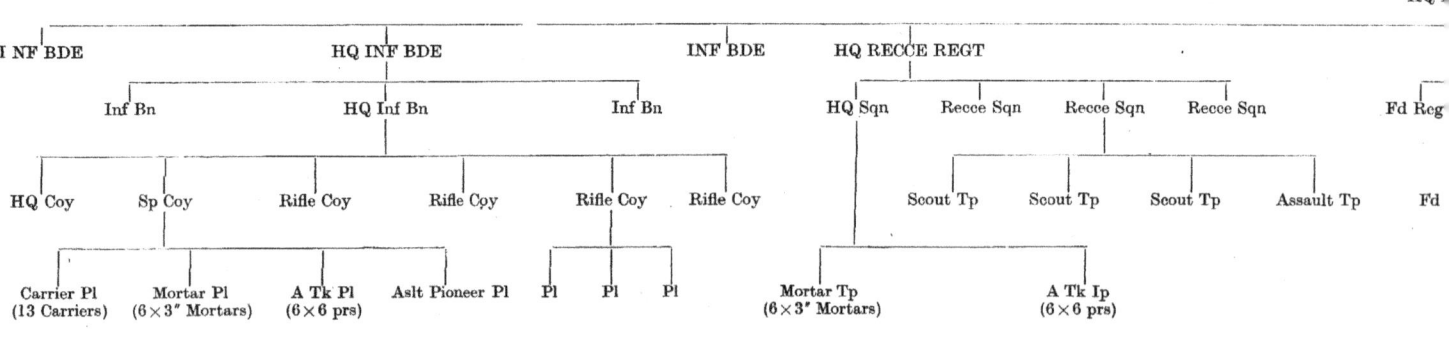

NO

1. Total strength of par
   (i.e. Div less Sigs
2. No weapon smaller t

...NADIAN/POLISH DIVISION (JULY 1944)

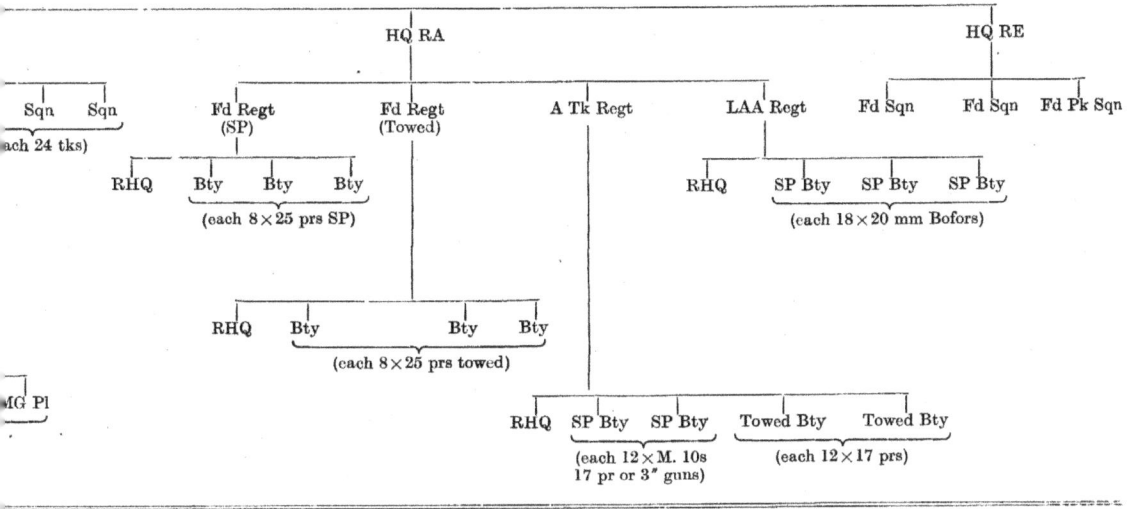

INDEPENDENT ARMOURED BRIGADE

The organisation of the Independent Armoured Brigade was similar to that of the Armoured Brigade in the Armoured Division, except that it had no Motor battalion.

...SH/CANADIAN INFANTRY DIVISION (JULY 1944)

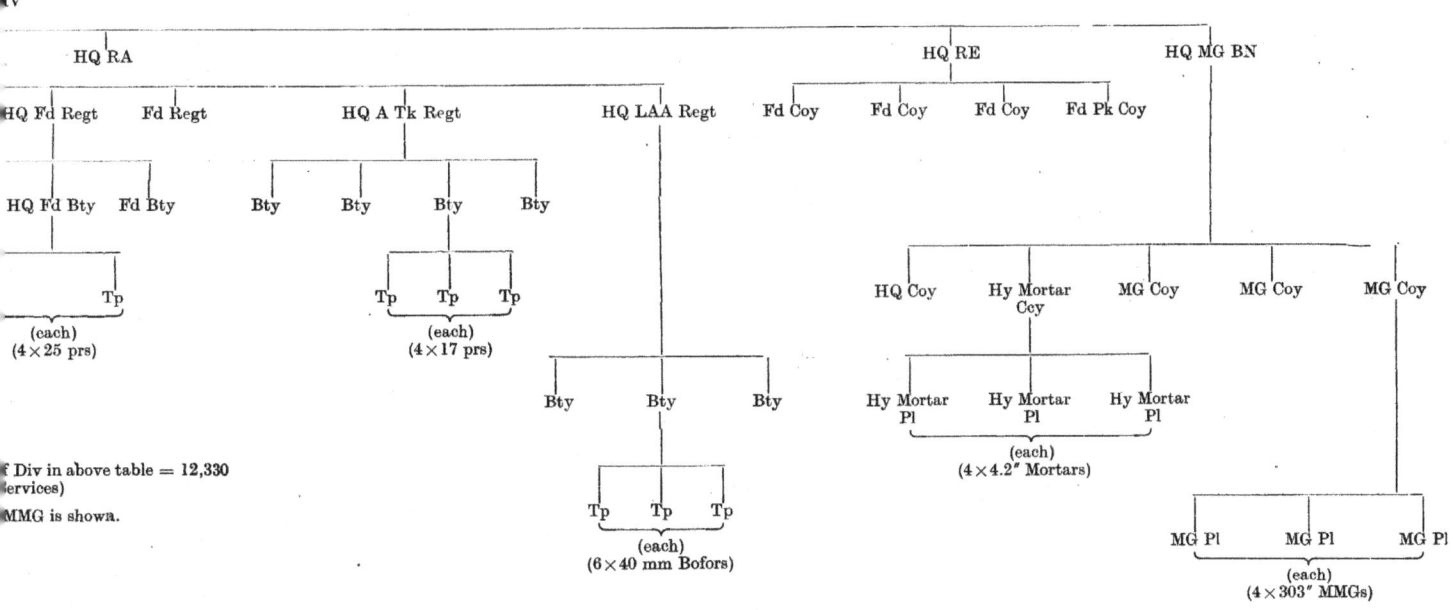

TABLE 7 — GERMAN PA

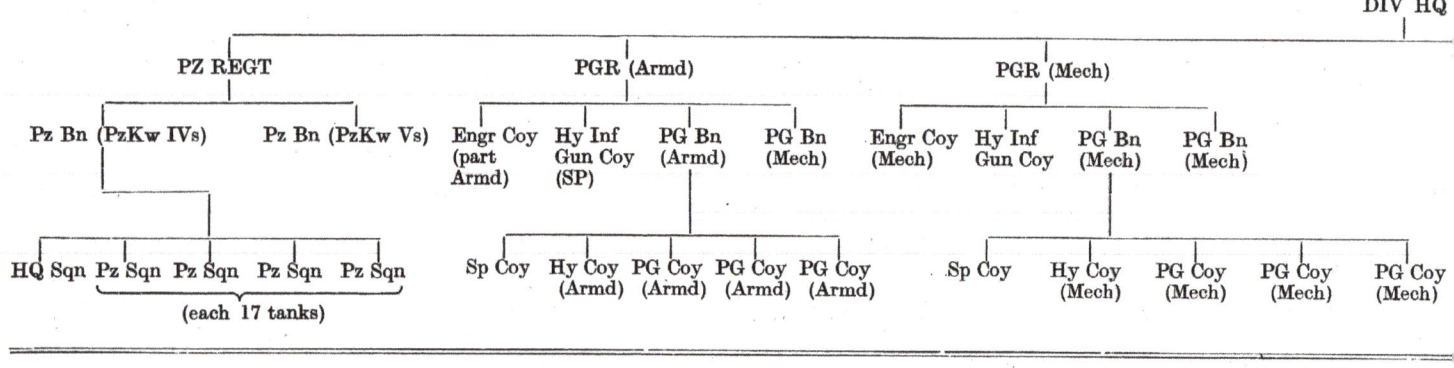

NOTES

1. Approx total strength (WE) of the Arm
2. Strength of fighting tanks in the Armd/

TABLE 8 — PROBABLE OR

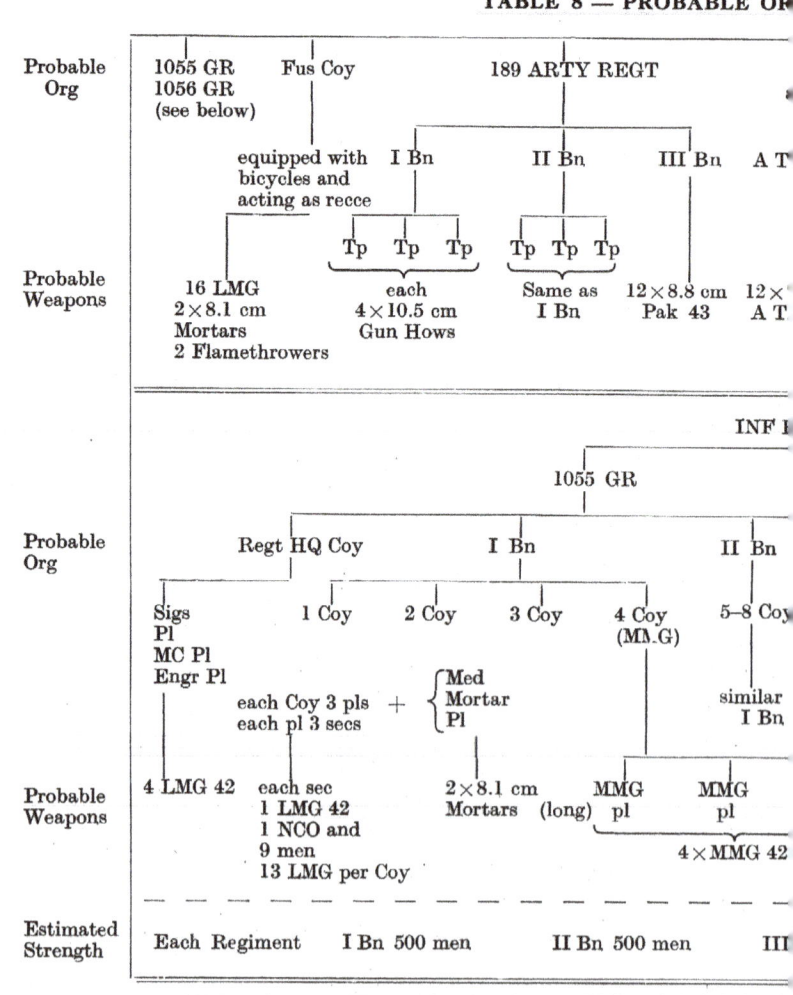

TABLE 8a — PERSO

Men 10,550;   Horses 2,650;   M.T. 900;   LMGs 350;
10.5 cm Gun Hows 24;   7.5 cm A Tk Guns 18;   8.8 cm A Tk

NZER DIVISION

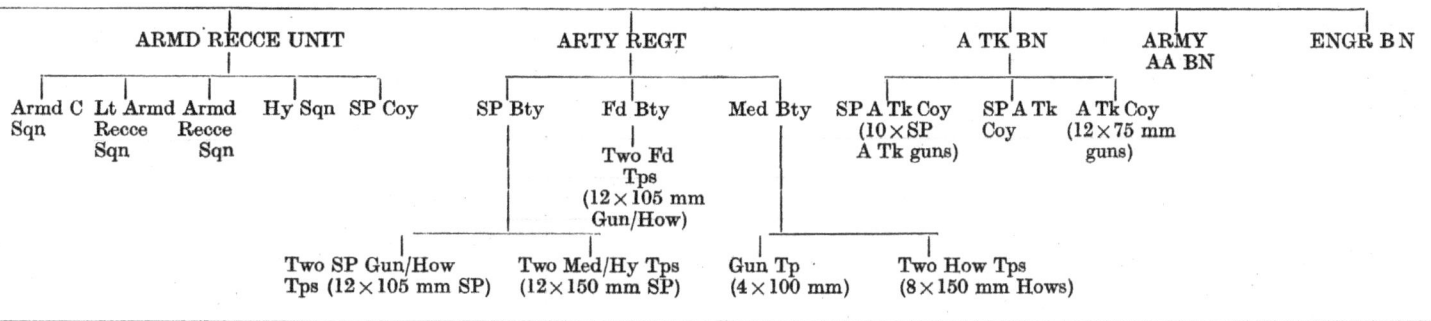

	BRITISH	GERMAN
/Pz Div	13,500	14,000
z Div	259	160

GANISATION OF 89 INF DIV

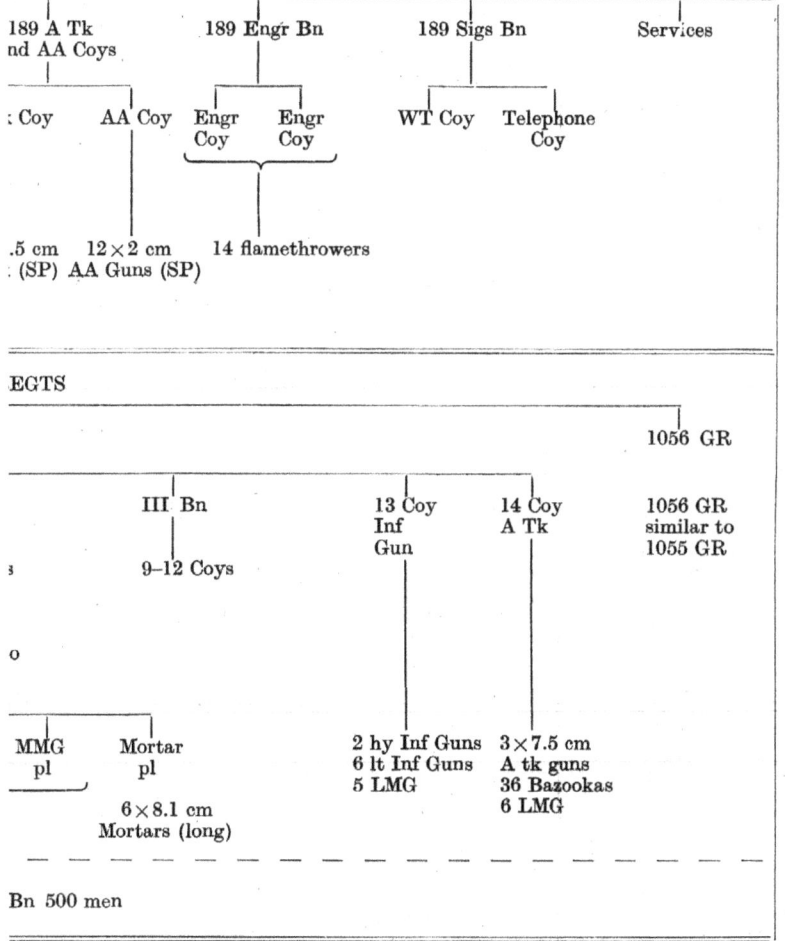

EGTS

```
                                                    1056 GR
                III Bn          13 Coy    14 Coy    1056 GR
                                Inf       A Tk      similar to
                9-12 Coys       Gun                 1055 GR
```

```
MMG    Mortar            2 hy Inf Guns   3 × 7.5 cm
 pl      pl              6 lt Inf Guns   A tk guns
                         5 LMG           36 Bazookas
       6 × 8.1 cm                        6 LMG
       Mortars (long)
```

Bn 500 men

NNEL AND WEAPONS

HMGs 76 ; 8.1 cm Mortars 78 ; Lt Inf Guns 12 ; Hy Inf Guns 4 ;
Guns 12 ; 8.8 Basookas 72 ; 2 cm AA Guns 12 ; Flamethrowers 16 .

APPENDIX "C"

LIST OF REFERENCE MAPS

1.	FRANCE	1 : 250,000	CHERBOURG and CAEN	SHEET	3A and 8
2.		1 : 100,000	CAEN and FALAISE	SHEET	7F
3.		1 : 50,000	CAEN		7F/1
			TROARN		7F/2
			AUNAY SUR ODON		7F/3
			ST PIERRE SUR DIVES		7F/4
			FLERS		7F/5
			FALAISE		7F/6

Sheets 7F/1 7F/2 7F/3 and 7F/4 join at TILLY LA CAMPAGNE.

4.		1 : 25,000	CAEN	40/16 SW
			BRETTVILLE SUR LAIZE	40/14 NW
			POTIGNY	40/14 SW
			ST PIERRE	40/14 SE
			MEZIDON	40/14 NE

APPENDIX "D"

Copy No.
TOP SECRET
8-1/Ops

Main Headquarters
2nd Canadian Corps

5 Aug 44

2 CDN CORPS OPERATION INSTRUCTION No. 4
OPERATION "TOTALIZE"

Reference maps : FRANCE 1/50,000 sheets 7 F1, 7 F2, 7 F3, 7 F4, 7 F5, 7 F6

INFORMATION

1. **Enemy**

   As in 2 Cdn Corps Intelligence Summaries and as shown on defence overprints to be issued separately.

2. **Own Troops**

   Additional troops :

   (a) *Under Command :*
   - (i) 51 (H) Div.
   - (ii) 1 Polish Armd Div.
   - (iii) 33 Brit Armd Bde.

   (b) *In support :*
   9 AGRA.

   (c) Depending upon availability certain other troops from 79 Armd Div may be placed under command.

3. **Air**

   Considerable air forces will be available to support the operation.

4. **Boundaries**

   Present RIGHT and LEFT inter-corps boundaries.

INTENTION

5. To break through the enemy positions astride the CAEN–FALAISE road.

METHOD

6. The operation will be carried out in three phases :

   (a) *Phase I* — Break through the FONTENAY LE MARMION 0358–LA HOGUE 0960 position.
   (b) *Phase II* — Break through the HAUTMESNIL 0852–ST SYLVAIN 1354 position.
   (c) *Phase III* — Exploit as ordered by Commander 2 Cdn Corps.

TASKS

7. **2 Cdn Div**

   With under command 2 Cdn Armd Bde :

   (a) *Phase I*

   (i) Capture as first objective CAILLOUET 0555, GAUMESNIL 0755 and woods 0756.
   (ii) Mop up area MAY SUR ORNE 0259–FONTENAY LE MARMION 0358–CAILLOUET–GAUMESNIL–ROQUANCOURT 0558.
   (iii) Reorganise in area ST ANDRE SUR ORNE 0261–MAY SUR ORNE–FONTENAY LE MARMION–CAILLOUET–GAUMESNIL–VERRIERES 0560 to protect RIGHT flank and form firm base for launching of Phase II.

(b) *Phase II*

   Maintain firm base in area ST ANDRE SUR ORNE–FONTENAY LE MARMION–CAILLOUET–GAUMESNIL–VERRIERES.

(c) *Phase III*

   Relieve 3 Cdn Inf Div at BRETTEVILLE SUR LAIZE 0553.

8. **51 (H) Div**

   With under command 33 Brit Armd Bde.

   (a) *Phase I*

   (i) Capture as first objective LORGUICHON Wood 0757–CRAMESNIL 0856–ST AIGNAN DE CRAMESNIL 0956 and woods to SOUTH 0856, 0855–GARCELLES SECQUEVILLE 0858.

   (ii) After capture of first objective, capture in succession SECQUEVILLE LA CAMPAGNE 0959 and wood area 1160–1159–1058.

   (b) *Phase II*

   Exploit to secure POUSSY LA CAMPAGNE 1356–BILLY 1457–CONTEVILLE 1257.

   (c) *Phase III*

   Relieve 3 Cdn Div at ST SYLVAIN 1354.

9. **4 Cdn Armd Div**

   (a) *Phase I*

   Remain in area VAUCELLES.

   (b) *Phase II*

   Attack on axis road CAEN–FALAISE and capture HAUTMESNIL 0852 and high ground NW of BRETTEVILLE LE RABET 1050.

   (c) *Phase III*

   (i) Advance on axis HAUTMESNIL 0852–point 180 0747–point 206 0943.

   (ii) Position itself facing WEST and SOUTH on high ground point 180 0747–point 195 0864–point 206 0943.

   (iii) Patrol to gain or maintain contact within the arc including road FONTAINE LE PIN 0844–MESLAY 0043–including road FALAISE 1435–ARGENTAN 2618.

10. **3 Cdn Div**

   (a) *Phase I*

   Remain concentrated in area CAEN.

   (b) *Phase II*

   (i) Following in rear of 4 Cdn Armd Div, secure the RIGHT flank by clearing and forming a firm base about BRETTEVILLE SUR LAIZE.

   (ii) Secure LEFT flank by clearing and forming a firm base about woods 1054–1055.

   (iii) Be prepared to exploit from woods 1054–1055 to ST SYLVAIN.

   (c) *Phase III*

   Upon being relieved by 2 Cdn Div and 51 (H) Div in BRETTEVILLE SUR LAIZE and ST SYLVAIN re-position brigades in areas HAUTMESNIL, BRETTEVILLE LE RABET and high ground point 140 1347.

11. **1 Polish Armd Div**

   (a) *Phase I*

   Remain in concentration area.

   (b) *Phase II*

   Move to forward concentration area on orders Commander 2 Cdn Corps.

   (c) *Phase III*

   (i) Advance on axis QUESNAY 1047–point 165 1443–point 159 1438.

   (ii) Position itself facing EAST and SOUTH on high ground point 170 1442–point 159 1438.

   (iii) Patrol to maintain or gain contact within the arc excluding road FALAISE–ARGENTAN including road MONTBOINT 1446–CONDE SUR IFS 1952.

12. **Start Line**

    Line of road ST ANDRE SUR ORNE–HUBERT FOLIE 0662–SOLIERS 0862.

13. **Corps Report Lines**

    (a) Road LAIZE LA VILLE 0157–FONTENAY LE MARMION 0358–ROQUANCOURT 0558–GARCELLES SECQUEVILLE 0858–road junction 105605–VIMONT 1461, code word McDONALD.

    (b) Road BRETTEVILLE SUR LAIZE 0553–ST AIGNAN DE CRAMESNIL 0956–ARGENCES 1761, code word LAUGHTON.

    (c) Road LA LONDE 0748–GRAINVILLE LANGANNERIE 0949–BRETTEVILLE LE RABET 1050–ST MARTIN DES BOIS 1354–AIRAN 1858, code word DRESSLER.

    (d) Track BRAY EN CINGLAIS 0745–AISY 0945–OUILLY LE TESSON 1246–MAIZIERES 1749–CONDE SUR IFS 1952, code word VALENTINO.

    (e) Road from road junction 107400–SOULANGY 1241–road and track junction 154424–road and track junction 177433–SASSY 1845–ERNES 2049, code word HENIE.

    (f) Road LE MESNIL JACQUET 0434–FALAISE 1435–DAMBLAINVILLE 2038–Bridge 2240, code word LOMBARD.

14. **Grouping and Boundaries**

    (a) Inter divisional boundary 2 Cdn Div–51 (H) Div inclusive 2 Cdn Div CAEN–FALAISE road, to exclusive 2 Cdn Div railway bridge 068583–thence line of railway to track 068573–incl 2 Cdn Div point 122 0756–road and track junction 078553–thence road CAEN-FALAISE.

    (b) At commencement of Phase III 51 (H) Div and 33 Brit Armd Bde will revert to command 1 Brit Corps, the latter corps assuming responsibility for protection of EASTERN flank of 2 Cdn Corps NORTH of River LAISON. At this stage inter-corps boundary will become all inclusive to 2 Cdn Corps present boundary to railway at 082651–069585 thence track junction 076567–track junction 084549–point 82 1053–wood 119525–SOIGNOLLES 138509–BOUT DU HAUT 1648.

15. **Timings**

    (a) D Day Monday 7 August 1944.

    (b) H hour :—

    (i) Phase I — 2300 hrs.

    (ii) Phase II — 1400 hrs D plus 1.

    (c) D day and H hour will be confirmed by message not later than 071830B August.

16. **Artillery**

    (a) *Phase I*

    (i) NO preliminary bombardment.

    (ii) Rolling barrage opening at H hour advancing at a rate of 100 yards per minute to first objectives.

    (b) *Phase II*

    (i) Divisional artilleries under divisional control.

    (ii) AGsRA on call to 4 Cdn Armd Div and 3 Cdn Div.

    (c) *Phase III*

    (i) Divisional artilleries under divisional control.

    (ii) Each armoured division to have one medium regiment under command.

    (iii) AGsRA will be available for support after pause to "step up".

    (d) 12 and 1 Corps artillery are providing support on RIGHT and LEFT flanks respectively.

    (e) Details being issued separately.

17. **Searchlights**

    Will be employed under direction of CCRA. No illumination before H hour.

18. **Engineers**

    Issued separately.

19. **Air**

   Issued separately.

20. **Aids to Navigation in Phase I**
   (a) Leading tanks will have positions and bearing of thrust lines fixed by survey.
   (b) Bofors barrage, co-ordinated by CCRA 2 Cdn Corps, will be fired over divisional thrust lines.
   (c) Wireless directional beams, two per divisional front, under direction CSO 2 Cdn Corps.
   (d) Target indicator shells will be fired under divisional arrangements on thrust lines. 2 Cdn Div RED indicators, 51 (H) Div GREEN indicators.

ADMINISTRATION

21. Administrative order issued separately.

22. **Traffic**

   Special instructions to be issued separately.

INTERCOMMUNICATION

23. (a) Axis of advance 2 Cdn Corps—road CAEN–FALAISE.
   (b) Commanders' Command Post and Signal Centre at 052652.
   (c) Headquarters locations :
      (i) 2 Cdn Corps Main–970743
      (ii) 4 Cdn Armd Div–063681
      (iii) 2 Cdn Div–029667
      (iv) 3 Cdn Div–to be notified
      (v) 51 (H) Div –044647.
   (d) Code words already issued.
   (e) Signals instruction issued separately.

Brig
C of S 2 Cdn Corps

APPENDIX "E"

TOP SECRET
8-1/Ops
Main Headquarters
2nd Canadian Corps
6 Aug 44
Copy Number

OPERATION "TOTALIZE"

Reference 2 Cdn Corps Operation Instruction No. 4 issued 051200B Aug.

1. As a result of the rapidly changing enemy situation a conference was called by GOC 2 Cdn Corps at 061000B August. The following notes are issued as confirmation thereof:

2. There is no change in the basic plan as set forth in Operation Instruction Number Four. The alterations which have been made are designed to:

   (a) Take advantage of the lesser opposition expected on the Corps front during Phase I.

   (b) Take advantage of the D plus 1 air effort and mainted the momentum by launching 4 Cdn Armd and 1 Polish Armd Divs directly through to their final objectives in Phase II.

3. Divisional tasks may now be summarised as follows:

   (a) **2 Cdn Div**

   (i) No change in Phase I.

   (ii) During Phase II carry out the task previously allotted to 3 Cdn Div–namely to secure the RIGHT FLANK by clearing and forming a firm base about BRETTEVILLE SUR LAIZE.

   (b) **51 (H) Div**

   (i) No change in Phase I.

   (ii) During Phase II carry out the task previously allotted to 3 Cdn Div–namely to secure the LEFT FLANK by clearing and forming a firm base about woods 1054–1055.

   (c) **4 Cdn Armd Div**

   (i) During Phase I to move up behind 2 Cdn Div so as to be positioned on the Corps start line by morning D plus 1.

   (ii) As Phase II, pass through 2 Cdn Div and go directly to final objective—namely position itself facing WEST and SOUTH on high ground point 180 0747–point 195 0846–point 206 0943; and patrol to gain or maintain contact within the arc including road FONTAINE LE PIN 0844–MESLAY 0034–including road FALAISE 1435–ARGENTAN 2618.

   (d) **1 Polish Armd Div**

   (i) During Phase I to move from present concentration area so as to be positioned behind 51 (H) Div on the corps start line by morning D plus 1.

   (ii) As Phase II to pass through 51 (H) Div and go directly to final objective—namely position itself facing EAST and SOUTH on high ground point 170 1442–point 159 1438; and patrol to maintain or gain contact within the arc excluding road FALAISE-ARGENTAN including road MONTBOINT 1446–CONDE SUR IFS 1952.

   (e) **3 Cdn Div**

   (i) During Phase I to remain in its present concentration area.

   (ii) Follow the move forward of 1 Polish Armd Div to a forward concentration area NORTH of CAEN.

   (iii) Be prepared to move forward on orders of Commander 2 Cdn Corps to take over areas HAUTMESNIL, BRETTEVILLE LE RABET and high ground point 140 1347.

4. Artillery tasks may now be summarised as follows :—

    (a) *Phase I*—No change

    (b) *Phase II*

        (i) AGsRA on call to 4 Cdn Armd Div and 1 Polish Armd Div.

        (ii) Two medium regiments will be moved forward by 4 Cdn Armd Div. Upon these regiments coming into action one will be in support of each armoured division.

5. **Searchlights**

Illumination will be controlled by CCRA. NO illumination until opening of artillery barrage.

6. **Timings**

For both Phase I and Phase II :—

    (a) H hour will be the time at which the leading troops cross the corps start line.

    (b) H hour will be confirmed by message not later than 071830B August.

7. **Acknowledge**

                                                      For Brig
                                                   C of S 2 Cdn Corps.

APPENDIX "F"
(less Trace P)

TOP SECRET
2CD/G/1-C
GS 2 Cdn Inf Div
7 Aug 44
Copy No.

2 CDN INF DIV OO No. 2 OPERATION "TOTALIZE"

Ref Maps : FRANCE 1/25,000, Sheets 40/16 SW 40/14 NW

INFM

1. **Enemy**

As given in int summary att and def overprint issued separately.

2. **Own Tps**

2 Cdn Corps is attacking with 2 Cdn Inf Div, 51 (H) Div to secure area CAILLOUET 0555–pt 122 0756–CRAMESNIL 0856–ST AIGNAN DE CRAMESNIL 0956–and exploit with 4 Cdn Armd Div and 1 Polish Armd Div as ordered by Comd 2 Cdn Corps.

4 Cdn Armd Div will move to SL in lanes ot 2 Cdn Armd Bde at 080100B.

Air : Considerable air forces will be available to sp the op.

Additional tps under comd 2 Cdn Inf Div :

      2 Cdn Armd Bde
      1 LOTHIANS less one sqn
      56 A Tk Bty (SP)
      74 A Tk Bty (17 pdr RAM towed)
      79 Assault Sqn RE (AVRE)
      A Sqn 141 Armd Regt.

INTENTION

3. 2 Cdn Inf Div will attack and secure the posn CAILLOUET 0555–pt 122 0756– BRETTEVILLE SUR LAIZE 0552.

METHOD

4. Attack will take place in two stages :

Stage I. In artificial and natural moonlight.

2 Cdn Armd Bde with under comd :
    4 Cdn Inf Bde (in armd tp carriers)
    8 Cdn Recce Regt (14CH)
    one coy MG (TOR SCOT (MG))
    one pl hy mortars (TOR SCOT (MG))
    56 A Tk Bty (SP)
    74 A Tk Bty (17 pdr RAM towed)
    1 LOTHIANS, less one sqn (a)
    79 Assault Sqn RE (AVRE)
    one pl 2 Cdn Fd Coy RCE
    ASSU Tel

will advance down two lanes.

(a) 1 LOTHIANS, less one sqn, upon completion of Stage I will come under comd 4 Cdn Armd Div.

Objectives, bdys, assembly areas and SL—see Trace P att.

H hr To be notified by 071300B hrs.

Air bombing Hy bombers will engage for 40 mins at 072130B hrs or 072300B hrs the following targets:

      Target No. 1—02345915
      Target No. 3—03185831

Rate of adv 100 yds in one min.

5 Cdn Inf Bde with under comd:
- 10 Cdn Armd Regt, less one sqn
- one coy MMG (TOR SCOT (MG))
- one pl hy mortars (from 080200B hrs)
- 56 A Tk Bty (SP) (from time of comn Stage 1 by 2 Cdn Armd Bde).

will be prepared to:
(a) restore momentum of attack, if lost, and capture any of the objectives of 2 Cdn Armd Bde.
(b) move, on orders of GOC 2 Cdn Inf Div, between the lanes of armd colns to area 0556-0656 preparatory to attacking and capturing BRETTEVILLE SUR LAIZE 0552. Details of plan to be settled on the ground.

6 Cdn Inf Bde with under comd:
- one coy MMG (TOR SCOT (MG))
- three pls hy mortar (TOR SCOT (MG))
- two btys 2 Cdn A Tk Regt
- one sqn 141 Armd Regt (Crocodiles)

will mop up area between excl CAEN–FALAISE rd and excl R ORNE as far SOUTH as Northing 575. Mopping up to commence at H hr.

Arty. Fd and med barrage at H plus 15. Med arty 400 yds in adv of fd arty. Opening line through junc 60 grid line and CAEN-FALAISE rd, and at right angles to it.

    Rate of adv—100 yds per min
    Superimposed concs on selected targets
    Barrage will NOT be stopped except on orders of Corps Comd.
    Arty sp, by 2 Cdn Inf Div Arty and one AGRA, available on call except during timed programme.

LAA. 4 Cdn LAA Regt will fire directional barrage along lanes, 6 rpg every 4 mins.

SLs. Eight SLs will light at H plus 15 from areas 9964 and 0065.

Stage 2

6 Cdn Inf Bde will re-org on gen line MAY SUR ORNE 0259–FONTENAY LE MARMION 0358–ROQUANCOURT 0558.

5 Cdn Inf Bde, on orders of GOC 2 Cdn Inf Div, will attack and secure BRETTEVILLE SUR LAIZE 0552 not before 1400 hrs D plus 1.

2 Cdn Armd Bde will be prepared to sp 5 Cdn Inf Bde.

Arty. 2 Cdn Inf Div Arty and 12 Corps Arty will sp the attack. Predicted smoke screen will cover right flank if required.

Air. Hy bombers will engage BRETTEVILLE SUR LAIZE 0552 at 1400 hrs.

Moves of 4 Cdn Armd Div

Routes: (A) VAUCELLES 0366–FLEURY 0264–PIDGEON
         (B) VAUCELLES 0366–rd CAEN–FALAISE–MOON route–EAGLE.

Timings Head not past pts 022642 and 048643 before 080100B hrs.
         Head at SL by 080600B hrs.

Assembly Areas WEST Pt 67 0163–houses 030613–X rds 0361–Pt 67.
                 EAST Area NORTH and EAST of IFS.

All Stages

A Tk. One bty 2 Cdn A Regt will be in res.
Upon completion of Stage 1 by 2 Cdn Armd Bde, 56 A Tk Bty (SP) will come under comd 5 Cdn Inf Bde and will be replaced by one bty 2 Cdn A Tk Regt.

LAA To be controlled by 2 Cdn Inf Div Arty.

   RCE   Tasks: (i) Open routes CHARLIE, HORN, EAGLE

           (ii) Clearance of rds of mines.

           (iii) Assist bdes in clearing mines and booby traps.

ADM

5. Issued separately.

INTERCOMN

6. **Div Comd Post** opens 072000B hrs map ref 038635.

7. **5 Cdn Inf Bde Comd Post** will be est map ref 038635 by 072300B hrs.

8. **6 Cdn Inf Bde Comd Post** will be est map ref 038635 by 072300 hrs.

9. **2 Cdn Armd Bde Tac HQ** moves behind leading sqn of Cdn Armd Regt in Fortress Force.

10. **Code words.**   Att

   Code word followed by ABLE means leading tps on objective.
   Code word followed by BAKER means rest of comd incl sp arms is on the objective.
   Code word followed by CHARLIE means the posn is organised, disposed to withstand a counter-attack and ready to dig in.

11. **Identification.** Vehs and fwd sub-units will carry YELLOW smoke and YELLOW celanese triangle strips for identification to friendly aircraft.

12. **Synchronisation.** BBC time sigs.

13. **Tels.** ASSU tels are allotted to :   HQ 2 Cdn Inf Div
              5 Cdn Inf Bde
              6 Cdn Inf Bde
              2 Cdn Armd Bde
   One VCP on ASSU net will be deployed area 0261.

   ACK

Method of Issue: LO	Lt-Col
Time of Signature: 071300B hrs.	GS 2 Cdn Inf Div

APPENDIX "G"

TOP SECRET
Copy No.
6 Aug 44

51 (H) DIV OO No. 6 OPERATION "TOTALIZE"

Ref Maps 1/25,000 Sheets 40/16 SW—40/14 NW

INFORMATION

1. **Enemy**

   As in 51 (H) Div Intelligence Summary and as shown on Def overprints both to be issued separately.

2. **Own Troops**

   (a) 51 (H) Div is now under comd 2 Cdn Corps, and is taking part in op "TOTALIZE" with the object of breaking through the enemy posns astride the CAEN—FALAISE rd.

   (b) Additional tps under comd 51 (H) Div :

           33 Armd Bde
           33 Bty 6 Cdn A tk Regt
           103 Bty 6 Cdn A tk Regt
           22 Dgns (Flails)
           80 Assault Sqn RE (AVRE)
           "B" Sqn 141 RAC Regt (Crocodiles)

3. **Boundaries**

   Between 2 Cdn Div and 51 (H) Div, incl 2 Cdn Div, CAEN-FALAISE rd to excl rly br 068583—thence line of rly to track 068573–pt 122 0756—rd and track junc 078553—thence rd CAEN-FALAISE.

INTENTION

4. 51 (H) Div will seize and hold the area LORGUICHON WOOD 0757–CRAMESNIL 0856–ST AIGNAN DE CRAMESNIL and woods to SOUTH 0856–0855–GARCELLES SECQUEVILLE 0858–subsequently capturing SECQUEVILLE LA CAMPAGNE 0959 and the wooded area 1160–1159–1058, prior to further exploitation.

METHOD

5. **Preliminary conc**

   See 51 (H) Div Mov Instr for Op "TOTALIZE" issued separately.

6. **Grouping**

   (a) 33 Armd Bde with under comd   22 Dgns
                                                    80 Assault Sqn RE

   (b) 152 Bde with under comd   243 A Tk Bty
                                                    One pl 275 Fd Coy
            and in sp   "A" Coy 1/7 Mx
                                                    275 Fd Coy less one pl.

   (c) 153 Bde with under comd   242 A Tk Bty
            and in sp   103 Bty 6 Cdn A Tk Regt
                                                  274 Fd Coy RE

   (d) 154 Bde with under comd   241 A Tk Bty
                                                    33 Bty 6 Cdn A Tk Regt
                                                  276 Fd Coy RE
                                                "B" Coy 1/7 Mx

7. **Phases**

   The Op will be carried out in three phases.

   (a) *Phase I*

   The capture of LORGUICHON WOOD 0757–CRAMESNIL 0856–ST AIGNAN DE CRAMESNIL 0956–GARCELLES SECQUEVILLE 0858–SECQUEVILLE LA CAMPAGNE 0959–wooded area 1160–1159–1058.

   (b) *Phase II*

   Exploitation to secure POUSSY LA CAMPAGNE 1356–BILLY 1457–CONTEVILLE 1257.

   (c) *Phase III*

   Relief of 3 Cdn Div at ST SYLVAIN 1354.

TASKS

8. **154 Bde, with in sp 33 Armd Bde**

   (a) *Phase I*

   (i) Capture and hold area CRAMESNIL–ST AIGNAN DE CRAMESNIL–woods 0856–0855–GARCELLES SEQUEVILLE.

   CODEWORD—LINER

   (ii) Start Line—rd ST ANDRE SUR ORNE–HUBERT FOLIE–SOLIERS.

   (iii) "H" hr—2300 hrs 7 Aug.

   (iv) This op will be carried out by two armd cols by-passing TILLY LA CAMPAGNE on either flank.

9. **152 Bde**

   (a) *Phase I*

   Capture, mop-up and hold :—

   (i) TILLY LA CAMPAGNE—with one bn. This attack will commence at "H" hr (see para 8(a)(iii)) to take advantage of the Corps Barrage.

   CODEWORD—SLOOP

   (ii) Area LORGUICHON village and wood and rly cutting in sq 0658—with one bn.

   CODEWORD—YAWL

   In addition to the above tasks 152 Bde will be prepared to :

   (iii) Complete the occupation of the area given in para 8 (a) above. If necessary, the whole Bde may be required to ensure the completion of this task.

   (iv) Provide one bn if required to assist 154 Bde to complete their task.

   (v) Occupy and clear SECQUEVILLE LA CAMPAGNE and wooded areas in 0959 and 1058.

   CODEWORD—BRIG

   This op will NOT commence until the area stated in para 8 (a) is firmly held. "B" Sqn 141 RAC Regt will be available to sp this op.

   (b) *Phase II*

   Dependent on the situation, 152 Bde will be prepared to exploit to secure POUSSY LA CAMPAGNE–BILLY–CONTEVILLE.

10. **153 Bde**

    (a) *Phase I*

    (i) Hold a firm base in area GRENTHEVILLE–FOUR–SOLIERS–BOURGUEBUS, until relieved of this responsibility (not before 0800 hrs 8 Aug).

    CODEWORD—YACHT.

    On vacating firm base, 103 Bty 6 Cdn A Tk Regt will remain in situ, reverting to comd 2 Cdn Corps.

(ii) After the capture of SECQUEVILLE LA CAMPAGNE by 152 Bde, to clear the wooded area 1060–1160–1059–1159. For this op tanks and crocodiles will be made available if required.

CODEWORD—CANOE.

11. **Vehicles**

   (a) (i) Sufficient "Priests"—Scout Cars and carriers are being provided to lift 154 Bde to their objective.

   (ii) After debussing and as the situation permits, all vehs less those mentioned in (iii) and (iv) below will be despatched in small convoys to a Div Collecting Centre in area 055643. The Centre will be controlled by an offr to be detailed by 2 Derby Yeo who will despatch the "Priests" to a rep of 3 Cdn Inf Div at 045650.

   (iii) 154 Bde will retain four scout cars per bn for the evac of casualties.

   (iv) 154 Bde will send six half track scout cars to Main HQ 33 Armd Bde at first light 8 Aug. These vehs will be used as amn carriers until the situation allows of three-tonners to be used.

   (v) All vehs supplied by 2 Derby Yeo and RA 51 (H) Div will be returned to the Div Collecting Centre as soon as possible for refitting. Half tracks supplied by Cdn Corps will be retained for the purpose outlined in sub paras (iii) and (iv) above.

   (b) A/Q will provide 20 × 3 ton lorries to be held by 153 Bde for the purpose of ferrying fwd units when necessary.

12. **RA**

   (a) No preliminary bombardment.

   (b) A Corps Fd and Med Barrage is being fired starting at "H" hr, astride the CAEN–FALAISE rd, advancing at the rate of 100 yds per min to the first objective.

   (c) RA Inf trace to be issued separately.

13. **RE**

   (a) CRE will recce two routes each of 4 lanes from 154 Bde conc area in CORMELLES to the start line. These routes will be clearly marked and lit as follows :—

   (i) Right pair of lanes of each route—GREEN.

   (ii) Left pair of lanes of each route—AMBER.

   (b) Routes SOUTH from start line to objective will proceed in a straight line on a fixed bearing.

14. **MG**

   1/7 Mx less "B" Coy will cover the left flank during the adv to the first objective from the area 083612, and thereafter as required.

15. **Recce**

   2 Derby YEO will remain in present locn until further orders.

16. **141 RAC**

   "B" sqn 141 RAC will remain in area 0565 until called fwd.

17. **Aids to Navigation**

   (a) The navigation of cols to debussing pts will be the responsibility of tk comds.

   (b) LAA will fire over each route from the start line to the objective.

   (c) Wireless directional beams will cover each route.

   (d) GREEN target indicator shells will be fired by Div arty on each route.

   (e) Diffused light will be produced by searchlights. No illumination before "H" hr.

18. **Air**

    (a) Hy bombers will "obliterate" areas—MAY SUR ORNE–FONTENAY LE MARMION—and woods 1160–1159–1058 by bombing starting before "H" hr. No bombs are to fall in the lane between Grid line 04 Easting and rd FOUR–LA HOGUE–SECQUEVILLE LA CAMPAGNE.

    (b) ASSU tentacles allotted to :
           33 Armd Bde
           153 Bde
           154 Bde

INTERCOMN

19. **Div Axis**

Right route from start line to first objective.

20. **Locn of HQ**

    (a) Main HQ 51 (H) Div opens area CORMELLES pm 6 Aug.

    (b) Rear HQ 51 (H) Div opens area BIEVILLE pm 6 Aug.

    (c) 51 (H) Div Comd Post opens am 8 Aug in BRAS, later moving to rly cutting in sq 0658.

    (d) Main HQ 2 Cdn Corps—970743.

    (e) 2 Cdn Div—029667.

21. **CODEWORDS**

See Appx "B". Addressees will reproduce only those codewords actually required to cover their own tasks.

Time of Signature 0905 hrs.

                                                                         Lt-Col
                                                                          GS

Method of Despatch : by LO and SDR.

APPENDIX "H"

TOP SECRET
6 Aug 44

ADDENDUM No. 1 to 51 (H) DIV OO No. 6

Ref Para 13 (b). Details of routes are as under

WEST ROUTE "A"

Forming up pt at 04976472–to start pt on Start Line at 05736173–thence on Grid Bearing 154°, to debussing pt 08005700.

EAST ROUTE "B"

Forming up pt at 06606498–to start pt on Start Line at 07196240–thence on Grid Bearing 160°, to debussing pt at 08845779.

Lt-Col
GS

BLA
PWS

APPENDIX "J"
(less air programme and trace at para 2)

TOP SECRET
Copy No.
7 Aug 44

ADDENDUM No. 2 to 51 (H) DIV OO No. 6

AIR

1. Cancel para 18.

2. Air programme 8–1/Ops dated 7 Aug with trace showing bombline and target areas is att.

3. The complete garrison of BOURGUEBUS will be withdrawn NORTH of the bombline before bombing commences.

TIMINGS

4. Cancel para 8 (*a*) (iii).

5. Timings for the bombing to commence, and "H" hr (i.e. time at which leading tps cross the start line) depend on the result of experiments with marker shells.

   (*a*) **If marker shells NOT satisfactory:**
   (i) Bombing will commence (i.e. "first bomb") in Phase 1 at 2130 hrs D day.
   (ii) Bombing will cease (i.e. "last bomb") at 2210 hrs.
   (iii) "H" hr will be at 2300 hrs.
   (iv) Arty barrage and illumination of searchlights will be at 2313 hrs.

   (*b*) **If marker shells prove satisfactory,** the following timings will apply:
   (i) First bomb   2300 hrs
   (ii) "H" hr   2330 hrs
   (iii) Last bomb   2340 hrs
   (iv) Opening of arty barrage and illumination of lights 2343 hrs (THIS TIME WILL BE CONFIRMED WHEN "H" hr is CONFIRMED.)

6. If marker shells are used to identify aiming pts for the RAF, UNDER NO CIRCUMSTANCES WILL THESE BE FIRED FOR ANY OTHER PURPOSE UNTIL AFTER LAST BOMB.

7. Whether or not marker shells are to be used will be notified to all concerned immediately a definite decision has been made, by 1830 hrs at the latest.

VEHICLES

8. Ref para 11 (*a*) (ii).

"Priests" will NOT now be returned to the rep of 3 Cdn Div at 045650, but will be handed over to 153 Bde, who will arrange for an offr to be at the Div Collecting Centre in area 055643 by 1000 hrs 8 Aug.

141 RAC

9. B Sqn 141 RAC Regt under comd 33 Armd Bde until further notice.

10. One additional sqn 141 RAC Regt, now under comd 2 Cdn Div, will come under comd 33 Armd Bde prior to commencement of Phase II. Arrangements have been made for this sqn to come up on the frequency of "B" sqn immediately after being released by 2 Cdn Div.

22 DGNS

11. 22 DGNS pass to comd 1 Polish Armd Div on completion of Phase I. 33 Armd Bde are responsible for rallying the Regt as soon as possible after completion of their task and for their replenishment.

TRAFFIC

12. (a) During Phase I, 1 Polish Armd Div will concentrate behind 51 (H) Div with head on the Corps start line by morning D plus 1, prior to passing through to their objectives.

(b) All traffic SOUTH of the R ORNE will be frozen from 072400B hrs Aug and restrictions will not be lifted before 081400B hrs. This does not incl mov of leading tps in the fwd area.

(c) The following route will be closed to all traffic from "H" minus 140 mins to "H" minus 40 mins for the passage of the armd col on Route "A". Rd 060657–thence SW to track junc 056650–051652. APM to arrange.

ACK.

For Lt-Col
GS

Time of Signature 1330B

Method of Despatch : LO : ELS

APPENDIX "K"

(NOTE: Appendices A and B only have been reproduced as an addendum to this instruction)

TOP SECRET

ROYAL CANADIAN ARTILLERY
2 CDN CORPS OPERATION INSTRUCTION No. 5.

Ref Maps — FRANCE : 1/50,000 SHEETS — 7F1, 7F2, 7F3, 7F4
                1/25,000 SHEETS — 40/16/SW 40/14/NW

INFORMATION

1. **OWN TPS.** — Additional Arty available.

   (a) Under comd 2 Cdn Corps

      51 (H) Div Arty -   126 Fd Regt
                                 127 Fd Regt
                                 128 Fd Regt

      Polish Armd Div Arty -   1 Fd Regt (SP)
                                 2 Fd Regt

   (b) In sp 2 Cdn Corps (with reservation)

      49 Div Arty -   143 Fd Regt
                                 185 Fd Regt
                                 150 Fd Regt

      3 AGRA
      4 AGRA
      2 Cdn & 109 Hy AA Regts

METHOD

2. **GENERAL** — Outline plan, phases, etc. (issued with 2 Cdn Corps Operation Instr No. 4 for Operation "TOTALIZE").

ALLOTMENT

3. (a) **Phase I**

     (i) 2 Cdn Inf Div (with under comd 2 Cdn Armd Bde)

        in sp. 2 Cdn Inf Div Arty
                2 Cdn AGRA

        Additional Arty (with reservations)
           3 AGRA
           2 Cdn & 109 Hy AA Regts

     (ii) 51 (H) Inf Div (with under comd 33 Armd Bde)

        in sp 51 (H) Inf Div Arty
               4 Cdn Armd Div Arty
               9 AGRA

        Additional Arty (with reservations)

           49 Inf Div Arty
           4 AGRA.

     (iii) On completion of Phase I, on orders from Comd 2 Cdn Corps, the sp of 2 Cdn and 9 AGRA passes to 4 Cdn Armd Div and Polish Armd Div. Codeword—"MAPLE", to code sign followed by the time will indicate the transfer.
         Example—"MAPLE TO QUC 1200."

(b) **Phase II**

4 Cdn Armd Div on the RIGHT and Polish Armd Div on the LEFT form up behind 2 Cdn Inf Div and 51 (H) Inf Div respectively.

Both Armd Divs adv simultaneously through the inf divs astride the main axis.

(i) *4 Cdn Armd Div*

Under comd 4 Cdn Armd Div Arty (incl 19 Cdn Fd Regt)
One med regt (9 AGRA)

in sp 9 AGRA

(ii) *Polish Armd Div*

Under comd Polish Div Arty
One med regt (2 Cdn AGRA)
in sp 2 Cdn AGRA

(iii) *3 Cdn Inf Div*

Under comd 3 Cdn Inf Div arty (less 14 Cdn Fd Regt)
One med regt 2 Cdn AGRA—if necessary.

(c) **Special Timings for Phase II**

(i) Gun recce parties from one med regt 9 AGRA will report to HQ RCA 4 Cdn Armd Div in the conc area behind 2 Cdn Inf Div (HQ RAC 4 Cdn Armd Div to pass location) before 080600 B hrs.

(ii) Gun recce parties from one med regt 2 Cdn AGRA will report to HQ Arty Polish Armd Div in conc area behind 51 (H) Inf Div before 080800 B hrs.

(iii) All guns of 4 Cdn Armd Div Arty and the two med regts referred to will remain in sp of inf divs as detailed for Phase I until released by Comd 2 Cdn Corps.

CONTROL

4. (a) **Reps**

(i) RCA 2 Cdn Inf Div—to be provided by
2 Cdn AGRA
3 AGRA

(ii) RA 51 (H) Div—to be provided by
RCA 4 Cdn Armd Div
9 AGRA
4 AGRA
RA 49 Div

(iii) RCA 4 Cdn Armd Div—to be provided by
9 AGRA

(iv) Arty Polish Armd Div—to be provided by
4 Cdn Armd Div
2 Cdn AGRA

Times for reps to report will be notified by fmns concerned.

(b) **FOOs**

To be arranged between fmns as required.

(c) **LOs (with wireless sets)**

(i) RA 51 (H) Div—to be provided by
RCA 2 Cdn Inf Div

(ii) RCA 2 Cdn Corps—to be provided by
RCA 2 Cdn Inf Div
RCA 4 Cdn Armd Div
RA 51 (H) Div
2 Cdn AGRA
9 AGRA
344 SL Bty
Arty Polish Armd Div

to report to CCRA's Report Centre at 062678 by 071800B.

TASKS

5. (a) **Phase I**

   (i) A barrage will move in front of the attack across a frontage of 4050 yards to a depth of 6000 yards. Rate of adv 100 yds in one minute—moving in lifts of 200 yds.

   The barrage will commence at (H plus 15 mins on right)
   (H plus 13 mins on the left).

   the following guns being employed:
   - 2 Cdn Inf Div Arty
   - 4 Cdn Armd Div Arty
   - 51 (H) Div Arty
   - 2 Cdn AGRA
   - 9 AGRA
   - Two med regts 4 AGRA

   Details of the barrage will be produced by HQ RCA 2 Cdn Corps in trace and task table form, to be issued separately.

   (ii) Areas requiring special treatment as selected by 2 Cdn Inf Div and 51 (H) Div will be dealt with by guns of flanking AGsRA or Hy AA regts. Details of these concs will be produced by HQ RA of the div concerned. These concs are shown on the corps trace.

   (iii) Pre-arranged DF and DF (SOS) tasks are also shown on the corps trace.

   (iv) In the event of a check the div concerned may remove its own fd guns from the barrage on authority of the GOC of the div concerned. The med guns will remain on the barrage and fire to conclusion.

   (b) **Phase II**

   HQ RCA 4 Cdn Armd Div will prepare a list of selected concs on call. List of co-ordinates of these concs, are shown on the printed sheet att to corps trace.

   (c) **Phase II**

   HQ Arty Polish Armd Div will issue a further list of selected concs on call for their adv and exploitation. This list will be made available at a later date.

CB

6. Comd 2 Cdn AGRA will be responsible for all CB activity on 2 Cdn Corps front. Flanking fmns have contracted to deal with HBs on their respective fronts (1 & 12 Corps) and will conform to timings for the pre-arranged CB bombards. Appendix "A" att outlines the CB policy and amn expenditure.

SURVEY

7. CO 2 Cdn Svy Regt will co-ordinate all svy tasks, priorities as follows:

   (a) Gun areas

   (b) Tp leaders tanks—2 and 33 Armd Bdes

   (c) DF base for wireless beam

   (d) S.rg

   (e) F.sp

   Svy dets must be prepared to

   (i) move fwd on very short notice with 4 Cdn Armd Div Arty—AGsRA—3 Cdn Inf Div Arty—Polish Div Arty.

   (ii) Regimental Svy Report Centre will be est at 045650 by H hr.

A TK

8. Btys of 6 Cdn A Tk Regt will be disposed as follows:

Under comd 2 Cdn Inf Div	56 A Tk Bty 3" M10 SP
	74 A Tk Bty 17 pr tank towed.
Under comd 51 (H) Div	33 A Tk Bty 3" M10 SP
	103 A Tk Bty 17 pr tank towed.

   103 A Tk Bty is presently deployed in area 4 Cdn Armd Div and will remain there when 51 (H) Div takes over, passing under comd with the area.

LAA

9. Sub area 107 has taken over responsibility for everything north of R ORNE other than rear installations belonging to fwd fmns which will still be their own responsibility.

OC 6 Cdn LAA Regt will co-ordinate LAA def of main gun areas and area along the south bank of R ORNE.

AOP

10. Some additional AOP flts have been made available permitting sp as follows:

2 Cdn Inf Div	A Flt 660 Sqn
3 Cdn Inf Div	C Flt 660 Sqn
4 Cdn Armd Div	B Flt 660 Sqn
51 (H) Div	C Flt 652 Sqn
2 Cdn AGRA	C Flt 661 Sqn
9 AGRA	Flt 661 Sqn
CBO 2 Cdn Corps	C Flt 661 Sqn

Fmns must keep AOP pilots informed about shooting restrictions.

AIDS TO KEEPING DIRECTION

11. Certain navigational aids are being provided to assist movement at night during Phase I. All aids are a div responsibility.

   (a) Bofors tracer—during rolling barrage.
   2 Cdn Inf Div—six rds from three bofors every 4 mins.
   51 (H) Div—five rds from two bofors every 5 mins.

   (b) Night marker shells (coloured 25 pr base ejection flares) 2 Cdn Inf Div will fire "green" marker shells on to a feature near the inter-div bdy. Arrangements between 2 Cdn Inf and 51 (H) Divs. Times to be issued later to 2 Div through "G".

PRODUCTION OF FIRE PLAN DATA

12. (a) **2 Cdn Corps**

   (i) Barrage trace and task table.

   (ii) List of tgts on call for 2 Cdn Inf Div, 51 (H) Div and 4 Cdn Armd Div.

   (b) **2 Cdn Inf Div**

   (i) Prearranged timed concs—(tgts for 3 AGRA to be passed to 2 Cdn AGRA and Hy AA regts in case of 3 AGRA not being available).

   (ii) Tasks for own div arty and 2 Cdn AGRA after barrage.

   (c) **51 (H) Div**

   (i) Prearranged timed concs for 49 Inf Div Arty and 4 AGRA.

   (ii) Tasks for own div arty and 9 AGRA after barrage.

   (d) **CBO 2 Cdn Corps**

   Task tables for CB periods: (A) H plus 100 to H plus 120
   (B) H plus 7 hrs to H plus 7 hrs 20 mins.

   (e) **Distribution**

   All fire plans will be delivered by LO to HQ RAC 2 Cdn Corps MR 966742 by 071200B in packets prepared and labelled for distribution. LOs will remain and pick up fire plans for their own fmns, at 1300 hrs.

CONTROL OF OBSERVED FIRE AND TGT NUMBERS

13. (a) CsRA—2, 3 and 4, Cdn Divs and 51 (H) Div may call for VICTOR tgts on CCRA's net.

CCRA 2 Cdn Corps	1—10
CRA 2 Cdn Inf Div	11—20
3 Cdn Inf Div	21—30
4 Cdn Armd Div	31—40
Polish Div	41—50
51 (H) Div	51—60

(b) ML Targets
    2 Cdn Corps   1—199
    2 Cdn Inf Div   200—299
    3 Cdn Inf Div   300—399
    4 Cdn Armd Div   400—499
    51 (H) Div   900—999
    Polish Div   800—899

(c) DF and DF(SOS). Normal div numbering.

SLs

14. (a) 344 SL Bty will be deployed to provide artificial twilight across 2 Cdn Corps front.

    (b) Intensity of light will be controlled through CCRA's Report centre.

    (c) SLs expose at H plus 13 mins.

MOVEMENT

15. All movement behind rear div bdy of over 10 vhs to be authorised by "Q" Moves 2 Cdn Corps through HQ RCA 2 Corps or own fmn. (Except for maintenance traffic).

AMN

16. Allotment—see appx "B" att.

INTERCOMN

17. **Axis of Adv**—2 Cdn Corps—road CAEN-FALAISE.

18. **Locations**—See appx "C" att.

19. **Comn**—Line and wireless—see appx "D" att.

20. **Codeword "Chestnuts"**—will be used to notify all concerned when own tps are being shelled by own guns.

    Example "CHESTNUTS MR 123456 190 degrees 1605 hrs."

    ACK

Brigadier
CCRA 2 Cdn Corps

LIST OF APPENDICES

"A" CB Policy
"B" Amn Allotment
"C" Locations
"D" Line and Wireless.

APPENDIX "L"

Addendum "A" to RCA

Operation Instruction No. 5
dated 7 Aug 44

ROYAL CANADIAN ARTILLERY 2nd CANADIAN CORPS

COUNTER BATTERY POLICY—OPERATION "TOTALIZE"

1. No intensive CB programme before H hour. The present active policy will continue all during D day and amn at the rate of 30 rpg for 2 Cdn AGRA and 9 AGRA may be expended by the CBO.

2. (a) During Operation "TOTALIZE" two intensive CB bombardments will be carried out on known HBs at:

   (i) H plus 100 to H plus 120
   (ii) H plus 7 hrs to H plus 7 hrs and 20 mins.

   (b) Guns available for both of these prearranged bombards:

2 Cdn AGRA	Four med and one hy regt
9 AGRA	Three med and one HAA regt
2 Cdn Inf Div	Three fd regts
51 (H) Inf Div	Three fd regts
4 Cdn Armd Div	One fd regt (tractor drawn).

   Of this allotment 2 Cdn and 51 (H) Divs will retain a priority call over own div artys and one med regt from each of 2 Cdn and 9 AGRA.

   (c) Amn available

Fd Guns	50 rpg
Med and 7.2	30 rpg
155 mm	NIL—only for long range HBs
3.7	25 rpg.

   Further amn can be made available to CBO on request.

3. Flanking formations have contracted to deal with HBs on their respective fronts. Amn as follow has been made available on 2 Cdn Corps account for this purpose.

1 Corps	49 Div Arty	three fd regts	150 rpg
	4 AGRA	50 rpg 5.5 and 7.2	
		25 rpg 155 mm	
12 Corps	3 AGRA	50 rpg 5.5 and 7.2	
		25 rpg 155 mm.	

4. On completion of prearranged fire plan, all med and hy guns NOT otherwise employed will be available to fire CB tasks on call from CBO. Div concerned retain priority call.

5. "Apple Pie" bombardment will probably be required on occasion during D plus 1 and D plus 2. Requests will come from G2 Air 2 Cdn Corps.

6. Arty/R to be flown on D plus 1 and D plus 2 under arrangements 2 Cdn AGRA.

Addendum "B" to RCA
2 Cdn Corps Op Instr No. 5
dated 7 Aug 44

AMMUNITION

1. Allotment as under :

FMN	In sp of Attack	CB	On Call	TOTAL RPG
2 Cdn Inf Div Sector				
2 Cdn Inf Div 25-pr HE	400	50	200	650
25-pr (coloured flare)	80 (green)			
3 Cdn Inf Div	200		200	400
2 Cdn AGRA 5.5"	200	50	100	350
7.2"	100	50	50	200
155 mm		30	20	50
51 (H) Div Sector				
51 (H) Div 25-pr HE	400	50	200	650
4 Cdn Armd Div 25-pr HE	400	50	200	650
105 mm	400	50	200	650
Polish Armd Div 25-pr HE	200		400	600
49 Div		150	100	250
9 AGRA 5.5"	200	50	100	350
3.7"	50	50	50	150
4 AGRA 5.5"	100	50	100	250
7.2"	50	50	50	150
155 mm		25		25

2. Each fmn will ensure that total amount allotted is either dumped at gun posns or is available for its account in dumps SOUTH of the R ORNE by 1200 hrs 7 Aug 44.

3. Amn allotted to 3 AGRA, 4 AGRA, and 49 Div is for account of First Cdn Army.

4. 155-mm amn is available in limited quantity. 155-mm will be reserved for CB tasks out of range of other calibres and urgent demands from 4 Cdn Armd Div and Polish Armd Div on targets out of range of other calibres.

GUNS

FMN/Unit	Number and Type of Equipment						
	25-pr TD	25-pr SP	105-mm	5.5	7.2	155-mm	3.7
2 Cdn Inf Div	72						
3 Cdn Inf Div	48						
4 Cdn Armd Div (incl 19 Cdn A Fd Regt)	24	24	24				
1 Pol Armd Div	24	24					
51 (H) Inf Div	72						
49 (WR) Inf Div	72						
2 Cdn AGRA				64	8	8	
3 Brit AGRA				64	8	8	
4 Brit AGRA				64	8	8	
9 Brit AGRA				48			
2 Cdn HAA Regt							24
109 Brit HAA Regt							24
TOTALS	312	48	24	240	24	24	48

APPENDIX "M"

ACCOUNT BY BRIGADEFUHRER KURT MEYER COMD 12 SS PZ DIV.

In this interrogation report BRIGADEFUEHRER KURT MEYER, Commander 12 SS Pz Div, gives an outline account of the operations of his division, which owing to its reduced strength, had been organised into battle groups.

As soon as the news of the Allied attack reached MEYER, he issued orders to battle group WALDMULLER to take up positions astride the road CAEN–FALAISE at CINTHEAUX to prevent a break through down the main axis to FALAISE. He also ordered battle group KRAUSE, which was opposing the 12 Corps troops at BRIEUX, to return at once and prepare to launch a counter attack with WALDMULLER.

MEYER got into his car and drove to URVILLE where he met the Commander 89 Inf Div, who, as a result of the bombing, had little or no idea of the situation. MEYER went on up the main road and found himself in the middle of the shelling. In his own words he describes the situation. "I got out of my car and my knees were trembling, the sweat was pouring down my face, and my clothes were soaked with perspiration. It was not that I was particularly anxious for myself because my experiences of the last five years had inured me against fear of death, but I realised that if I failed now and if I did not deploy my division correctly, the Allies would be through to FALAISE and the German armies in the west trapped. I knew how weak my division was and the task which confronted me gave me, at that time, some of the worst moments I had ever had in my life."

Whilst on the main road alone, MEYER saw groups of men from 89 Inf Div, who had scattered in panic from the bombing, making their way back as quickly as possible. MEYER calmly lit a cigar, stood in the middle of the road and in a loud voice asked them if they were going to leave him alone to cope with the Allied attack. One look at this impressive thirty-five year old Commander was enough and the men turned round.

The tanks of battle group KRAUSE arrived during the morning 8 August and the counter-attack by the two battle groups on ST AIGNAN DE CRAMESNIL was launched about 1300 hours. This combined infantry and tank attack was not successful and the battle groups withdrew, KRAUSE to the south, WALDMULLER to the south east, both having suffered losses. Capt WITTMAN of 101 Hy Tk Bn was killed in this action. This officer held the record for the number of tanks knocked out by one individual. Since 1943, on the Russian front, he was officially credited with having knocked out one hundred and forty three tanks of all kinds.

Battle Group WALDMULLER successfully opposed the advance of 1 Polish Armd Div during the remaining hours of daylight. To assist it, it had twenty Panzer IVs from the anti-tank battalion of 12 SS Div, which, unable to move across at the time the division went into reserve owing to mechanical troubles, now emerged from the North East, all repairs completed. Battle Group KRAUSE, with the remnants of units of 89 Inf Div, were fighting astride the main axis, but were unable to prevent the capture of CINTHEAUX and HAUTMESNIL by last light.

It has not been possible to trace any reports or statements from officers of 89 Inf Div giving an account of this battle. The Grenadier Regiments resistance against the Canadian and British troops varied. There was at this time marked distrust between the SS and Army troops. The Army resented the preferential treatment and obviously better equipment afforded to the SS Div, and the feeling had grown, particularly amongst lower ranks, that the SS were kept in the rear areas, restricting their activities to a considerable extent to keeping the forwards troops in the line. Prisoners statements amplify this feeling. Two prisoners from 89 Div captured on 9 August state :—

"Yesterday morning the SS with pistols in their hands drove us into battle with the cry — 'Push on, you dogs' — threatening to shoot our corporal because he did not advance fast enough with his group."

It is not surprising therefore, in their first battle, that the mixed 89 Inf Div's morale was low and their resistance variable.

Photographs

3. A "Crocodile" Flamethrower mounted on a Churchill Mark VII

4. A Sherman "Flail"

1. A Sherman Mark Vc

2. An Assault Vehicle, Royal Engineers (AVRE)

5. A "defrocked Priest", used as an Armoured Personnel Carrier (7 August 1944)

6. Another view of the "Priest"

7. *A 3-in. SP Anti-tank gun the M. 10*

8. *A German 88 mm. dual purpose gun*

9. A German Pz KW VI (TIGER)

10. A German Pz KW V (PANTHER)

www.ingramcontent.com/pod-product-compliance
Lightning Source LLC
Chambersburg PA
CBHW042302010526
44113CB00048B/2777